Emily Bridger shows us the creativity and the boldness with wh... ...men remade gender norms in order to become comrade... ...king study of gender in the context of the strug...

...rd

A pioneering exploration of young wome... ...vism in Soweto, in the difficult and critical period of ... ...ous. Through sensitive analysis of oral histories, it sheds new ... ...wo understudied questions in South African historiography. Most urgently, this book asks: In a struggle led publicly by young men, what roles did young women play? The author argues that while young women were always a minority of comrades, their actions were integral to township struggles: they debated at COSAS meetings, enforced boycotts, smuggled arms, recruited into the ANC underground, and punished criminals and spies in their community. Young women's activism was both similar to young men's activism, and marked by their gendered experiences of everyday life in Soweto: young women used activism as a way to take leadership in student circles, to get out of overprotective homes, and to protect themselves from sexual violence on the streets. Thus the book also addresses a second question that scholars have neglected: How did young women experience township life, in an era of States of Emergency and multiple forms of political and personal violence? In my view, the author's contribution to our knowledge of female students' experiences is particularly significant, and timely amidst a new wave of student activism in South Africa in which young women have played key roles. ... original and compelling.

Meghan Healy-Clancy, Bridgewater State University

This study contributes another important element to the literature on the anti-apartheid struggle, but does so in a highly distinctive manner. It tells the story of the gender struggle within the political struggle – the story of those women who became political activists and fought, often quite literally, on the frontline in the townships. Based around a unique and quite remarkable collection of oral histories, the voices of these young women dominate this text and give it immense authority and authenticity. This is no artificial academic presentation of feminist theory, but instead tells the gritty story of struggle in tooth and claw, through personal and often highly emotional accounts of personal suffering, hardships, and loss. ... This is a truly important study.

David Anderson, University of Warwick

An important contribution to the study of gender and political resistance in South Africa. Aside from raising the voices of often-forgotten women actors in the 1980s struggles, it offers fresh insights into the lived experiences of politicised youth. ... an outstanding, textured, fascinating study.

Clive Glaser, University of the Witwatersrand

Young Women against Apartheid

Gender, Youth and South Africa's Liberation Struggle

Emily Bridger

 JAMES CURREY

James Currey
is an imprint of
Boydell & Brewer Ltd
PO Box 9, Woodbridge
Suffolk IP12 3DF (GB)
www.jamescurrey.com
and of
Boydell & Brewer Inc.
668 Mt Hope Avenue
Rochester, NY 14620–2731 (US)
www.boydellandbrewer.com

First published 2021
Paperback edition 2023

ISBN 978-1-84701-263-0 (James Currey hardback)
ISBN 978-1-84701-273-9 (James Currey Africa-only paperback)
ISBN 978-1-84701-362-0 (James Currey paperback)

A CIP catalogue record for this book is available
from the British Library

For Heidi Pasques (1963–2017)
Who acted as a mother, sister, and great friend to me over the course of researching this book.

Contents

Acknowledgements

This book's greatest debt is to the former comrades of Soweto whose stories are told within its pages. Without their help and support this research would never have been possible. These men and women not only shared their detailed and at times difficult memories with me, but also invited me into their homes and treated me as a fellow comrade. Particular thanks go to Musa, Lucy, Florence, Makgane, and Daniel for all the hard work they put in to helping me find interviewees and navigate Soweto over the course of my research.

This research was made possible by the financial support of multiple organisations. I am extremely grateful to the University of Exeter's College of Humanities and the Social Sciences and Humanities Research Council of Canada for funding the initial research for this book. Many thanks also go to the Maple Leaf Trust and the generous support of their Canadian Centennial Scholarship Fund. Travel to overseas conferences where I initially presented some of this research was made possible by the Royal Historical Society and the African Studies Association Women's Caucus. Most recently, a UKRI Future Leaders Fellowship has provided me with the time and funding to see through the final stages of this project.

Two academic institutions have been foundational to the writing of this book. I began this project in 2013 as a doctoral student at the University of Exeter, the same institution to which I returned in 2017 to take up my first academic position as a lecturer. Stacey Hynd has provided invaluable guidance from the outset of this research, first as my supervisor and later as a wonderful friend and colleague. No words can adequately express how grateful I am for her support and encouragement. Martin Thomas has long acted as my unofficial mentor, always offering probing and insightful questions (many of which I am still trying to answer). I would like to thank Exeter's Centre of Imperial and Global History for providing me with an intellectual home while I completed this book. At Exeter I have also benefitted from the support and friendship of wonderful colleagues. To Charmian Mansell, Josh Rhodes, Hannah Charnock, Angela Muir, Anna Jackman, Fred Cooper, Michelle Webb, and Tom Chadwick – thank you for making the PhD years not only bearable but actually rather enjoyable. To James Davey, Beccy Williams, Gemma Clark, Miguel Hernandez, Tawny Paul, Tim Reece, Gajendra Singh, and Richard Ward, thank you for providing the office corridor chats and after-work pints which served as welcomed procrastination from the writing process. I would also like to thank my students, especially those who enrolled in my third-year module on South Africa over the past few years; discussing the key themes of this book with you and hearing your perspectives has helped beyond measure.

While conducting the research for this book in South Africa from 2014 to 2019, the University of the Witwatersrand and the wonderful staff of its History Workshop provided a welcoming and stimulating academic home. I am particularly grateful to Anne Heffernan, Franziska Rueedi, Laura Philips, Clive Glaser, Noor Nieftagodien, and Srila Roy for their advice and support. Special thanks also go to the staff at the Historical Papers Research Archive at Wits. Zofia Sulej and Gabi Mohale greatly aided the research process and also provided an uplifting atmosphere to work in.

This book has benefited from the advice and wisdom of many other scholars: Gary Kynoch first inspired my interest in South African history at Dalhousie University in 2009, and has continued to provide invaluable advice and support ever since; David Anderson provided much needed guidance on the publication process; Jonny Steinberg has taught me so much about the art of interviewing; Rebekah Lee acted as a wonderful PhD examiner; and Sarah Duff, Megan Healy-Clancy, and Rachel Johnson have helped me to think more critically about gender and generation in South African history. To Kate Bruce-Lockhart, George Roberts, and Sacha Hepburn, thank you for reading so much of this book in its early drafts and helping me to navigate the publication of my first book – your support and friendship over the last few years has been invaluable.

Many other people have worked tirelessly behind the scenes to support this book's publication. I would like to thank Jaqueline Mitchell and her team at James Currey; Kate Kirkwood for producing the book's map; Thabiso Mareletsa who helped with translation; and Judy Seidman for allowing the use of her wonderful artwork for the book's cover. Special thanks also go to James Bridger for always being an enthusiastic proof reader of my work.

Finally, conducting this research and writing this book would not have been possible without the social and emotional support of friends and family across three continents, provided in the form of great conversation and delicious food and drink. In South Africa, thank you to Micah and Tessa Reddy, Nicole Beardsworth, and Karliene Dempsey; in Canada to Kate Pelsoci, my brothers, and parents; and in the UK to Liz Gourd, Jazz Jagger, Hannah Corkery, and the Giblin family.

Emily Bridger, Exeter, 2020

Acronyms and Abbreviations

ANC	African National Congress
ANCWL	African National Congress Women's League
ANCYL	African National Congress Youth League
AZASM	Azanian Students' Movement
BCM	Black Consciousness Movement
COSAS	Congress of South African Students
DET	Department of Education and Training
DPSC	Detainees Parents Support Committee
FEDTRAW	Federation of Transvaal Women
FLN	National Liberation Front (Algeria)
FMLN	Farabundo Marti National Liberation Front (El Salvador)
FSLN	Sandinista National Liberation Front (Nicaragua)
FRELIMO	Mozambique Liberation Front
LTTE	Liberation Tigers of Tamil Eelam (Sri Lanka)
MK	*Umkhonto we Sizwe* (The Spear of the Nation)
PAC	Pan Africanist Congress
PWV	Pretoria-Witwatersrand-Vereeniging region (now Gauteng)
SACP	South African Communist Party
SAHA	South African History Archive
SAYCO	South African Youth Congress
SOSCO	Soweto Student Congress
SOYCO	Soweto Youth Congress
SRC	student representative council
TPLF	Tifray People's Liberation Front (Ethiopia)
TRC	Truth and Reconciliation Commission
UDF	United Democratic Front

Glossary

baferekanyi	terrorist
comtsotsi	a blend of 'comrade' and *tsotsi*; a criminal or gangster operating under the guise of political activism during the township uprisings
dagga	marijuana
emoyeni	'in the air'; used by comrades to refer to hiding places where they would sleep when trying to avoid police detection
impimpi	a police informer, sell-out, collaborator, or spy
iphekula	terrorist
jolling	to party or have a good time
klap	to slap or hit
kombi	a minivan
nyaope	a street drug generally made of low-grade heroin, cannabis, and other materials
shebeen	a drinking establishment, often in a private home, where liquor is sold and consumed
siyayinyova	'we will destroy'; a slogan often chanted by comrades which came to be used as a name denoting young activists
sjambok	a heavy whip used for punishment
takkies	a sport or running shoe
toyi-toyi	a military dance step or march characterised by high knee movements, often performed while moving forwards in protest gatherings or marches. Generally accompanied by singing and chanting of slogans
tsotsi	a young gangster or criminal in South Africa's townships
umrabulo	a political discussion, seminar, or debate
vuilpop	someone considered dirty or uncouth, a 'dirty little scoundrel'

Map of Soweto

Introduction

Vicky was seventeen years old when, in 1983, police came knocking on the door of her family home in Diepkloof, Soweto – a township located fifteen kilometres from central Johannesburg. It was the middle of the night and Vicky's family – her mother, two sisters and three brothers – were all asleep in their small two-bedroom house. Vicky lay beside her sisters. Her hair, which she wore in short tight curls during the day, had been neatly plaited into braids by her mother before bed. The police burst into the house searching for Vicky, shouting for the *lang en skraal meisei met krullerige hare* (the tall and slim girl with curly hair), as she had been described to them by a local informer. But in her night-time braids Vicky was indistinguishable to the police from her sisters. The officers returned to their van and brought in the youth who had informed them that Vicky was involved in anti-apartheid student politics in the area, demanding that he point her out to them. With the correct sister in their grasp, the police took Vicky, along with six young men they had also rounded up that night, to Moroka Police Station.[1]

At the time of Vicky's arrest, South Africa was still in the midst of apartheid. Yet after two decades of heavy suppression, the country's anti-apartheid activists were beginning to feel a faint sense of hope. New resistance organisations were forming, township communities were organising against local grievances, and the apartheid government was beginning to implement a number of concessions and reforms. In the same year as Vicky's encounter with the police, activists came together to form the United Democratic Front (UDF), which helped to inspire a new period of mass insurrectionary politics. By the end of 1984, many South African townships were engaged in uprisings against the state and its local allies. This year marked the beginning of an unprecedented period of protest and political violence, as burgeoning activism was met by the state's increased militarisation and use of coercive tactics against township residents.

During these township uprisings, which lasted in various forms until the country's formal transition to non-racial democracy in 1994, it was often African children, students, and youths who became the vanguards and shock-troops of the anti-apartheid struggle. These young people – loosely referred

---

[1]   Interview with Vicky, Diepkloof, 14 May 2014.

to as 'the comrades' – joined the struggle as members of student and youth organisations such as the Congress of South African Students (COSAS) or South African Youth Congress (SAYCO), or simply as unaffiliated individuals drawn to escalating conflict in township streets. In July 1985, the state declared the first of multiple, successive states of emergency, which gave the security forces new powers to invade the townships and detain and arrest activists. That same year, the African National Congress (ANC) shifted its strategy towards 'people's war' and called on those within the townships to 'render South Africa ungovernable'. This message was intoxicating to many urban activists – especially the youth – and violence intensified as those in the townships heeded this call.[2] As students and youth increasingly engaged in militant confrontation with state security forces, they also suffered the bulk of retaliation from state agents. Of the 49,000 people detained in the country from 1985 to 1990, approximately 40 per cent were under the age of eighteen.[3]

Vicky was one of the first comrades and members of COSAS to be detained in Soweto in 1983. Her fate was something that thousands of other children and youths in the township would come to experience over the subsequent years. When she arrived at Moroka Police Station that night, however, she was initially relieved: her father – a local policeman – was on duty. Surely her father would release her, she thought. Yet instead he was furious at the sight of his daughter amongst the night's catch of young activists. 'You know what happened?' Vicky asked me during our 2014 interview. 'Right there in the charge office? My father beat me up!' To her father, Vicky's transgression was two-fold: first, in joining the liberation struggle she was fighting on the opposite side as him and causing trouble for the police; and second, she had done this as a girl. 'What's wrong with you?' He shouted at her. 'Why don't I get your brothers here? I only get you here, hey? You're a woman! How can you do this?' The next day, Vicky's gender again became the subject of discussion. When it came time to be charged and taken to prison, she was offered the help of a lawyer. Seeing her as the only girl amongst a group of boys he asked the police if they had made a mistake; surely this skinny teenage girl could not have been involved in politics or public violence alongside these young men? The police agreed, and Vicky was released.

The assumption made by these police officers – that African girls and young women were not active agents in student politics and the township uprisings of the 1980s – has since been repeated by historians, journalists,

[2]   Hilary Sapire, 'Township Histories, Insurrection and Liberation in Late Apartheid South Africa,' *South African Historical Journal* 65:2 (2013): 167–198.

[3]   Christopher Merrett, 'Detention without trial in South Africa: The abuse of human rights as state strategy in the late 1980s,' *Africa Today* 37:2 (1990): 53–66.

and other commentators on South Africa's past. Popular depictions of young activists as brave and militant, combined with ungendered uses of the terms 'children' or 'youth', have led to a common assumption that the 'comrades' were an exclusively male group. As township politics grew increasingly confrontational during the mid-1980s, girls and young women were thought to have been largely demobilised from the struggle. Scholars presumed that due to parental concerns over their safety and respectability, boys' disparaging attitudes towards them, and the increasingly violent nature of township politics, girls and young women were marginalised from the liberation struggle during these years and increasingly confined to the home.[4] Where girls do appear in either public or academic narratives of the period they are generally painted as peripheral participants, silent bystanders, or victims of male-instigated violence.[5] Despite repeated evidence that African girls and young women were involved in the key moments in South Africa's liberation struggle – the 1976 Soweto Uprisings, the township revolt of the 1980s, and the transition conflict of the early 1990s – we are rarely given insight into their lives or perspectives and almost never hear their voices. Stock depictions of black girls as peripheral victims are not limited to South African history but are symptomatic of much of African and Global history. Due to their triple marginalisation on account of their age, gender, and race, black girls have been excluded from centres of power and silenced in practices of record keeping, leaving persistent paucities in our historical understandings of race, youth, and gender.[6] Following a new trend in the historiography to try to counter such marginalisation, this book asks: where were the girls and young women?[7]

Young Women against Apartheid tells the stories of a group of girls and young women who came of age during the final years of South Africa's liberation struggle. This book is about what life was like for African girls under apartheid, why some chose to join the liberation struggle, and how they navigated the benefits and pitfalls political activism posed to young people during

---

[4] Jeremy Seekings, 'Gender Ideology and Township Politics in the 1980's,' *Agenda* 10 (1991): 77.

[5] See Jeremy Seekings, *Heroes or Villains? Youth Politics in the 1980s* (Johannesburg: Raven Press, 1993); Clive Glaser, *Bo-Tsotsi: The Youth Gangs of Soweto, 1935–1976* (Oxford: James Currey, 2000).

[6] Mary Jo Maynes, 'Age as a Category of Historical Analysis: History, Agency, and Narratives of Childhood,' *The Journal of the History of Childhood and Youth* 1:1 (2008): 115.

[7] Abosede George, *Making Modern Girls: A History of Girlhood, Labor, and Social Development in Colonial Lagos* (Athens: Ohio University Press, 2014), 17; Carolyn Nordstrom, *Girls and Warzones: Troubling Questions* (Uppsala: Life and Peace Institute, 1997), 10.

these years. These were young women who, as teenagers and secondary school students, made an unconventional choice to join student organisations, engage in public protest, and take up arms against the state and its allies. They often did so against their parents' wishes and in contravention of societal norms that confined girls to the home and made township streets dangerous places for female students. They describe themselves as active, politically curious 'tomboys' who wanted to participate in the struggle alongside young men rather than separately from them. Having eschewed women's organisations in favour of student ones, they identified as 'comrades' more so than as girls or women and did not organise specifically around gender issues. They participated in both non-violent and violent forms of political action, including attending marches and rallies, throwing stones or petrol bombs at police vehicles or homes, punishing suspected informers and other offenders, and even joining underground guerrilla armies. Rather than shying away from violence, they actively participated in political confrontations with security forces, local councillors, and township residents suspected of collaborating with the state or jeopardising the struggle. Thousands of these young women were eventually detained by the state, and in police and prison cells across the country were subjected to solitary confinement, beatings, interrogation, and torture. At the heart of this monograph lies the life histories of these female comrades themselves, who are now in their forties and fifties. In interviews, these women repudiate any notion of themselves as powerless or marginalised, instead constructing themselves as decisive actors in South Africa's liberation struggle.

But this book seeks to do much more than simply address the silences and gaps in South African historiography. As Belinda Bozzoli writes of her own work with women's testimonies, 'this book will have failed…if it is read as yet another contribution to the detailed understanding of "what happened".'[8] Primarily a work of oral history, this book is not only concerned with what female comrades did, but equally with how these now middle-aged women reflect on and recall their time as activists: how they reconstruct their pasts; relate their personal experiences to collective histories of the struggle; and insert themselves into a historical narrative from which they have been excluded. Within these women's narratives are details and perspectives central to key topics in South African history and debates in the country today, including gender inequality and sexual violence, the history of the liberation struggle and the role of political violence within it, and connections between the past and the present. By listening to and analysing these women's narratives, we

---

[8]   Belinda Bozzoli with Mmantho Nkotsoe, *The Women of Phokeng: Consciousness, Life Strategy and Migrancy in South Africa, 1900–1983* (London: James Currey, 1991), 7.

can challenge conventional historiography and foster a better understanding of why young people joined the struggle, why and how they decided to employ political violence, and how they managed their overlapping and at times conflicting identities as activists, children, students, friends, and workers. The history of female comrades thus offers new perspectives on and contributes to recent debates and developments in wider histories of South Africa's liberation struggle, social histories of gender and generation in the townships, and cultural histories of memory and violence.

South Africa's Liberation Struggle

Today, South Africa's liberation struggle is mythologised and celebrated by national leaders, international audiences, and the country's heritage industry. The ANC was just one of multiple (and at times competing) organisations involved in the struggle against apartheid. But over its long period in government since 1994, it has entrenched narratives of its predominance and continues to draw strength from its historical role in the struggle.[9] Yet this is a history that remains heatedly contested and marked by persistent silences. The dominant narrative of the country's past is a romantic and triumphant account of good versus evil, of the 'masses' struggling against the 'system'. But this history promotes simplified, teleological accounts of the struggle against apartheid at the expense of highlighting the complexities and fissures of the liberation movement. It has also created a 'resistance paradigm' which privileges histories of protest and dissent over those of quiescence or collaboration. As Jacob Dlamini argues, 'this master narrative would have us believe that black South Africans, who populate struggle jargon mostly as faceless "masses of our people", experienced apartheid the same way, suffered the same way and fought the same way against apartheid. That is untrue.'[10]

Despite the nearly three decades that have passed since the end of apartheid, and vested interested by academics, politicians and the general population in the country's past, large gaps remain in our understanding of the liberation struggle. Early work produced by social historians within the country during the 1980s and early 1990s did much to uncover resistance 'from below' engaged in and organised by people within the townships.[11] There was a 'clear emanci-

---

[9]   Chris Saunders, 'Liberation Struggles in Southern Africa: New Perspectives,' *South African Historical Journal* 62:1 (2010): 5.

[10]   Jacob Dlamini, *Native Nostalgia* (Johannesburg: Jacana, 2009), 18.

[11]   Jeremy Seekings, 'Quiescence and the Transition to Confrontation: South African Townships, 1978–1984' (DPhil thesis, University of Oxford, 1990); Tom Lodge and Bill Nasson, *All Here and Now: Black Politics in South Africa in the*

pationist agenda' behind much of this work, as scholars sought to counter state portrayals of activists as either criminal, anarchic, and violent or as puppets of an ANC-lead conspiracy.[12] These scholars critically enquired into a wide range of structural, demographic and educational factors that helped to explain the new upsurge in youth radicalism. Yet, as Jeremy Seekings admits, their work was 'somewhat sanitised' and tended to gloss over internal conflicts within the struggle and the involvement of young activists in various forms of violence.[13] Like the dominant narrative of the country's past, this research also priori-tised protest over inaction and contributed to the resistance paradigm through which histories of the later apartheid years are still often viewed. The 2000s witnessed renewed interest in struggle histories, marked by the publication of the state-sponsored, seven-volume *The Road to Democracy in South Africa*.[14] While this helped to fill many empirical gaps in historical knowledge, the series largely focused on decision-making, ideology, and (predominantly male) leadership – taking a very different approach from the social history writing of the 1980s and 1990s. The series tended to place the ANC at the centre of events, and prioritised histories of exile, armed struggle, and elites above those of localised activists and protestors within the country.

This book is part of a recent move away from either romanticised, trium-phant narratives of the past or top–down histories of ideology and leadership. Dismantling these narratives, historians have recently demonstrated the muta-bility of the categories of 'resistor' and 'collaborator', highlighted the liberation movement's lack of any coherent strategy or omnipresent leadership, and explored struggle history beyond the confines of the ANC and its affiliates.[15]

1980s (London: C. Hurst and Company, 1992); Colin Bundy, 'Street Sociology and Pavement Politics: Aspects of Youth and Student Resistance in Cape Town, 1985,' *Journal of Southern African Studies* 13:3 (1987): 303–330; Charles Carter, 'Comrades and Community: Politics and the Construction of Hegemony in Al-exandra Township, South Africa, 1984–1987,' (DPhil thesis, Oxford University, 1991); Ineke van Kessell, *'Beyond our Wildest Dreams': The United Democratic Front and the Transformation of South Africa* (Charlottesville: University Press of Virginia, 2000); Jonathan Hyslop, *The Classroom Struggle: Policy and Resistance in South Africa 1940–1990* (Pietermaritzburg: University of Natal Press, 1999).

12 Sapire, 'Township Histories,' 186.

13 Jeremy Seekings, 'Whose Voices? Politics and Methodology in the Study of Polit-ical Organisation and Protest in the Final Phase of the "Struggle" in South Africa,' *South African Historical Journal* 62:1 (2010): 13.

14 SADET, *The Road to Democracy in South Africa*, Volumes 1–7 (Johannesburg: Unisa Press, 2005–2017).

15 Key works in these recent developments include Jacob Dlamini, *Askari: A Story of Collaboration and Betrayal in the Anti-Apartheid Struggle* (New York: Oxford University Press, 2015); Hilary Sapire and Chris Saunders (eds), *Southern African*

There is now an increasing awareness amongst historians that 'apartheid did not always produce resistance, and that resistance was not always occasioned by apartheid.'[16] Scholarship is turning away from organisational histories towards histories of local, everyday resistance by ordinary South Africans, exploring the meanings of and motivations for protest and violence.[17] Other historians are shifting their attention towards quiescence, exploring the lives of those who chose not to engage in the struggle.[18] Yet we still know too little about the lives people led and the choices they made during these years – about how ordinary men, women, and children coped with the increasing violence in their communities and decided whether or not to participate in protests, throw stones, or seek out and join political organisations.

Young Women against Apartheid contributes to this trend by arguing for the need to step beyond a strict resistance paradigm, and to view social histories of township life and histories of the liberation struggle within a single frame. By doing so, we can understand how experiences beyond the struggle moulded people's pathways to activism and shaped the roles they took on within the struggle. Previous histories of the township uprisings have at times been so preoccupied with political resistance that they have tended to 'neglect other forms of consciousness and culture resulting in a distorted and one-sided view of the township and the people who inhabited them.'[19] Early histories of the 1980s township uprisings and young people's roles within them often conformed to these critiques. They explained the rise of the comrades through structural factors or a political economy approach, arguing that this new demographic of young activists emerged due to the contracting economy, rising inflation, and mass expansion of secondary schooling.[20] In doing so, they were

---

Liberation Struggles: New Local, Regional and Global Perspectives (Claremont, South Africa: UCT Press, 2013); Thula Simpson, *Umkhonto we Sizwe: The ANC's Armed Struggle* (Cape Town: Penguin Books, 2016).

[16] Gary Minkley and Ciraj Rassool, 'Orality, Memory, and Social History in South Africa,' in Sarah Nuttall and Carli Coetzee (eds), *Negotiating the Past: The Making of Memory in South Africa* (Oxford: Oxford University Press, 1998), 94.

[17] Franziska Rueedi, '"Siyayinyova!": Patterns of Violence in the African Townships of the Vaal Triangle, South Africa, 1980–86,' *Africa* 85:3 (2015): 395–416; Belinda Bozzoli, *Theatres of Struggles and the End of Apartheid* (Athens, Ohio: Ohio University Press, 2004).

[18] Dlamini, *Native Nostalgia*; Rebekah Lee, *African Women and Apartheid: Migration and Settlement in Urban South Africa* (London: IB Tauris, 2009); Clive Glaser, 'Soweto's Islands of Learning: Morris Isaacson and Orlando High Schools under Bantu Education, 1958–1975,' *Journal of Southern African Studies* 41:1 (2015): 159–171.

[19] Sapire, 'Township Histories,' 169.

[20] Bundy, 'Street Sociology and Pavement Politics'; Shaun Johnson, '"The Soldiers of Luthuli": Youth in the Politics of Resistance in South Africa,' in Shaun Johnson

criticised for portraying the comrades as a 'monolithic bloc', and failing to see the differences occasioned by class, race, level of education, or organisational affiliation.[21] The complexities of children and youths' lives were often neglected in these accounts, as they were seen simply as activists or students, rather than as children, siblings, friends, or workers. There was little understanding of comrades' lives beyond their involvement in resistance, with few attempts to join together discussions of youth politics with broader works on childhood, juvenile delinquency, and generational divides.[22] This historiographical approach also led to the complete neglect of female comrades; without attention to the individual lives and trajectories of activists, it was assumed that all young resistors were male. Joining the struggle and participating in political violence was largely seen as a means of proving one's masculinity or gaining status in society. Descriptions of the comrades as 'hard, ruthless and disciplined with no time to rest and no time for pleasure, as living under the constant threat of death, and prepared to sacrifice their very lives for the struggle,' conjured up images of young men that did not sit easily alongside dominant images of girls as passive victims of violence or bystanders confined to the home.[23]

But when girls and young women who did join the struggle are examined more closely, we can gain a better understanding of why young people chose to participate in the liberation movement, and what exactly it was that they were resisting. As Frederick Cooper contends, 'resistance' against colonial rule is often taken as unproblematic in African history, when in reality 'what is being resisted is not always clear.' Under the resistance framework that developed in African history during the 1970s and 1980s, conflicts within colonised populations – over age, gender, and class – were 'sanitised'.[24] This paradigm thus blinded historians to 'the tangled layers of political relations

(ed), *South Africa: No Turning Back* (Bloomington and Indianapolis: Indiana University Press, 1989), 94–152.

21   Kumi Naidoo, 'The Politics of Youth Resistance in the 1980s: The Dilemmas of a Differentiated Durban,' *Journal of Southern African Studies* 18:1 (1992): 145. For further critiques of Bundy's work see Seekings, *Heroes or Villains*; Ari Sitas, 'The Making of the "Comrades" Movement in Natal, 1985–91,' *Journal of Southern African Studies* 18:3 (1992): 629–41.

22   One exception to this is Marks' work, which does discuss the family lives and backgrounds of young activists. Monique Marks, *Young Warriors: Youth Politics, Identity and Violence in South Africa* (Johannesburg: Witwatersrand University Press, 2001); see also Clive Glaser, 'Youth and Generation in South African History,' *Safundi* 19:2 (2018): 117–138.

23   Catherine Campbell, 'Learning to Kill? Masculinity, the Family and Violence in Natal,' *Journal of Southern African Studies* 18:3 (1992): 624.

24   Frederick Cooper, 'Conflict and Connection: Rethinking Colonial African History,' *The American Historical Review* 99:5 (1994): 1532–1533.

which animate social protest.'[25] In South Africa, scholars have often created a sharp distinction between women organising against national oppression and those campaigning against gender oppression, seeing the two struggles as competing forces. Yet as Shireen Hassim argues, this differentiation obscures the interconnected experiences that motivate women's political action, and 'does not allow us to understand the complex processes by which gender consciousness emerges in situations where there are sharp inequalities of race and class as well as gender.'[26] Hassim and her colleagues demonstrate how, in joining the broader nationalist struggle, women shared many political interests with men. However, they still acted as gendered beings, and their positions and responsibilities within the household and community still shaped their demands and actions.[27] This book develops this argument further and argues for the need to take both gender and generation into account when examining women's political action.

South Africa's female comrades joined the liberation struggle as a means of addressing the multiple injustices they faced, not just on account of race and class but also their gender and generation. Distinctly gendered inequalities intersected with other societal cleavages and the broader goals of liberation to motivate their involvement in the struggle, as their adolescent experiences of inferiority and victimisation shaped how and why they engaged in collective action. Their activism and political violence were not only used to rebel against the apartheid state, but also to resist the confines placed on African girls' behaviour, contest gendered township geographies that confined girls to the home, and fight against their subordination and maltreatment. By stepping beyond the resistance paradigm, we can see how the gendered and generational power relations that shaped girls' lives are central to understanding why young women joined the struggle, the roles they played, and the meanings they attach to their former activism in the present.

Furthermore, female comrades were not only activists, but also students, workers, friends, sisters, daughters, and mothers. These different identities combined and clashed to motivate and complicate young women's involvement in the liberation struggle. Previous histories of women's resistance in South Africa have tended to focus on women's organised, structured opposition to

[25] Lynn M. Thomas, "'Ngaitana (I will circumcise myself)": The Gender and Generational Politics of the 1956 Ban on Clitoridectomy in Meru, Kenya,' *Gender & History* 8:3 (1996): 341.

[26] Shireen Hassim, *Women's Organizations and Democracy in South Africa: Contesting Authority* (Madison: University of Wisconsin Press, 2006), 34–35.

[27] Jo Beall, Shireen Hassim and Alison Todes, "'A Bit on the Side"?: Gender Struggles in the Politics of Transformation in South Africa,' *Feminist Review* 33 (1989): 33–47.

the apartheid state or the denial of women's rights. In doing so, this work has neglected how everyday realities and identities shape women's political activities. But as Nthabiseng Motsemme writes, 'if we are to fully grapple with the politicization and responses of ordinary township women, we have to look to everyday life, practices and daily encounters with apartheid to formulate a fuller picture.'[28] This book thus focuses on less organised and more dispersed forms of resistance that often occurred beyond organisational structures or control. It combines socio-cultural histories of township life with histories of the liberation struggle, seeing the two as inseparable in explaining how and why South Africans took to the streets or picked up arms during the late-apartheid period. It seeks to shed light on what township life was like for African girls, the multiple problems they faced, and the different coping strategies they developed to address their overlapping inequalities. This approach helps to open up liberation histories beyond their conventional focus on organisations, leadership, and strategy, and offers a better understanding of meanings of and motivations for the everyday resistance of ordinary South Africans.

Gender and Generation in South African History

Focusing on gender and generation within the liberation struggle, this book asks how being young, black, and female shaped one's experience of living under and resisting apartheid. Over recent decades, historians have elucidated much about both African women and youths during apartheid, two groups neglected in the country's early historiography, which tended to focus on race and class rather than gender and generation. Women's history took hold in South Africa later than elsewhere in the world. Due to the endurance of apartheid and lack of a significant feminist movement in the country, it was not until the late 1970s that efforts were first made to detail the history of women's roles and organisations within the liberation movement.[29] A generation of gender historians followed in the 1980s and 1990s who made the important argument that due to their subordinate legal status and position within the home and family, African women experienced apartheid differently from men, and thus responded to it or rebelled against it for different reasons

---

28   Nthabiseng Motsemme, 'The Mute Always Speak: On Women's Silences at the Truth and Reconciliation Commission,' *Current Sociology* 52:5 (2004): 919.

29   Cherryl Walker, *Women and Resistance in South Africa* (London: Onyx Press, 1982); Belinda Bozzoli, 'Marxism, Feminism and South African Studies,' *Journal of Southern African Studies* 9:2 (1983): 139–171; Julia C. Wells, 'The History of Black Women's Struggle against Pass Laws in South Africa, 1900–1960,' (PhD thesis, Columbia University, 1982).

and through different means.[30] Histories of women's resistance against pass laws or beer halls and their navigation of urbanisation have provided us with rich insight into the gendering of survival or resistance strategies during the segregationist and apartheid periods, and the complex space between victim-hood and agency that women occupied.[31]

But persistent gaps in this history remain. Few historians have placed women into historical narratives beyond the 1960s. In particular, women and girls' involvement in the 1976 Soweto Uprisings and township conflicts of the 1980s remain largely ignored.[32] Monograph-length works on women's involvement in the liberation struggle have tended to focus on key women's organisations and their ideologies or strategies, rather than on 'ordinary' women in the townships who had weaker organisational ties or who were drawn to the struggle for reasons other than supporting the women's move-ment.[33] Further, women's involvement in the struggle has predominantly been seen as an extension of their roles as mothers and wives, with their political agency most frequently 'couched in the presiding ideology of motherhood.'[34] We thus have little knowledge of women who did not join the struggle as women or mothers primarily, but rather as students, trade unionists, or soldiers. Such an overwhelming focus on motherhood as wom-en's main public political identity has also obscured the histories of younger

---

30 Beall et al, 'A Bit on the Side,' 30–56.
31 Philip Bonner, "'Desirable or Undesirable Basotho Women?" Liquor, Prostitution and the Migration of Basotho Women to the Rand, 1920–1945,' in Cherryl Walker (ed), *Women and Gender in Southern Africa to 1945* (London: James Currey, 1990), 221–250; Helen Bradford, "'We are now the men": Women's Beer Protests in the Natal Countryside, 1929,' in Belinda Bozzoli (ed), *Class, Community and Conflict: South African Perspectives* (Johannesburg: Ravan Press, 1987), 292–323; Anne Mager and Gary Minkley, 'Reaping the Whirlwind: The East London Riots of 1952,' in Philip Bonner, Peter Delius and Deborah Posel (eds), *Apartheid's Genesis: 1935–1962* (Johannesburg: Witwatersrand University Press, 1993), 229–251; Bo-zzoli, *Women of Phokeng*; Lee, *African Women and Apartheid.*
32 Important exceptions to this include Debby Bonnin, 'Claiming Spaces, Chang-ing Places: Political Violence and Women's Protests in KwaZulu-Natal,' *Journal of Southern African Studies* 26:2 (2000): 301–316; Janet Cherry, "'We were not afraid": The Role of Women in the 1980s Township Uprising in the Eastern Cape,' in Nomboniso Gasa (ed), *Women in South African History: They remove boulders and cross rivers* (Cape Town: HSRC Press, 2007).
33 Walker, *Women and Resistance*; Hassim, *Women's Organizations and Democracy in South Africa*. A recent exception to this is Leslie Hadfield, *Liberation and Devel-opment: Black Consciousness Community Programs in South Africa* (East Lansing: Michigan State University Press, 2016).
34 Anne McClintock, "'No Longer in Future Heaven": Women and Nationalism in South Africa,' *Transition* 51 (1991): 116.

women who did not yet occupy societal positions as mothers or wives, and histories of women's involvement in political violence, as images of women as combatants do not always sit easily alongside societal expectations of their mothering roles.[35]

Histories of childhood and youth too have been slower to develop in South Africa than elsewhere on the continent. Over recent decades, historical explorations of childhood and youth have burgeoned in response to new conceptualisations of these age categories as culturally and historically specific, defined more by social, cultural, and political traits rather than by strict biological age. From the 1990s, a rich body of literature on generational conflict, child labour, and youth cultures emerged in Africa, spurred by concerns over shifting demographics and the increasing precariousness of conventional transitions from childhood to adulthood based on wage labour, marriage, and establishing an independent household.[36] But such studies were more limited in South Africa, where the main focus due to the rise of the comrades in the 1980s was on youth as political actors. Outside of the resistance paradigm, little was written on 'ordinary' or non-politicised young people in the country.[37] When scholars, journalists, and humanitarian workers increasingly turned their attention to children and youth in the 1990s, they viewed them as objects of concern, afraid that prolonged violence and disrupted education had produced a 'lost generation'.[38] With the exception of Clive Glaser's work on youth gangs and Anne Mager's on rural youth socialisation, little historical work was produced on youth as anything other

---

[35] The key exception to this is Jacklyn Cock, *Colonels and Cadres: War and Gender in South Africa* (Cape Town: Oxford University Press, 1991).

[36] Alcinda Honwana and Filip de Boeck (eds), *Makers & Breakers: Children and Youth in Postcolonial Africa* (Oxford: James Currey, 2005); Richard Waller, 'Rebellious Youth in Colonial Africa,' *The Journal of African History* 47:1 (2006): 77–92; Lynn M. Thomas, *Politics of the Womb: Women, Reproduction, and the State in Kenya* (Berkeley: University of California Press, 2003); Andrew Burton and Helene Charton-Bigot (eds), *Generations Past: Youth in East African History* (Athens: Ohio University Press, 2010); Paul Ocobock, *An Uncertain Age: The Politics of Manhood in Kenya* (Athens: Ohio University Press, 2017).

[37] Jeremy Seekings, 'Beyond Heroes and Villains: The Rediscovery of the Ordinary in the Study of Childhood and Adolescence in South Africa,' *Social Dynamics* 32:1 (2006): 1–20.

[38] Sandra Burman and Pamela Reynolds (eds), *Growing Up in a Divided Society: The Contexts of Childhood in South Africa* (Johannesburg: Ravan Press, 1986); Jeremy Seekings, 'The "Lost Generation": South Africa's "Youth Problem" in the Early 1990s,' *Transformation* 29 (1996): 103–125; Gill Straker, *Faces in the Revolution: The Psychological Effects of Violence on Township Youth in South Africa* (Cape Town: David Philip, 1992).

than activists or victims, leaving their other identities as students, children, siblings, workers, or parents unexplored.[39]

Yet a larger, more pressing gap in our historical understanding exists at the intersection of these two bodies of historiography. African girls have been persistently excluded from both categories, conforming to neither the focus on motherhood that pervades women's history, nor the masculine images of activists, delinquents, and gangsters that characterise histories of childhood and youth. Girlhood is currently a budding and promising field of historical inquiry yet has been particularly slow to develop in South Africa. Scholars across the globe are seeking to locate girls' voices in a creative range of sources, as girls are typically absent from conventional historical records. In Africa, as Abosede George argues, 'girls have been doubly marginalized as subjects of historical inquiry' on account of their race and gender.[40] Existing works on South African girlhood have predominantly focused either on the pre-1948 segregationist period, or on contemporary issues sparked by post-1994 HIV/AIDS prevalence.[41] Social histories of township life during apartheid have thus far excluded African girls. Works on youth and generation in the townships have been male-centric, exploring how young people navigated everyday life under apartheid exclusively through the prism of male experience. In more specific accounts of the 1980s girls are also largely absent. Where they do appear, they do so through stock depictions as victims of male-instigated violence or marginalised bystanders, confined to the private sphere. These

[39] Glaser, *Bo-Tsotsi*; Anne Mager, *Gender and the Making of a South African Bantustan: A Social History of the Ciskei* (Portsmouth, NH: Heinemann, 1999).

[40] George, *Making Modern Girls*, 14.

[41] Sarah Emily Duff, *Changing Childhoods in the Cape Colony: Dutch Reformed Church Evangelicalism and Colonial Childhood, 1860–1895* (Basingstoke: Palgrave Macmillan, 2015); Deborah Gaitskell, '"Christian Compounds for Girls": Church Hostels for African Women in Johannesburg, 1907–1970,' *Journal of Southern African Studies* 6:1 (1979): 44–69; Meghan Healy-Clancy, *A World of Their Own: A History of South African Women's Education* (Charlottesville: University of Virginia Press, 2013); Lynn M. Thomas, 'The Modern Girl and Racial Respectability in 1930s South Africa,' *The Journal of African History* 47:3 (2006): 461–490; Rachel Johnson, '"The Girl About Town": Discussions of Modernity and Female Youth in Drum Magazine, 1951–1970,' *Social Dynamics* 35:1 (2009): 36–50; Deevia Bhana, '"Girls are not free" – In and Out of the South African School,' *International Journal of Educational Development* 32:2 (2012): 352–358; Rachel Jewkes and Robert Morrell, 'Sexuality and the Limits of Agency among South African Teenage Women: Theorising Femininities and Their Connections to HIV Risk Practises,' *Social Science & Medicine* 74:11 (2012): 1729–1737; Relebohile Moletsane, 'South African Girlhood in the Age of AIDS: Towards Girlhood Studies?' *Agenda* 21:7 (2007): 155–165.

tropes obscure the complexities not only of girls and young women's lives, but also of township politics and gender ideologies on a much wider scale. Seeing girls only as victims ignores how they developed a wide variety of strategies – ranging from acquiescence to manipulation to outright resistance – to cope with the daily injustices they faced living under apartheid. While this book offers the first detailed exploration of African girlhood during apartheid, it focuses on girls and young women who made the unconventional decision to join the liberation struggle, through COSAS or other ANC-aligned student and youth groups, as a means of addressing multiple grievances, not all of which were explicitly political or directed at the state. In doing so, it does not deny that many girls in the townships chose alternative paths, avoiding political conflict at all costs, focusing on their education and future careers, pursuing other leisure activities, or performing caring duties in the home.

This book demonstrates how the liberation struggle, despite being a male-dominated arena, could provide girls and young women with a sense of accomplishment, agency, and empowerment. Such feelings were difficult for African girls to otherwise attain in a patriarchal society in which they were largely confined to the private sphere, seen as the inferior sex, and rendered highly susceptible to sexual violence. The struggle opened new spaces in which girls could challenge their subordination and enjoy themselves through collective action. Previous literature on the comrades has identified a particular 'struggle masculinity' espoused by young male activists in the 1980s and 1990s, characterised by political militancy and an anti-authority stance. 'During those days,' writes Thokozani Xaba, 'being a "comrade" endowed a young man with social respect and status within his community. Being referred to as a "young lion" and a "liberator" was an intoxicating and psychologically satiating accolade.'[42] Yet no comparative theorisations have been made about new femininities emerging amongst young female activists at this time. This book argues that just as the struggle offered young men a means of asserting their masculinity, so too did it offer young women a channel through which they could challenge hegemonic or emphasised femininities and construct an oppositional, militarised femininity that defied social expectations and limitations of girlhood. This oppositional gender identity, which I term 'struggle femininity', was characterised by many of the same characteristics as 'struggle masculinity', including a public performance of bravery, aggression, and the willingness to use violence or die for the struggle. Yet it was also

---

[42]   Thokozani Xaba, 'Masculinity and its Malcontents: The Confrontation between "Struggle Masculinity" and "Post-Struggle Masculinity" (1990–1997),' in Robert Morrell (ed), Changing *Men in Southern Africa* (Scotsville: University of Natal Press, 2001), 108.

marked by female comrades' flouting of parental concerns, challenging of the normalisation of sexual violence, and their purposeful and effective defiance of political, social, and cultural constraints on girls' behaviour. These young activists emphasised their rejection of both traditional, conservative femininities that confined girls to the private sphere and more 'modern' femininities associated with consumerism, dating, and beauty pageants. They wore trousers instead of skirts or dresses, kept predominantly male company, and engaged in collective action and political violence in male-dominated public spaces. Through such actions, they gained a sense of agency in their relationships with men, parents, and the apartheid state, and achieved greater freedom of movement and expression than was typical for young women in South Africa's townships at the time. Yet performing this new heroic role brought difficulties and challenges too, as young women struggled to balance being a 'good' activist and a 'good' daughter, faced stigma from their communities, and left themselves little room to express or display vulnerability.

Memory and Oral History

In constructing this history, this book draws predominantly on oral history interviews with both male and female former comrades. Written sources on the comrades are scarce. Following the banning of COSAS in August 1985, the organisation was forced to operate underground, and thus committed very little to paper. Documents confiscated by the security forces may likely have been destroyed as part of the National Party's purge of its archives in the lead up to the 1994 elections.[43] A few pamphlets and documents from student and youth organisations are available at Historical Papers at the University of Witwatersrand and the South African History Archive. Although scant, these are triangulated with oral history interviews and media reports throughout this book to allow for an analysis of the tensions between COSAS policy and practice, public discourses of gender equality and private practices of sexism, and narratives recorded in the 1980s and those told thirty years after comrades' involvement in the struggle.

Due to the scarcity of documentary sources from this period, most of the previous work on the township uprisings has similarly relied on oral sources. The earliest works in this field were based on interviews with almost exclusively male activists conducted while the struggle was still ongoing; interviews which were often not recorded or transcribed in full due to

---

[43] Verne Harris, "'They Should Have Destroyed More'": The Destruction of Public Records by the South African State in the Final Years of Apartheid, 1990–94,' *Transformation* 42 (2000): 29–56.

security concerns. Such methodological challenges led scholars at times to take an uncritical approach to oral history. This was a time of exciting new developments within the field as oral historians in Europe and South Africa pioneered new ways of interpreting memory and oral traditions.[44] Yet academics investigating township politics tended to take male activists' narratives as fact with little analysis of why these young men might narrate their political involvement in particular ways.[45] Despite most scholars' reliance on oral sources, memory itself was rarely taken seriously as a theoretical concept in initial works on the township uprisings. Interviews were used as a supplement to fill the archive's gaps and access history 'from below', and thus became 'a source, not a complex of historical narratives whose form is not fixed.'[46]

Yet when oral history is used simply as evidence from which to pick facts like 'currants from a cake', one misses the methodology's greatest strength: the value of the subjective.[47] Rather than seeing oral sources as literal recollections of the past, this book values them for the unique insight into the subjective meaning of history they provide: what is remembered, by whom, and, most importantly, why. It is less interested in historical 'truth' than it is in misremembering, embellishment, secrets, or lies. As Alessandro Portelli writes, 'Oral history approaches truth as much when it departs from "facts" as when it records them carefully, because the errors and even the lies reveal, under scrutiny, the creative processes of memory, imagination, symbolism and interpretation that endow events with cultural significance.'[48] Oral history cannot provide us with direct access to the past lives, experiences, or emotional states of South Africa's comrades. Yet it can illuminate how these

[44] For excellent South African works of oral history from these years see Bozzoli, *Women of Phokeng*; and Isabel Hofmeyr, *'We spend our years as a tale that is told': Oral Historical Narrative in a South African Chiefdom* (Portsmouth: Heinemann, 1994). For key international works of oral history see Alessandro Portelli, *The Death of Luigi Trastulli and Other Stories: Form and Meaning in Oral History* (New York: State University of New York Press, 1991); Luisa Passerini, *Fascism in Popular Memory: The Cultural Experience of the Turin Working Class* (Cambridge: Cambridge University Press, 1987); Alistair Thomson, *Anzac Memories: Living with the Legend* (Clayton: Monash University Press, 1994); Paul Thompson, *The Voice of the Past: Oral History* (Oxford: Oxford University Press, 1978).

[45] Seekings, *Heroes or Villains*; Carter, 'Comrades and Community'.

[46] Minkley and Rassool, 'Orality, Memory, and Social History,' 91; 99.

[47] Elizabeth Tonkin, *Narrating Our Pasts: The Social Construction of Oral History* (Cambridge: Cambridge University Press, 1992), 6.

[48] Alessandro Portelli, *The Text and the Voice: Writing, Speaking, and Democracy in American Literature* (New York: Columbia University Press, 1994), 53.

activists see themselves today, how they wish to be seen, and how they situate their involvement in the struggle within wider socio-political contexts
and collective memories of the liberation movement.

Both male and female interviewees were generally enthusiastic in retelling their pasts. This book has benefitted greatly from their interest in this
project and their passion for having their stories told – without their collaboration it would not have been possible. Women in particular demonstrated
a belief that they played an important role in South Africa's history which
needed to be shared, and this shaped the type of narratives they constructed.
Like Bozzoli's women from Phokeng, they 'construct the past in ways that
place them at the centre of important events and convey to us what they
think is important about their lives', whether this be their bravery, trauma, or
resilience.[49] On the whole, the stories they tell are ones that emphasise their
agency and empowerment. The emotional qualities of their narratives, in
which women laugh, shout, and tell animated, enthusiastic stories, reveal the
seductive feelings of camaraderie, agency, and pride that engagement in the
liberation struggle could bring for young women. Their narratives suggest
that they remain nostalgic for their time as activists and continue to identify
as 'comrades' today as a means of holding on to the feelings of potency that
their involvement in the struggle gave them.

However, these romanticised narratives of young women's liberation need
to be examined more closely for which aspects of the struggle they emphasise
and which they silence or conceal. For the empowerment girls gained through
their activism was (and still is) fragile, and consistently challenged by some male
comrades' derogatory attitudes, women's continued experiences of violence, and
post-apartheid history-making which has erased these women's experiences
from dominant narratives of the liberation movement. By casting themselves as
heroes of the liberation struggle, female comrades seek to make their empowerment lasting rather than transitory, and to hide or shield from view their
post-apartheid disempowerment and disappointments. When analysed more
closely, their narratives also reveal the lingering difficulties former activists or
combatants face in post-apartheid South Africa and provide evidence of a more
conflicted relationship between the past and the present for these women. An
exploration of these oral histories thus offers scholars far more than a new,
untold perspective on South Africa's past; it also complicates existing historical
narratives, projecting a more challenging and nuanced account of what it was
like to participate in the struggle and live with the consequences of this in its
aftermath, and offering a messier, more ambiguous depiction of the past.

---

[49] Bozzoli, *Women of Phokeng*, 11.

While conducting this research, I sought to interview anyone who had been a member of student or youth organisations in Soweto during the 1980s and early 1990s. Over the course of three years, from 2014 to 2016, I formally interviewed forty-nine people: twenty-eight female comrades; twenty male comrades; and one woman who grew up in Soweto during the 1980s but did not join the struggle. Initial contact was made through one male interviewee, Makgane, who was a COSAS leader in the 1980s and had been involved in Monique Marks' research in the early 1990s.[50] I first met Makgane at a fortuitous moment in 2013, when he and some of his former associates were involved in the Each One Teach One Foundation, an organisation of former COSAS members from Soweto founded in 2012, which works to preserve and promote their contributions to the struggle and further the goals of the Freedom Charter.[51] The foundation and I thus shared a similar desire to record and publicise the history of Soweto's comrades. Makgane and his associates agreed to provide me with names and phone numbers of their former fellow activists. I got the sense that these initial contacts did much more than help with logistics; they also acted as key gatekeepers to their communities and social networks. After meeting with me and vetting me they seemed to communicate their approval to their friends and comrades and encourage them to speak to me. However, in these interactions, which I did not see or hear, I also got the feeling that these former male leaders were providing some instructions to other comrades about what to say and not to say in their interviews. However, I was largely allowed to pursue my research uninhibited by the Foundation's members. Several of the former comrades I met and interviewed later played key roles in this research: Lucy helped to organise interviews with female comrades; Florence served as a research assistant for a couple of months, accompanying me on interviews, guiding me around Soweto and helping with translation when needed; and Musa introduced me to many comrades, and also acted as a key local guide.

Although this book is primarily about female comrades, I also wanted to interview former male comrades to understand how these two groups interacted, and to analyse the similarities and differences between their accounts. Both groups were first interviewed using a life history approach, before being asked more specific questions relating to gender and the involvement of female comrades in the liberation movement. As the following chapters will demonstrate, the agency female comrades accorded to themselves in their narratives did not always align with how men described the roles they played (or supposedly did not play) during the struggle. I met with many of these comrades

[50]   Marks, Young Warriors.
[51]   Each One Teach One Foundation, <http://www.eotof.org.za/> [accessed 2 April 2014].

more than once while conducting the research for this book, often speaking with their families too, and towards the end of the research conducted group interviews with activists who had gone to the same schools or lived in the same neighbourhoods. Most interviews were conducted in former comrades' own homes in Soweto – sometimes the same multi-generational houses they had lived in as young activists. Others were held at people's workplaces or occasionally in malls and cafes. All interviewees were offered the choice to remain anonymous in this research. However, the majority wanted their names used in order to have their stories acknowledged. As a compromise between protecting their identities and abiding by their wishes, only their first names, or in some cases preferred nicknames, have been used here, and some other identifying details have been removed. Two female interviewees did wish to be anonymised, and they have been given pseudonyms.[52]

The oldest interviewee was born in 1963 and the youngest in 1976, with the majority being born between 1967 and 1972. All interviewees were secondary school students in their teens when they joined the liberation movement – ranging in age from twelve to nineteen when they became involved in township politics. They were all participants in Congress-aligned student or youth organisations and saw the ANC as their parent organisation within the wider liberation struggle. At the time of interviews, they all remained deeply loyal to the ANC, with many still participating in local politics. This group of activists come from a range of economic backgrounds, from more impoverished to emerging middle-class. During the 1980s, many of their parents were factory workers, shop workers, or domestic servants. All lived in Soweto for at least part of their teenage years, and the majority were born there and still reside there today. A large percentage of these interviewees were from Diepkloof, located on the north-eastern edge of Soweto.[53] But interviewees were also drawn from Orlando East and West, Naledi, Pimville, Zola, and Jabavu. More than half were un- or under-employed at the time of their interviews, surviving largely through government grants and work in the informal sector. All interviewees were classified as 'black' under apartheid's racial hierarchy.

Conducting interviews as a foreign researcher with a group of people who have lived through multiple violent and traumatic experiences posed a number of methodological and ethical difficulties. My position as a white middle-class female from a British university (though with a North American accent) naturally affected the content of interviewees' recollections and shaped the nature of our relationships. I was reminded throughout the research process of Portelli's

---

[52]   Short biographies of each interviewee can be found in the book's bibliography.
[53]   For Diepkloof's history see Marks, *Young Warriors*.

counsel that there are always two subjects in an interview whose roles are not fixed to 'observer' and 'observed', but oscillate between the two.[54] As I listened to these former comrades and analysed the stories they told, so too did they study me and make careful decisions about what to divulge based on their assumptions about my identity, motivations, and personal politics. Certain stories in this book, particularly those relating to gender relations as discussed in chapter four, have been shaped by their narrators specifically for an international and presumably progressive audience. There were also many stories that clearly went untold in these interviews, particularly relating to acts of violence engaged in by the comrades and traumas experienced in detention, as chapters five and six explore.

Yet acknowledging this shifting relationship between researcher and the researched is not to deny the unequal power dynamics inherent in these interviews. I never assumed a shared commonality with my female interviewees based on our common identities as women; while our differences in race, generation, and class marked us apart, it was also clear that we did not necessarily share similar conceptualisations of feminism or gender equality.[55] This book attempts to acknowledge the interaction and dynamics of these oral history interviews throughout its chapters, instead of treating these sources as unmediated extractions. Yet I recognise that this process in and of itself means that the ultimate power of telling these women's histories rests with me and my analysis, not with these South African women themselves. A limitation in the book lies in its reliance on English as the main language of communication with interviewees. All interviews were conducted primarily in English, with the occasional use of Zulu, Xhosa, or Afrikaans phrases and expressions. This has restricted linguistic analysis of interviewees' specific words and statements and made it challenging to discern if a quiet interviewee was reticent because of their discomfort with sharing certain memories, or discomfort with expressing these in a secondary language. Nevertheless, the majority of interviewees were confident narrators who were eager to participate in this project and ensure that their stories were incorporated into the wider histories this book addresses.

Young Women against Apartheid begins by exploring what life was like for young people growing up in apartheid's townships in the 1970s and 1980s, providing a historical overview of childhood and youth during this period.

---

[54]   Portelli, *The Death of Luigi Trastulli*, 30.
[55]   See Daphne Patai, 'U.S. Academics and Third World Women: Is Ethical Research Possible?' in Sherna Berger Gluck and Daphne Patai (eds), *Women's Words: The Feminist Practice of Oral History* (New York: Routledge, 1991), 144.

Chapter one demonstrates how, even for those who avoided political confrontation, children and students' lives were increasingly shaped by violence and conflict during these years. It asks what factors led some within this generation to join the liberation struggle and outlines the history of student and youth activism. It then explores how gender identities intersected with generational ones for township youth, making girls' experiences of adolescence markedly different from boys'. Through a study of women's own narratives of their time as girls it highlights how girls' lives were shaped by the constant threat of sexual violence, the inferiority complexes instilled in them from a young age, and the gendered expectations placed on their behaviour by parents, boys, and township communities. As the rest of the book demonstrates, these inequalities would become a central motivating factor behind girls' decisions to join the struggle.

The book then moves on to a series of chapters which are organised according to the various township spaces in which female comrades were active: the school, the home, the meeting, the street, and the prison cell. Dlamini criticises urban histories of the liberation struggle for talking about townships vaguely as 'sites of struggle' without due attention to the multiple, specific places and spaces of these communities.[56] Structuring these chapters in this way demonstrates how different township spaces offered girls different opportunities to challenge both the apartheid state and the limitations of girlhood in various ways. Simultaneously, it highlights the restrictions girls' activism faced in these spaces, and how female comrades created different gender identities in different locations to try to overcome these challenges.

Chapter two charts female comrades' initial encounters with the struggle at school, detailing how and why they chose to join the liberation movement through student organisations. Schools represented one particular space where girls could gain exposure to politics. While they were generally protected from political activities by their parents in the home and had less access to public spaces in the township where political mobilisation tended to occur for boys, at school they could seek out political organisations and begin to develop their own political understandings. Upon joining student organisations, female students felt a new sense of purpose and belonging. Engaging in the student struggle provided them with potent feelings of agency and allowed them to not only challenge the injustices they witnessed at school, but also to begin constructing an alternative, political girlhood that helped to mitigate their adolescent experiences of inferiority and vulnerability.

---

[56] Dlamini, *Native Nostalgia*, 153.

But once girls became committed to the student struggle, their lives changed dramatically. Chapter three explores how becoming a female comrade impacted girls' lives at home, and changed their relationships with their parents, families, friends and neighbours. It asks how girls and young women's overlapping identities as activists, daughters, and labourers within the home intersected and clashed. Previous histories of the township uprisings have predominantly focused on the public spaces of protest and violence, ignoring how activism was lived day-to-day in the townships' private domains. Yet such a focus often excludes the full range of girls' activism from view and reinforces a false binary between public and private spaces. For female comrades, the home was an important space in which they challenged the expected norms of African girlhood by abandoning their household duties and defying parental authority. Yet they could not fully escape the intersecting gendered and generational social hierarchies of the home that cast them within certain roles and bestowed particular responsibilities on them. This chapter demonstrates how girls' positions and responsibilities within the home shaped their activism in ways that were both empowering and restricting, enabling them to politicise their households in new ways but simultaneously damaging their relationships with parents and the wider community, and limiting their long-term engagement in the struggle.

Chapter four takes a different approach; rather than addressing a concrete, physical space, it addresses more of a conceptual one – 'the meeting'. It asks how gender relations between young women and men were negotiated and contested within the ideological space of student organisations' meetings. In interviews, both men and women at first constructed the meeting as an idealised, utopian space of gender equality, one in which the patriarchal problems plaguing township society did not intrude. However, this construction was often challenged later in interviews as men demonstrated their discriminatory views and women acknowledged instances of their unequal treatment or abuse. This chapter highlights the discords between young activists' espousal of gender equality on paper and their actual treatment of female comrades in practice. It explores how wider township gender ideologies affected the student movement and shaped the ideas and practices of young activists.

Where female comrades' narratives often became most animated was in describing their involvement in political confrontations in Soweto's streets, and it is these narratives which chapter five explores. Township streets during the 1980s were sites of masculine power and were generally spaces in which girls were victimised or excluded. For female comrades then, engaging in protest and political violence in the streets – whether this meant throwing stones at police vehicles, punishing residents who contravened the consumer boycott, or beating suspected informers and gangsters – was not only a means by which they could heed the ANC's call to make the townships ungovernable, but was also a way of challenging dominant gender ideologies and claiming new feelings of freedom and empowerment. Nevertheless, the masculine nature of these spaces posed significant challenges to female comrades, who had to constantly prove their worth and bravery, and demonstrate that their involvement in confrontation and violence was not limited by their gender like male comrades presumed.

Chapter six examines female comrades' experiences of arrest, detention, and torture. Both male and female comrades were pursued by the security forces, and if found were detained for periods ranging from two weeks to over six months. Within apartheid's carceral spaces – whether township police stations or larger prisons – young activists experienced violation and trauma; they were beaten, interrogated, psychologically abused, and tortured. Yet these experiences had particularly gendered meanings. Female comrades who had struggled so hard to empower themselves against feelings of powerlessness could not hide from the vulnerability they faced in detention. These feelings of vulnerability were deliberately amplified and exploited by warders and police to target female comrades' gendered and political identities. In narrating such experiences, female comrades lose their previous fluency and self-assurance, as their narratives become disjointed and interspersed with silences. Nevertheless, oral testimonies of detention recount more than just brutality and ill treatment, as many women also focus on their strategies of resistance in detention, feelings of camaraderie, or how their political identity was strengthened by knowing the threat they posed to the apartheid state. By focusing their contemporary narratives of detention on resistance rather than victimisation, they seek to transform their traumatic memories into meaningful and redemptive narratives and transform the prison cell from a space of trauma to one of resistance and political growth.

The final chapter of this book shifts the lens to contemporary South Africa and 'the interview' as a space for reminiscence and memory making, exploring in greater detail the life stories former comrades create to make sense of their involvement in the liberation struggle – involvement which at times brought them significant hardship, pain, and stigmatisation, and is yet to be acknowledged in dominant historical narratives. This chapter first explores female comrades' post-apartheid lives before analysing how their present circumstances may affect and shape their recollections of the past. For most female comrades, their involvement in the struggle has both helped and hindered their post-apartheid lives, and often in contradictory ways. While they today feel empowered, enlightened and more resilient because of their past activism, they are also tired of struggling, disappointed with the lack of wider change in the country, and saddened by the opportunities they missed because they dedicated their teenage years to the liberation movement. Their recollections of the past are marked by similar contradictions: while they are incredibly proud of the roles they played and celebrate their heroism, they simultaneously still struggle to come to terms with some of the actions they engaged in or the violence they experienced. These ambiguities reflect the competing needs these women face in the present to have their involvement in the struggle more widely acknowledged on the one hand, while gaining a sense of composure and accepting post-apartheid disappointments on the other.

Young Women against Apartheid is not intended to provide a comprehensive history of girls' political activism in South African history. Nor is it a political, organisational history of COSAS. Readers may note that it pays little attention to political strategy or ideology, offering a socio-cultural history of young female activists rather than a more traditionally political one. This largely reflects the content of female comrades' own recollections, and where they chose to focus their narratives. Furthermore, the oral history the book draws on was limited to Soweto. Yet the fragmentary research available on female comrades from other areas, including Alexandra and the Eastern Cape, corroborates the findings discussed here.[57] Moreover, the book's locational specificity allows for a more detailed analysis of identity and subjectivity. It enables us to see the liberation struggle from the micro-perspectives of those who were engaged in it on the ground, who may have not been in leadership positions or involved in strategic decision-making, but who were nonetheless indispensable to the struggle, and also deserve to have their memories shared and stories told.

[57] Charles Carter, "'We Are the Progressives": Alexandra Youth Congress Activists and the Freedom Charter, 1983–85,' *Journal of Southern African Studies* 17:2 (1991): 215; Cherry, 'The Role of Women in the 1980s Township Uprising in the Eastern Cape.'

1

African Girlhood under the Apartheid State

Describing her childhood in the South African township of Soweto during the final decades of apartheid, Redi Tlhabi writes in her memoir, 'to be a girl meant to be powerless.'[1] Born in 1978, Tlhabi's childhood coincided with the township uprisings. The now-renowned journalist and writer grew up in Orlando East, just down the street from many of the women interviewed for this book. She narrates her adolescence in Soweto with a mix of longing and lamentation, describing the township as:

> ...certainly, a perplexing place. The palpable jubilation and energy on the streets was no veneer; it was genuine. There were choir competitions, games in the streets and dancing at weddings, all of which offered some respite from the quagmire of suffering and oppression of the black nation...People made the best of an enervating situation and got on with life, work, childrearing and church...But poverty and unemployment lurked everywhere, always threatening to bring weary men and women to their knees. And the deprivation and violence brutalised many, crushing dreams and swallowing innocence.

Despite the increased interest in global histories of childhood and youth over the past few decades, we still know very little about childhood and youth in apartheid South Africa beyond the resistance paradigm. Given the emphasis placed on the histories of young activists, it is difficult to ascertain what a 'normal' adolescence was for African children and youth in apartheid South Africa. But primary and secondary sources alike demonstrate that during the 1970s and 1980s, young people's lives were increasingly shaped by escalating political conflict and violence. As Tlhabi acknowledges, 'The Soweto in which I grew up in the eighties was very different from that of my father's day. Political violence was now the norm; young men and women disappeared, swallowed up by the never-ending struggle.' Tlhabi's memoir

---

[1] Redi Tlhabi, *Endings and Beginnings: A Story of Healing* (Johannesburg: Jacana, 2012), 40.

25

offers a rich personal narrative of how young people's lives came to be distinctly shaped by the liberation struggle – even for those who stayed far away from politics themselves. She writes of the interruptions caused by 'comrades' at school who would 'barge into our classrooms and order us home'. She grew accustomed to the large army tanks that patrolled Soweto's streets, and found herself fascinated by the 'menacing soldiers with their big guns'. Despite the endurance of family life, school, and leisure activities that Tlhabi describes, childhoods in South Africa's townships were ones increasingly wrought by violence, conflict, and disruption during these years.[2]

Yet Tlhabi's narrative also demonstrates how gender identities intersected with generational ones for Soweto's youth, making experiences of childhood and adolescence very different for African girls and boys. Tlhabi's youth was also marked by the strict limitations placed on her freedom of movement in Soweto due to marauding gangsters, the 'sheer torment' of being harassed and threatened by boys on the way to school, and the blame and responsibility placed on her own shoulders to ensure she did not fall victim to sexual assault or pregnancy. This chapter paints a preliminary picture of how young people navigated adolescence in South Africa's townships during the late-apartheid period. It reviews the rise of the comrades and explores what drew young people to join the liberation struggle during these years. It asks what life was like for African girls during these turbulent times: their experiences of violence; how they navigated township spaces; and the expectations placed on them by parents and boyfriends. These insights provide the foundations for understanding female comrades' stories of their involvement in activism and violence which this book subsequently tells. As the rest of this book will demonstrate, female comrades joined the struggle in part to overcome or address these inequalities of their girlhoods. Yet such experiences were not easily forgotten or erased, and girls' resentment at their feelings of vulnerability and inferiority continued to shape why they joined the liberation movement, the roles they played, and how they now reflect on their time as comrades.

Childhood and Youth in Late-Apartheid South Africa

The terms 'childhood' and 'youth' defy easy categorisation. While international bodies tend to take a 'strict 18' definition of childhood, this can be an arbitrary dividing line that does not reflect the realities of young people's lives. Particularly in the African context, the end of childhood is often not marked by age but rather by marriage, motherhood, or economic independence. Furthermore, childhood

[2]   *Ibid.*, 11–33.

is not necessarily a period defined by innocence or incompetence.[3] Defining 'youth' is an even more difficult task given the political and racial assumptions tied to the term. Although it connotes age or a period in one's life, definitions of youth based on age or biology alone tend to be trans-historical, and ignore the ways in which youth is historically, socially and culturally constructed.[4] Furthermore, youth is not a fixed social category, and transitions to adulthood are rarely 'neat moments of permanent and irreversible change.'[5] The boundaries between childhood, youth, and adulthood are both permeable and blurred. In Africa today, many people are considered youth long past the numerical ages that typically mark the transition to adulthood in the West. The transition from youth to adulthood is marked by various social signifiers such as education, employment, financial independence, marriage, or political experience. As many of the more traditional paths to adulthood have become barred due to economic decline, political turmoil, and shifting demographic trends, youth, for many, has become a life stage indefinitely prolonged. As Rachel Johnson states, youth is a 'constructed identity, imposed upon, rejected, embraced or aspired to by people, not all of whom are necessarily young.'[6] The student activists who are the main focus of this research could be considered both children and youths according to these ambiguous definitions. All were in their teenage years and attending secondary school when they joined the liberation movement – although some continued their participation after leaving school, moving from student to youth political organisations.

In South Africa, the events of the 1980s gave rise to particular stereo-typed constructions of youth as potential sources of either heroic liberation or violent destruction.[7] Seeking to complicate these over-simplifications, academic research has predominantly focused on politicised youth, exploring the composition, motivations, and actions of student and youth activists. But this has left us with a very poor understanding of what life was like for the average adolescent growing up in South Africa's townships during the 1970s

[3] Afua Twum-Danso, 'The Political Child,' in Angela McIntyre (ed), *Invisible Stakeholders: Children and War in Africa* (Pretoria: Institute for Security Studies, 2005): 10–13.
[4] Jean Comaroff and John Comaroff, 'Reflections on Youth: From the Past to the Postcolony,' in Alcinda Manuel Honwana and Filip de Boeck (eds), *Makers and Breakers: Children and Youth in Postcolonial Africa* (Oxford: James Currey, 2005), 19.
[5] Rachel Bray et al., *Growing Up in the New South Africa: Childhood and Adolescence in Post-Apartheid Cape Town* (Cape Town: HSRC Press, 2010), 40.
[6] Rachel E. Johnson, 'Making History, Gendering Youth: Young Women and South Africa's Liberation Struggles after 1976,' (PhD thesis, Department of History, University of Sheffield, 2010), 19.
[7] Seekings, *Heroes or Villains*, 1–19.

and 1980s. Due to the increasing prominence of young people as the drivers of protest and rebellion, images and narratives of childhood under the apartheid state have been shaped by three primary discourses. First, children and youth have been seen as heroic activists at the forefront of the country's liberation struggle; as selfless 'young lions' who acted when older members of their communities failed to. But within their roles as political militants, youth were also seen (predominantly by the state and conservative media) as 'apocalyptic' – as savage, violent and destructive.[8] Lastly, children were constructed as innocent yet brutalised; a 'lost generation' who, because of the violence of the apartheid state, were robbed of an idealised childhood. From 1976 onwards, concerned humanitarian organisations declared that South Africa was a country at war with its children. Frank Chikane, an anti-apartheid leader who himself grew up in Soweto, characterised the world of the township child as 'extremely violent'. He explained:

> It is a world made up of teargas, bullets, whippings, detention, and death on the streets. It is an experience of military operations and night raids, of roadblocks and body searches. It is a world where parents and friends get carried away in the night to be interrogated. It is a world where people simply disappear, where parents are assassinated and homes are petrol bombed. Such is the environment of the township child today.[9]

According to Western standards of childhood as a period of innocence, dependence, and naivety, African children in apartheid South Africa were hardly 'children' at all. Delegates at an international conference on children and apartheid in Harare, Zimbabwe in 1989 were asked to consider what kind of society could '[compel] its children to assume the adult risks of protest and resilience, to forgo their childhood?'[10] From a young age most township children witnessed and learned how to negotiate or avoid political conflict and criminal violence. Chikane wrote of his amazement at children's resourcefulness, as on days of large political funerals in Soweto they would strategically line the streets with buckets of water to mitigate the effects of potential teargas attacks.[11] Another township resident stated, 'When my two-year-old daughter

---

[8]   *Ibid.*

[9]   Frank Chikane, 'Children in Turmoil: The Effects of the Unrest on Township Children,' in Sandra Burman and Pamela Reynolds (eds), *Growing up in a Divided Society: The Contexts of Childhood in South Africa* (Johannesburg, Ravan Press, 1986), 342–343.

[10] Victoria Brittain and Abdul S. Minty (eds), *Children of Resistance: On Children, Repression and the Law in Apartheid South Africa. Statements from the Harare Conference* (London: Kliptown Books, 1988), 9–10.

[11] Chikane, 'Children in Turmoil,' 343.

sees a military vehicle passing, she looks for a stone.'[12] The existing historiography has painted township life for children and youth as being dominated by political struggle from a remarkably young age. As Shaun Johnson narrated:

> The four or five year-old playing on the streets of Soweto played games involving the struggle, singing about Mandela, about Tambo, chanting slogans…I would ask them – these very young fellows – what is the struggle?, and they would say the struggle *ke ntwa*! The struggle is fighting! It is shocking the extent to which children turned into daredevils. Soldier meant only teargas to them, police only enemy target.[13]

Yet such language comes from those who spoke for or about children at the time, rather than from young people in South Africa's townships themselves. We know very little about the experiences of childhood outside of this discourse of violence and brutalisation, created by psychologists, human rights activists, and global anti-apartheid groups concerned at the time with apartheid's 'war against children'.

Outside of these political and violence paradigms, we also know very little about older 'children' – students and youths in the townships during these years. Gill Straker, a psychologist working with youth refugees of violence during the 1980s, argues that young people who did not participate in political uprisings in the townships were the exception.[14] However, the validity of this statement has been questioned by historians who have highlighted that stories of 'ordinary' childhood and adolescence from this period remain to be told.[15] As Glaser argues, 'even during these increasingly polarized times, substantial pockets of young people attended school in spite of prevailing boycotts, attended a-political church groups, hung out in gangs and generally tried as far as possible to avoid induction into comrade culture.'[16] Both Glaser and Seekings acknowledge that most young people's lives in the township were likely predominated by violence, school boycotts, and political conflict during these years; but 'how these affected most young people's lives, and how they responded, remains largely unknown.'[17]

What we do know is that increasing numbers of young people attended and stayed longer in secondary schools during these years. In the six years leading up to the Soweto Uprisings of 1976, enrolment in Bantu Education secondary

12   *Ibid.*
13   Johnson, 'The Soldiers of Luthuli,' 113.
14   Straker, *Faces in the Revolution*, 19.
15   Seekings, 'Beyond Heroes and Villains', 4.
16   Glaser, 'Youth and Generation in South African History,' 127.
17   Seekings, 'Beyond Heroes and Villains,' 3.

schools increased from 122,000 to 389,000. In 1984, over one million Africans were enrolled in secondary school. By the time of the township uprisings then, secondary education was no longer just the preserve of the African elite, but had become a mass phenomenon – though still far fewer African children attended school than other racial groups, with only 35 per cent of fifteen to nineteen year olds enrolled in secondary school in 1980.[18] Yet despite this expansion of African education, the quality of schooling declined as classrooms grew increasingly overcrowded, teachers were often underqualified, and textbooks and other necessities were rarely adequately supplied. This was reflected in the falling matric pass rate, which was only 48.3 per cent in DET schools in 1983. Despite reforms to African education in the 1980s, and the increased spend per African student committed by the state, Bantu Education was still very much in place, with African students' education geared towards preparing them for the semi-skilled workforce. In Soweto, some schools had notoriously bad infrastructure – particularly Diepdale High and Bopasenatla in Diepkloof, which many interviewees attended – with one student explaining that 'our schools are worse than prisons.'[19] Schools were often sites of violence too, with authoritarian principals and teachers regularly using corporal punishment against both male and female students. One male comrade recalled a particularly violent teacher who beat him so hard he cried and stopped attending school.[20] From mid-1984, regular boycotts routinely disrupted secondary schooling in Soweto, and in response security forces assumed a greater presence in schools.[21] Thus, even the normalcy that education may have provided amid the turmoil of the 1980s was disrupted by the struggle.

At school, many students were also involved in various clubs and groups such as debating organisations and athletics teams. Outside of schools, young men could often be found playing football, hanging out with friends on street corners, or engaging in gang cultures. Young women, on the other hand, tended to be more confined to the home and were often more active in local churches. With her interviewees in Diepkloof in the early 1990s, Marks found that most youths spent their leisure time listening to radio, talking with friends, doing homework, or being with a boyfriend or girlfriend. Weekends were often spent attending both weddings and funerals. Home lives for many young people were disrupted or dysfunctional; many had fathers who were

---

18   Bundy, 'Street Sociology and Pavement Politics,' 311–312; Hyslop, *The Classroom Struggle*, 169.

19   Marks, *Young Warriors*, 27–28.

20   Interview with Sello, Diepkloof, 14 May 2014.

21   Clive Glaser, 'Learning Amidst the Turmoil: Secondary Schooling in Soweto, 1977–1990,' *South African Historical Journal* 68:3 (2016): 426.

absent throughout their lives and lived in female-headed households or with grandparents. Those whose mothers did live with a male partner regularly witnessed domestic violence towards both women and children.[22] Yet as historians, we have very few insights into how these experiences were actually lived by young people, the identities they formed, or how they felt about the political events unfolding around them.

The Comrades

What we do know more about are the 'comrades' – those young people who participated in the liberation struggle. The term 'comrades' itself gained currency in 1985 and was used imprecisely to refer to 'practically any black youngsters engaged in resistance.'[23] It could denote both school-goers and slightly older or unemployed 'youths' no longer in school. Despite its ambiguity, the term became an important self-label for young people in the struggle, many of whom still identify as 'comrades' today. To those who were committed activists, 'comrade' denoted more than just being young and loosely involved in politics; it referred to 'resourceful and determined idealists' who belonged to particular groups and whose dedication to the struggle was known in their communities.[24]

Many scholars have sought to understand why young people were drawn to political resistance in such large numbers during the 1970s and 1980s. The poor quality of Bantu Education alone is not enough to explain the massive upsurge in student protest, as the racialised education policy operated for over twenty years prior to the 1976 uprisings with little unrest.[25] Before 1976, boys and young men tended to find gang culture much more attractive than politics when looking for an alternative form of youth socialisation.[26] But a combination of shifting demographics, economic decline, and the expansion of secondary schooling in the 1970s produced a new, larger cohort of young people with shared experiences of oppression and deprivation. Youths were now better educated than their parents, yet had little hope of finding secure

[22] Marks, *Young Warriors*, 24.
[23] Johnson, 'The Soldiers of Luthuli,' 118.
[24] Bozzoli, *Theatres of Struggle*, 94–95.
[25] Jonathan Hyslop, 'School Student Movements and State Education Policy, 1972–87,' in William Cobbett and Robin Cohen (eds), *Popular Struggles in South Africa* (London: James Currey, 1988), 183.
[26] Glaser, 'Youth and Generation in South African History,' 127.

jobs, as increasing numbers of school-leavers were confronted by a shrinking economy and rising unemployment.[27]

On 16 June 1976, African school students in the South African township of Soweto famously took to the streets in protest against the state's introduction of Afrikaans as the primary language of instruction in all schools. As they marched from their schools towards Orlando Stadium, they were met by heavily armed police who fired teargas and later live ammunition into the crowd of thousands of students. This moment sparked a country-wide revolt, largely led by students and youth, against many symbols of white rule in the townships.[28] June 1976 continues to occupy significant space in public memories of the anti-apartheid struggle and has come to be seen as a key turning point in South African history. Yet following the state's repression of student activists, South African townships experienced a period of relative quiescence, with many student leaders imprisoned or having joined the ANC in exile, and the organisations they had founded banned.

It was not long before the youth regrouped politically, this time under the banner of the Congress of South African Students (COSAS), formed in 1979 with the help of the ANC in exile. COSAS' primary purpose was to provide a national organisation for black secondary school students. In 1980, it declared its open support for the Freedom Charter (being the first mass organisation to do so since 1960), thus unofficially declaring its allegiance to the ANC rather than to any Black Consciousness organisations. The organisation's momentum was slow at first, in part due to the detention of most of its leaders shortly after its formation. But from 1980 onwards, renewed resistance – albeit localised, limited, and diverse – began to re-emerge in the country's townships. In 1982, COSAS limited its membership to current secondary school students only and helped to establish various youth group for its older or non-school attending supporters, such as the Soweto Youth Congress.[29] It was not until the resur-

---

[27]   Bundy, 'Street Sociology and Pavement Politics,' 310–313.

[28]   The 1976 Soweto Uprising is not discussed or analysed in any detail in this book. For more on 1976, see Alan Brooks and Jeremy Brickhill, *Whirlwind before the Storm: The Origins and Development of the Uprising in Soweto and the Rest of South Africa from June to December 1976* (London, International Defence and Aid Fund, 1980); Baruch Hirson, *Year of Fire, Year of Ash: The Soweto Revolt, Roots of a Revolution?* (London: Zed Books, 1979); Ali Khanqela Hlongwane et al, *Soweto '76: Reflections on the Liberation Struggles* (Johannesburg: Pan Macmillan, 2006); Helena Pohlandt-McCormick, *'I Saw a Nightmare—': Doing Violence to Memory: The Soweto Uprising, June 16 1976* (New York: Columbia University Press, 2007).

[29]   A national youth organisation, the South African Youth Congress (SAYCO) was not founded until March 1987, by which time it claimed to be the parent organisation to 1200 local affiliates. See Seekings, *Heroes or Villains*, 54.

gence of student protest and school boycotts in 1984 that COSAS became a mass organisation.[30] As COSAS came to represent the majority of dissatisfied African students it successfully re-orientated its strategy, and linked students' educational demands for greater provision of textbooks, an end to corporal punishment, and the establishment of student representative councils (SRCs), to wider local and national political grievances. In many townships its members were the motor of rebellion, helping to inspire other community groups into action. Members of COSAS worked alongside trade unions and other civic organisations, participating in rent boycotts, stayaways, and other forms of community protest. As Hylop writes, 'student protest provided the detonator for an explosion of worker and community struggle which confronted the dominant classes with their greatest challenge yet.'[31]

But the rising prominence of student activism occurred simultaneously to the increasing militarisation of township politics. From mid-1984, South Africa entered into a period of unprecedented political violence. The 'township uprisings', as events of these years came to be known, were first sparked in September, when an announcement of rent increases in the Vaal Triangle led to violent confrontations between protestors and police, resulting in the killing of a black local councillor. This event spilled over into a series of stayaways, demonstrations, and school boycotts, and eventually protest spread beyond the Vaal to the Eastern Cape, Free State, and Natal. Across numerous townships, escalating resistance was met with mounting state repression. In July 1985, the government declared a partial state of emergency across thirty-six magisterial districts in the Eastern Cape and Pretoria-Witwatersrand-Vereeniging (PWV) region, which granted the police the power to detain activists, enforce curfews, and control the media. But the partial state of emergency did not effectively impede resistance against apartheid in the townships. Rather, the militancy of the township uprisings only increased over the course of the next year, with frequent attacks on suspected informers, township police, and councillors, and boycotts of schools and white-owned businesses. In response to escalating unrest, the police employed tear-gas, rubber bullets, and even live ammunition indiscriminately against townships crowds.[32] In June 1986, a second state of emergency was declared, this time encompassing the whole country, and renewed each year until 1990.

In response to, and capitalising on, continued resistance in the townships, the ANC in exile called for a 'people's war' and began intensifying military action within South Africa and training new *Umkhonto we Sizwe* (MK) cadres

---

[30]   Hyslop, 'School Student Movements,' 191–193.
[31]   *Ibid.*, 183.
[32]   Sapire, 'Township Histories,' 172.

both in ANC camps abroad and in the townships themselves. Oliver Tambo, then ANC president, called on those within the country to 'render South Africa ungovernable'.[33] This message found particular traction amongst students and youth in the country's townships, who took on the roles of shock troops in the liberation movement. The ANC's successful manoeuvring during this period resulted in a new political culture in the townships, characterised by new expressions of allegiance to the ANC and its political strategies, as local protesters sang songs praising ANC leaders, invoked the discourse of the Freedom Charter, and circulated banned ANC literature and propaganda material.[34]

It was within this political climate that student and youth politics grew increasingly confrontational, with their activism being characterised primarily by a fierce willingness to oppose the police and attack any local residents seen as collaborators or deemed to be jeopardising the struggle. When the first state of emergency was declared in July 1985, COSAS members became the primary targets of detention without trial. In August, the organisation was officially banned. Yet by this point it had 'become too powerful to be stopped by decapitation', and its banning 'achieved only limited and temporary reductions in student action.'[35] In many townships, student activists simply rebranded themselves and formed new, more localised units, such as the Soweto Student Congress (SOSCO). Nevertheless, student activism during the latter 1980s faced significant challenges, including organisational weakness and the continued detention of its leadership, which opened COSAS and SOSCO up to exploitation by 'lumpen elements' and encouraged the increasing trend towards 'politically destructive violence' including revenge attacks and inter-group fighting.[36] One must acknowledge that the comrades were an incredibly heterogeneous group during these years, which included 'politically astute strategists as well as violent individuals, and many other young people besides.'[37] As comrade culture grew increasingly violent, it made normally non-violent people violent and attracted habitually violent people to street politics.[38] But most committed comrades saw themselves as the foot soldiers

[33] Oliver Tambo, 'Render South Africa Ungovernable,' *Sechaba*, March 1985, AG2918:9.13.3, KAIROS, Historical Papers (hereafter HP), University of the Witwatersrand, Johannesburg.

[34] Thula Simpson, '"Umkhonto We Sizwe, We Are Waiting for You": The ANC and the Township Uprising, September 1984 – September 1985,' *South African Historical Journal* 61:1 (2009): 173; Hyslop, 'School Student Movements,' 195.

[35] Hyslop, 'School Student Movements,' 195–196.

[36] *Ibid.*, 198.

[37] Seekings, *Heroes or Villains*, 56.

[38] *Ibid.*, 65.

of the wider liberation movement, and perceived their violent actions as a justified and rational response to the state's militarisation of the townships. They believed they were acting out the direct instructions of the ANC in exile, which they interpreted through listening to Radio Freedom or reading circulated banned literature from the liberation movement.

Comrades were millenarian in their belief that the end of apartheid was on the imminent horizon in the mid- to late 1980s, and that they had the ability to bring about a new, utopian South Africa.[39] Despite the dangers it posed, being a comrade could be immensely seductive to a young person. It provided feelings of camaraderie, potency, and authority, and gave many young people a sense of meaning and purpose when they had few other opportunities for social advancement in life. Comrades were thus drawn to the struggle not only by educational grievances or national political concerns, but also by more personal and subjective motivations such as a sense of adventure and feelings of belonging. Young political activists developed their own styles and repertoires, wearing political t-shirts, *toyi-toying* in township streets, singing freedom songs and publicly declaring their allegiance to the ANC and its armed wing MK.[40]

Where Were the Girls?

This dominant image of the archetypal comrade – a black youth chanting in the streets of Soweto, enforcing consumer and school boycotts, and singing songs praising Nelson Mandela and Oliver Tambo – is an overwhelmingly male one. In almost all of the histories of young people in South Africa – of victimised children, students, gangsters, and political activists – girls are invisible. They are excluded from the heroic, 'liberatory' images of *toyi-toying* comrades in township streets, and never mentioned in discussions of youth as a brutalised 'lost generation'. Even at the time there appears to have been little public or policy interest in young African women's lives, as girls rarely appear in the archives as objects of concern (let alone as agents in their own right). Various groups involved in the global anti-apartheid movement did show some concern for the plight of 'women and children', but the various publications they produced rarely included specific information on adolescent

---

[39] Belinda Bozzoli, 'Why were the 1980s "Millenarian"? Style, Repertories, Space and Authority in South Africa's Black Cities,' *Journal of Historical Sociology* 13:1 (2000): 78–110.

[40] Sitas, 'The Making of the "Comrades" Movement in Natal,' 634–636; Marks, *Young Warriors*.

girls.[41] Instead, they presented children as genderless victims, and women predominantly as vulnerable or aggrieved mothers. Girls' marginalisation has since continued in the historiography of this period. Because young women were rarely in leadership positions, and were less prominent in public spaces, they were less likely to be interviewed by academics. Their involvement in the struggle was also often more constrained or shorter than that of young men because of parental pressures and childcare responsibilities. Moreover, scholars documenting the rise of the comrades during the 1980s tended to be more concerned with race, class, and political economy than with gender. Where girls do appear in the historiography, they do so mostly as nameless, voiceless victims of sexual violence, and little to no attention has been paid to how they coped with and responded to the social, political, and economic shifts at play in township society during the 1970s and 1980s. Often, the existence of girls is conceptually denied in academic work, as young people are referred to through genderless terms of 'children', 'youth' or 'comrades'. Yet we must acknowledge that the experience of growing up in apartheid's townships during the 1970s and 1980s was a deeply and inescapably gendered one, in which one's schooling, play, home-life, freedom of movement, and vulnerabilities to violence were profoundly shaped by whether one was a boy or a girl.

In addressing this historical gap, we need to explore how women narrate their own experiences as adolescents. Doing so requires a tricky triangulation of the sparse sources available, of oral history interviews, media reports, and memoirs. Tlhabi's *Endings and Beginnings* is particularly useful in this endeavour, as the book provides details of her childhood in Soweto during the 1980s. Tlhabi and this book's interviewees describe their lives in the township in similar ways. They fondly reminisce about the joys of township life that continued despite increasing state repression. Like Dlamini does in *Native Nostalgia*, they demonstrate that there was much more to township life than just crime and deprivation.[42]

Yet violence was always an 'omnipresent spectre' in girls' lives.[43] Highlighting the contradictions of township life, Zintle, who grew up in Soweto in the 1980s but decided not to join the struggle, described of her childhood:

> I liked it. I liked my school, there was…a lot of playing, just games. In that sense, for a child it was very vibrant…Then there was also, you know, ya, South African things [laughs]. Like I remember there would be police

[41] See 'A Woman's Place is in the Struggle, Not Behind Bars', AG2523: M1.5, Detainees Parents Support Committee (hereafter DPSC), HP; *Cries of Freedom: Women in Detention in South Africa* (London, Catholic Institute for International Relations, 1988).
[42] Dlamini, *Native Nostalgia*, 156.
[43] Lee, *African Women and Apartheid*, 56.

who would come if maybe, like in Meadowlands, if there's one of the high schools that's decided to march or do whatever, then there would be police who will come to the school with guns and everything. But at the time I think it wasn't even funny or anything...you didn't think it was strange. It was just normal.[44]

When asked to describe their childhoods, many female comrades focused on memories of armoured vehicles, security forces, teargas, and rubber bullets. Almost all recalled specific details of how they experienced the 1976 uprisings, even though some were as young as four or five years old at the time. Tlhabi describes the normalisation of political violence and the presence of state security forces in the township, writing of how she 'got used to the big army tanks that patrolled our streets.' She recalls witnessing a necklacing on her walk home from school one day – a form of punishment that became increasingly used against suspected informers or sell-outs in South Africa during these years, in which a tyre was placed around a person's neck, filled with petrol, and set alight. But it was not only experiences of political violence that marked girls' lives growing up in the townships. The increasingly chaotic atmosphere in the townships also allowed gangsterism and criminality to flourish. Many female comrades recalled criminal violence as being more threatening to them as young girls than political violence. Tlhabi's parents did their best to shield her from the murders and turf wars that engulfed Soweto. But, as she comments, 'you couldn't grow up in Soweto and remain impervious to such goings on for long.'[45]

Both boys and girls in South Africa's townships would have shared this regular exposure to violence from an early age and been vulnerable to criminal and political violence. Yet experiences of township violence were profoundly gendered and had particular effects on African girls' mobility and sense of selves. By the 1980s South Africa already had a long history of violence against women, but the increasing militarisation of both the state and the internal liberation struggle during the 1980s bred wider cultures of violence and encouraged further and more widespread forms of gender-based violence.[46] Soweto's girls and young women thus faced particular vulnerabilities that were not shared by boys, and that greatly shaped their experiences of township life and adolescence.

[44] Interview with Zintle, Windsor West, 17 April 2015.
[45] Tlhabi, *Endings and Beginnings*, 29–33.
[46] Sheila Meintjes, 'Political Violence and Gender: A Neglected Relation in South Africa's Struggle for Democracy,' *Politikon* 25:2 (1998): 97–104; Graeme Simpson, 'Women and Children in Violent South African Townships,' 1993, AG3245: L2, Centre for the Study of Violence and Reconciliation, HP, 102.

Sexual Violence and the 'Female Fear Factory'

The form of violence most present in young women's lives was not political, but sexual. Girls' lives where shaped by the constant threat of sexual violence they faced across various township spaces – not only in the streets but also in schools, home, and *shebeens*. While abduction and rape had been regular features of life in Soweto since the 1940s, rates of rape and domestic abuse seem to have increased in the 1980s and early 1990s: 9365 cases of rape were reported to police in 1980, 19,368 cases in 1988, and 27,056 cases in 1993.[47] Tlhabi describes how the violation of girls and women was commonplace during the 1980s and early 1990s, yet was rarely the subject of public outrage: 'as horrendous as it was, the community seemed to treat rape as if it were just some minor inconvenience.'[48]

One particular factor that contributed to girls' fears of sexual violence during these years was the rise of 'jackrolling' – a form of very public gang rape. As Tlhabi describes, 'a group of guys would stumble upon a woman and kidnap her in broad daylight. She would then be repeatedly raped for as long as her captors felt like it, and only when they were good and ready would they let her go.'[49]

Jackrolling first emerged in Diepkloof, Soweto in 1987 and was then practised predominantly by one small gang. However, the practice soon became fashionable amongst certain township youth as a group activity that enabled young men to express their frustrations and conform to dominant masculine culture.[50] Mark Gevisser, documenting the rise of the jackrollers in the *Weekly Mail*, wrote of Orlando West, Soweto in 1989:

[47] It is important to note that this escalation reflects both an increase in reporting and in actual instances of sexual violence. Accurate statistics of gender-based violence are notoriously difficult to establish since assault and rape are rarely reported due to the normalisation of domestic violence, the inadequate responses of police, and the shame women can feel in disclosing such information. Vogelman and Eagle estimate that only one in twenty rapes in South Africa are reported, while the South African police estimate that for every rape reported, another thirty-five go unreported. As the 1995 Human Rights Watch Report concludes, 'there are no reliable figures, or even good estimates, of the number of rapes committed in South Africa.' These statistics are drawn from Human Rights Watch, 'South Africa: The State Response to Domestic Violence and Rape,' November 1995, <https://www.hrw.org/report/1995/11/01/violence-against-women-south-africa/state-response-domestic-violence-and-rape> [accessed 10 November 2014]; Lloyd Vogelman and Gillian Eagle, 'Overcoming Endemic Violence against Women in South Africa,' *Social Justice* 18:1 (1991): 210.

[48] Tlhabi, *Endings and Beginnings*, 39.

[49] *Ibid.*, 40.

[50] Steve Mokwena, 'The Era of the Jackrollers: Contextualising the rise of youth gangs in Soweto,' Paper presented at the Centre of the Study of Violence and Reconciliation, Johannesburg, 1991, <https://www.csvr.org.za/publications/1805-the-era-of-the-jackrollers-contextualising-the-rise-of-the-youth-gangs-in-soweto>

The 'jackroller' gangs are running riot. Their professed aim is to ensure that every girl in the township is raped and impregnated before the age of 26, and they have become so powerful that they walk into a classroom and select their victim in full view of the teacher. One girl is kidnapped and raped by five 'jackrollers', and reports it to the authorities. But on the day of the court case, she is taken to a field and, as punishment, raped again.[51]

The public nature and pervasiveness of jackrolling in Soweto cultured a constant state of anxiety in schoolgirls – who were gangsters' primary targets. As one young woman who was seventeen years old at the time commented, 'I am afraid of the jackrollers. They are affecting all of us girls. We are not safe anymore. We can't even walk in the streets without being harassed by hooligans.'[52] This ubiquitous fear was also described by Tlhabi, who writes, 'I'd known it happen to girls and young women around me, and I lived with the suffocating fear that one day it would be my turn.' She later reiterates, 'I lived with the fear of rape every day of my life, a fear that has never dissipated.'[53] Soweto's female comrades shared such dread as girls growing up in the township. Particularly those from Diepkloof narrate this fear as being a central facet of their adolescent lives. Thobile remembered the jackrollers as being worse than the police when it came to abuse and murder: 'they were jackrolling, they will take you, rape you. Sometimes you won't come back.'[54] Such fears of jackrolling shaped girls' relationships with township spaces. As Adam Ashforth writes, 'young women, especially, negotiate public space – streets, schools, and social gatherings – knowing they risk abduction and rape at any time.'[55] Simply walking through the township could be dangerous for girls; as one female interviewee explained, 'it was a risk to walk around, a big risk.'[56]

But it was not only in township streets where girls were vulnerable. Mary Mabaso, a community leader who organised Soweto's first march against sexual violence in 1990, commented on the inescapabilty of girls' insecurity:

When you leave your child alone in the home she is not safe. And in the street, she is not safe. And in the school she is not safe. There is nowhere that

---

[accessed 29 November 2014]; Diana E.H. Russell and Mary Mabaso, 'Rape and Child Sexual Abuse in Soweto: An Interview with Community Leader Mary Mabaso,' *South African Sociological Review* 3:2 (1991): 75.

51   Mark Gevisser, 'The war against women's bodies', *The Weekly Mail*, 6–12th September 1991, 13.
52   Mokwena, 'The Era of the Jackrollers.'
53   Tlhabi, *Endings and Beginnings*, 40.
54   Interview with Thobile, Diepkloof, 12 April 2014.
55   Adam Ashforth, 'Weighing Manhood in Soweto,' *Codesria Bulletin* 3–4 (1999): 54.
56   Interview with Nonkululeko, Diepkloof, 8 April 2014.

she can walk and be safe. Girls are afraid somebody in a car will stop them and say 'get in'. When they walk in the street they are raped by men with guns. Sexual abuse happens so much that some students stop going to school.[57]

As she states, even being in the home could not guarantee girls' protection. Tlhabi narrates one particularly harrowing incident in which she was sexually assaulted by a builder in her home as a child. 'From that day on' she writes, 'I delayed coming home, and spent my time playing with friends or visiting the local library until I was sure there'd be someone else at our house.'[58] Fathers, uncles, and half-brothers could all be potentially dangerous people for girls to be alone with in the home – as the numerous letters written by girls who had been raped by family members to the 'Dear Dolly' column of *Drum* magazine attest to.[59] Sexual violence within the family operated under a veil of secrecy during apartheid. Although public abductions of girls gained increasing media attention during these years, violence within the family did not. As Deborah Posel argues, 'Often, the more intimate the setting of the violence, the less the likelihood of its public recognition and acknowledgement.'[60] Child sexual abuse was shameful for a family, and thus parents would often be complicit in its concealment.

In schools too, girls were vulnerable to violence perpetrated by teachers, fellow pupils, or gangs who invaded classrooms. Robert Morrell and Relebohile Moletsane write of how girls 'contend[ed] daily with aggressive sexual advances' during apartheid and attended school in fear.[61] Violence against girls in school increased in the 1970s and 1980s, as the distinction between school-going youths and gang members blurred, and rape became a social, peer-approved action used to affirm masculinity. One woman who grew up in rural KwaZulu-Natal during the 1980s stated that 'going to school was a nightmare' as boys 'took advantage and physically abused girls who refused their attention.'[62] The late 1980s saw a drastic escalation of violence against

---

57 Russell and Mabaso, 'Rape and Child Sexual Abuse in Soweto,' 65.
58 Tlhabi, *Endings and Beginnings*, 42–43.
59 Jana Krige and Marcelyn Oostendorp, '"Too late for tears, dear sister": Constructing victims and perpetrators of rape in the advice column "Dear Dolly" from 1984 to 2004,' *Stellenbosch Papers in Linguistics Plus* 46 (2015), 7–23.
60 Deborah Posel, 'The Scandal of Manhood: "Baby Rape" and the Politicization of Sexual Violence in Post-Apartheid South Africa,' *Culture, Health and Sexuality*, 7:3 (2005): 242.
61 Robert Morrell and Relebohile Moletsane, 'Inequality and Fear: Learning and Working inside Bantu Education Schools,' in Peter Kallaway (ed), *History of Education under Apartheid, 1948–1994: The Doors of Learning and Culture Shall be Opened* (Cape Town: Peter Lang, 2002), 228.
62 Sithabile Ntombela and Nontokozo Mashiya, '"In my time, girls…": Reflections of African Adolescent Girl Identities and Realities across Two Generations,' *Agenda*

schoolgirls in Soweto, as increasingly brazen gangs waited outside school gates or even entered classrooms to find potential victims. Regular media reports referred to girls being 'dragged out of class and raped,' with many girls becoming so afraid that they stopped attending school altogether.[63]

Girls and women's vulnerability to sexual violence across all of these spaces helped to create what Pumla Dineo Gqola calls the 'female fear factory'.[64] Rape was (and still is) used as a method of social control to keep girls subordinate, and curtail their freedom of movement by keeping them in a constant state of fear.[65] It represented one extreme in a spectrum of abuse and harassment that girls and young women in Soweto were subjected to on a regular basis. Tlhabi describes how every girl had at least one local boy who would regularly threaten or sexually harass them as they attempted to walk to and from school, and the 'sheer torment' this caused. The fear she felt at these encounters is palpable in her book. Every time her personal 'tormenter', Siphiwe, appeared she would 'shake like a leaf': 'he was ugly and menacing, and I would break out in a sweat that trickled down my back and legs. I was beyond afraid; every time I encountered Siphiwe I thought my last day had come.'[66]

In the 1980s this 'fear factory' was reinforced by wider patriarchal cultures, domestic abuse, and the pervasive use of violence in young people's relationships. To be a 'real man' meant to be able to dominate others, particularly women, with or without their consent. Young men were raised to be assertive and masculine, while girls were taught to be obedient and subordinate.[67] Young men often felt entitled to girls' bodies, and girls' rejections of men's advances often meant little. Describing boys in her Pimville school, one interviewee explained, 'you know with guys, they would just want to be in love with ladies, and they will beat you if you don't want, they will take you even if you don't want.'[68] With her interviewees in Natal, Catherine Campbell found that girls commonly feared forced sex in their relationships. They saw male violence as undesirable, yet inevitable and unchangeable. As one stated, 'Of

23:79 (2009): 100.

63   *The Sowetan*, 26 January 1988; *The Sowetan*, 9 March 1989.

64   Pumla Dineo Gqola, *Rape: A South African Nightmare*, (MFBooks Joburg: Johannesburg, 2015) p. 78–79.

65   Russell and Mabaso, 'Rape and Child Sexual Abuse in Soweto,' 74.

66   Tlhabi, *Endings and Beginnings*, 48.

67   Graeme Simpson, 'Jack-asses and Jackrollers: Rediscovering Gender in Understanding Violence,' Research report written for the Centre for the Study of Violence and Reconciliation, 1992, <https://www.csvr.org.za/publications/1547-jack-asses-and-jackrollers-rediscovering-gender-in-understanding-violence> [accessed 29 November 2014].

68   Interview with Beatrice, Pimville, 23 May 2015.

course I don't like it when my boyfriend beats me. However there is no point in leaving him. I will probably just find someone worse.'[69] Their most common strategy for dealing with such violence was simply to 'talk calmly'.[70] Growing up, girls also regularly witnessed domestic violence in their homes and internalised this, later acquiescing to the same violence when used against them. One of Marks' female informants from Diepkloof believed that girls should be beaten by their boyfriends for any wrongdoing. She explained, 'If the guys beat the girls, they beat you with a reason.'[71]

Idealised Femininities and Gendered Geographies

In attempting to avoid such violence as best as possible, girls sought to conform their behaviour to idealised conceptions of femininity. As Richard Waller argues, female youth in African history have tended to bear the 'double burden of expectation and censure' and are generally chastised and controlled both by their elders and young men.[72] In South Africa, the ideal African girl was expected to be passive and innocent and was herself responsible for how she was treated by men.[73] South Africa's colonial and apartheid history produced societies in which women often did not have the means to be economically independent and were reliant on men for income and housing. This has promoted particular femininities that prize obedience and passivity, as well as acquiesce to male control and violence.[74] A 'good' girl during the 1980s was one who attended school and church but otherwise largely stayed at home to help with domestic chores and care for other children, who did not hang around with boys after a certain age, and who was chaste, respectable, and obedient. Only by behaving in these ways could young women have a 'bright future'.[75]

Young women's vulnerability to violence, combined with these expectations placed on their behaviour, meant that their freedom of movement in the townships was greatly restricted, and township geographies deeply gendered. Outside of school, boys and girls largely grew up in different spaces: whereas

---

[69] Campbell, 'Learning to Kill,' 625–627.
[70] Catherine Campbell, 'Identity and Gender in a Changing Society: The Social Identity of South African Township Youth,' (PhD thesis, Department of Psychology, University of Bristol, 1992), 121.
[71] Marks, *Young Warriors*, 25.
[72] Waller, 'Rebellious Youth in Colonial Africa,' 83.
[73] Jewkes and Morrell, 'Sexuality and the Limits of Agency,' 1730.
[74] Rachel Jewkes and Robert Morrell, 'Gender and Sexuality: Emerging Perspectives from the Heterosexual Epidemic in South Africa and Implications for HIV Risk and Prevention,' *Journal of the International AIDS Society* 13:6 (2010): 4.
[75] Campbell, 'Identity and Gender in a Changing Society,' 126.

boys were free to play and discuss politics in the street, girls were restricted to performing domestic duties in the home. More so than boys, they bore the burden of household labour, and were expected to return home quickly after school to cook and clean. As a male comrade explained, 'women are expected, by the time their parents come back home from work, there's fire, the pots are already in the stove or are waiting...everything is up and running.'[76] While most girls conformed to these expectations, they did not necessarily do so without grievance. Speaking about her adolescence, Tshitshi from Umlazi states, 'There were many things that I found frustrating. Top of the list was my responsibilities as a child minder...Household chores were a close second.' Even when her mother did not need her help, she was still required to perform these tasks as essential training for future married life.[77]

Girls' confinement to the home was thus not only or always about the necessity of their labour but was also about their safety and respectability. A document produced by the South African Youth Congress (SAYCO) on why women were less involved in youth politics stated that while boys are encouraged to go outside and play, girls are 'taught household chores and lectured a lot on how vulnerable [they are] to the outside world.'[78] Although girls were not immune from sexual violence in the home, they were certainly better protected there than in Soweto's streets. As one female comrade described it, because of such parental concerns over girls' vulnerability, girls were raised 'in a cocoon': 'what I've noticed from our communities, they don't care what boys do, only girl children, they will need to know where you're going. At times I don't even go to buy bread from the shops.'[79] Yet restrictions on girls' mobility were also due to dominant ideals of femininity. Campbell describes how township streets in the 1980s were 'clearly demarcated as the social territory of young men only,' and thus any woman who participated in street politics was 'invariably looked down on and regarded as sexually promiscuous.' She continues, 'A young woman on the streets might fall into the clutches of a propositioning male and the community might label her as loose, available and a man-chaser, reflecting badly not only on her womanhood but also on her family's dignity. In short such a young woman was "an embarrassment to her family."' As one of Campbell's female interviewees stated in defence of her reputation, 'I am not a hang-around girl. I am always behind my home

[76] Interview with Siphiwe, Pimville, 17 May 2015.
[77] Ntombela and Mashiya, 'Reflections on African Adolescent Girls,' 102.
[78] 'Organising Women,' Youth Focus, July 1989, AL2425: K1, South African Youth Congress, South African History Archive (hereafter SAHA), Johannesburg.
[79] Interview with Thabisile, Johannesburg, 25 May 2015.

gates.'[80] Girls' movement was monitored by both their families and by young men in their communities, particularly boyfriends and brothers. To them, it was important that girls remain at home for their own physical protection and to safeguard their reputations. The young men interviewed by Campbell emphasised that while it was okay for them to move around the township as they pleased, this was not the case for young women.[81]

The gendered geographies of township spaces and girls' socialisation towards the home had particular effects that ostracised girls from the rise of student politics in the 1980s. Although girls had some exposure to political discussion and debate at school, as the next chapter will discuss, at home they were largely shielded from politics by concerned parents. Many female comrades were curious about the struggle and asked their families to explain why the military had occupied the township or who Nelson Mandela was. Yet most were refused answers. As Penelope from Jabavu narrated, 'I will come home and ask, "what is *baferekanyi* [terrorist] mama?" Because I would want to understand. They talk about these people all the time on the radio.' But 'my mother would just brush you off and say, "Hey, you must clean that thing! You haven't cleaned and you ask too many questions!"'[82] Simultaneously, girls were discouraged from occupying public spaces, lingering in the streets, or leaving home late at night. As one of Campbell's female interviewees described, 'It's mostly boys who go to meetings, and not girls. I do not go to meetings… because it would take me away from home.'[83] Girls' involvement in COSAS was greatly restricted as they could often only attend meetings during the day due to parental constraints on their movement after dark. They were also rarely allowed to leave the house during the day if their chores were not complete. Siphiwe, a male COSAS member from Pimville, described, 'I think the parental pressure for women at the time was more than for men…It's difficult to explain, if you are a woman, to your parents that you can't sleep at home…it's difficult for them that they cannot take care of the household because they are busy with the struggle.'[84]

These restrictions on girls' mobility meant that they were mostly excluded from township streets, which became key sites of political mobilisation and organisation during these years. Describing youth culture in Alexandra in the 1980s, Bozzoli writes:

[80] Campbell, 'Identity and Gender in a Changing Society,' 125–126.
[81] *Ibid.*
[82] Interview with Penelope, Jabavu, 12 June 2015.
[83] Campbell, 'Identity and Gender in a Changing Society,' 321.
[84] Interview with Siphiwe, Pimville, 17 May 2015.

The highly structured little society of the township provided a number of environments in which a social and cultural life for young people was created. The streets were the most obvious. At home, rooms were so small and crowded that most people – especially youths who were out of school and unemployed – spent most of their time in Alexandra's street corner society, where neighbourhood and peer, mainly male, networks were rendered strong.[85]

As she notes, streets were spaces where male, not female, networks were formed. Subsequently, girls were excluded from the very spaces in which informal political education occurred and youths' consciousness was sharpened.[86] In contrast to girls, boys were 'having things easy', as one female comrade explained:

They don't have…chores that much, they've got all the time to themselves… That's why most of the time you'd find boys hanging around…on [street] corners. So it's easy for them to, to communicate. We used to say *umrabulo* [a political discussion or debate]…it was easy for them to *umrabulo*-ise, to make understand or make one politically aware. So it was easy because one guy would go chat, they'd start smoking, passing it, and chatting about whatever.[87]

The socialisation of girls towards the private sphere also contributed to what many interviewees themselves labelled as an 'inferiority complex' in girls. As one male comrade described, 'A female child, we are being taught from childhood that your duties are in the kitchen.' He continued, 'So that attitude makes these females to feel or to be inferior when compared to a male…So that thing makes females to be less effective when it comes to issues, especially around politics.'[88] Makgane, a COSAS leader from Diepkloof, discussed how he and his brother were absolved from household work while his sister was not. This had a distinctive affect when it came to the struggle: 'Because of those upbringings…it became easier to organise men, you know? It was more like a natural thing to do, to first start with men…Then look around and say hey, but we only have one woman.'[89] This inferiority complex was not merely something imposed on young women by their male peers, as the quotes above might suggest, but something that effected girls' own identities. When asked about why fewer girls than boys joined COSAS, one woman simply stated, 'I think it's us being female, we undermine ourselves.'[90]

[85] Bozzoli, *Theatres of Struggles*, 97.
[86] Bundy, 'Street Sociology and Pavement Politics,' 320.
[87] Interview with Florence, Diepkloof, 8 May 2014.
[88] Interview with Moses, Diepkloof, 19 April 2014.
[89] Interview with Makgane, Sandton, 17 April 2014.
[90] Interview with Nomsa, Diepkloof Extension, 19 April 2014.

It is important to resist the tendency to depict girls as merely passive victims of violence, and to ask how they responded to these overlapping forms of hierarchy and oppression that shaped their lives. However, their full range of strategies for contending with violence and subordination are difficult to access in the available sources. In his research on Soweto in the 1940s and 50s, Glaser found little evidence of young women building any type of defence networks to protect themselves. For most girls, he argues, marriage often provided the only escape from predatory male gangsters.[91] Tlhabi ultimately found some protection from township boys by growing close to one particularly notorious gangster whose reputation she used to ward off other young men.[92] Campbell notes that many of her female interviewees simply defied their families' control and travelled beyond their homes without parental permission, often to engage in romantic and sexual relationships with young men. But the young women who are the focus of this group chose another option: to join the liberation struggle. Although their activism put them at risk of other forms of violence, and could not wholly protect them from sexual violence, it did offer a partial escape from feelings of inferiority and helplessness.

Conclusion

This chapter has provided a preliminary sketch of what life was like for young people growing up in apartheid's townships during the 1970s and 1980s. Although much further research is needed to better understand how children and youth experienced and responded to segregation and repression, this chapter has demonstrated how young people's lives were increasingly shaped by political conflict and violence during these years, even for those who did their best to stay away from politics and comrade culture. It has also argued that experiences of childhood and youth were distinctly gendered in South Africa, with girls facing particular challenges that confined them to the home, instilled fear in them, and made them feel inferior and subordinate to young men. The various strategies that African girls developed to cope with, challenge, or acquiesce to the pressures, vulnerabilities, and expectations they faced during these years – beyond joining the liberation struggle – are yet to be extensively explored by academics.

As the rest of this book will demonstrate, some girls did choose to join the student movement and participate in political confrontation, despite the challenges they faced in doing so. While their decisions were spurred by numerous

---

[91] Clive Glaser, 'The Mark of Zorro: Sexuality and Gender Relations in the Tsotsi Subculture on the Witwatersrand,' *African Studies* 51:1 (1992): 60.

[92] Tlhabi, *Endings and Beginnings*, 55–56.

motivations, what these girls shared was a desire to challenge both the apartheid state and the inequalities and powerlessness they faced as African girls. By trading their skirts for trousers, housework for political meetings, and church-going for *toyi-toying*, they sought to be 'one of the boys' and escape the experiences of being a girl. Yet, the following chapters also demonstrate that these experiences of African girlhood – of violence, vulnerability, and inferiority – were not ones that could be completely erased by political activism. Throughout their time as student and youth activists, these women's adolescent experiences continued to shape why they joined the struggle and the roles they took on, and today are reflected in how these now-adults remember their time as comrades.

2

The School: Becoming a Female Comrade

'Nobody taught me politics,' Florence explained early on in our first meeting in 2014. At eight years old, Florence witnessed the chaos that engulfed Soweto in the wake of the 1976 student uprisings. Curious about what was happening, she constantly pestered her parents for answers and explanations, but they refused to give her any. 'You mustn't ask such questions, because you'll be arrested,' her mother told her. A year later, Florence opened a newspaper to see a picture of Winnie Madikizela-Mandela standing in front of her Brandfort home. 'She was so pretty,' she described, 'and I started reading because then, the only black pictures that we'd seen in the newspapers, they were adverts...and the prettiest ladies would be advertising Lux, the soaps, the creams.' But Florence did not understand the context of the article, which presumably detailed Madikizela-Mandela's banishment to Brandfort in 1977. Florence asked her mother and grandmother about Winnie and what had happened to her, but 'nobody could explain that because they were scared of explaining...And it started triggering something in my mind,' she said, 'why are these people not telling but I can see that there's something happening politically and people were dying?' It would be another seven years before Florence finally found the answers she was looking for – not in her home or in Soweto's streets but in her secondary school, Bopasenatla, at the age of sixteen. There, she met male students already politicised and heavily involved in COSAS. Rather than shooing her away, the male comrades she met at school encouraged her curiosity, answered her questions, and helped to equip her with the understanding necessary to recruit other girls into the student struggle. 'With COSAS,' Florence exclaimed, 'I felt I had a voice; as a human being, as a South African, and as a woman.'[1]

These stories from Florence's childhood are illustrative of how and why girls growing up in Soweto made the unconventional decision to join the liberation struggle while still teenagers and school students. They resented being shielded from politics and moments of political disruption in the townships. They could

---

[1]   Interview with Florence, Diepkloof, 8 May 2014.

see violence escalating around them, and yet were offered few answers at home as to why this was happening. Meanwhile their brothers and male schoolmates seemed to be at the centre of township politics; while they met on street corners to discuss the latest developments and plan action, girls were drawn increasingly into the home and told to focus on studies and their domestic chores rather than the 'nonsense' of politics. Florence's mentioning of Madikizela-Mandela in her account of her early politicisation is thus significant here. Seeing a young woman in the newspaper who was not a model or a beauty pageant contestant but an activist – and one so powerful that she had to be banished from Soweto – stirred something in Florence and helped her to realise that as a girl she too could be something other than a dutiful daughter and schoolgirl.

This chapter details female comrades' pathways to activism and explores how their experiences of girlhood in apartheid Soweto shaped their decisions to seek out and join student organisations as their first step into the wider liberation movement. It explores the opportunities and challenges that Bantu Education schools offered female students, highlighting their ambiguous nature as spaces of both empowerment and subordination. Like Florence, many female comrades recount being politically curious from a young age yet being denied the opportunity to engage in politics alongside boys. But as girls entered secondary school, this changed; while they were shielded from politics in the home, and strategically kept away from township streets, at school girls were surrounded by politicised students in a space less dangerous than the streets and with less parental supervision than the home. There, they were able to engage in political discussions and join student councils, and in doing so satiated their curiosity and felt part of something bigger than themselves. Initially, female comrades did not join student organisations out of a deep ideological commitment to the liberation struggle's cause. Rather, they saw student organisations as a means of addressing the immediate injustices they faced as students in Soweto. But they also found that student politics provided them with a sense of purpose and belonging at a time when girls had few social opportunities in the township other than church groups or beauty pageants. These emotional benefits of student activism – feelings of adventure, camaraderie, and purpose – were shared by male and female comrades; both groups recount the joy they felt in joining student organisations and taking up leadership roles in their schools and communities. Girls' participation – which often represented up to a third of COSAS membership at schools – was thus in part determined more by their identity as students and youth than by their gender.[2]

---

[2]   This estimate was made by interviewees, but supports what other researchers found in areas beyond Soweto too. See Carter, 'We are the Progressives', 215; Seekings, 'Gender Ideology and Township Politics', 81.

Yet the gratification they felt was, in part, a gendered experience. Girls and young women found that student politics allowed them to rebel against the confines of traditional femininities, and reject a girlhood predicated on housework, obedience, and political ignorance. Furthermore, many women recounted distinctly gendered motivations for seeking out political organisations at school. Most centred their narratives on key events in their adolescence which exposed the inequalities they experienced because of *both* their gender and generation: being corporally punished at school for not cleaning classrooms; feeling threatened in township streets because of gangsters known for gang-raping schoolgirls; or realising the injustice of their domestic work which kept them confined to the home while boys were free to play or discuss politics after school. Girls thus saw joining student organisations as an opportunity to better their lives on multiple fronts: to address the racial injustices they faced daily as Africans under apartheid; to confront educational and generational injustices at school and in their communities; and to construct a new political girlhood that mitigated their feelings of inferiority and vulnerability. As Florence explained, joining COSAS offered female students a voice – as students and community members, but also specifically as girls and young women.

Gendering Education under Apartheid

Within the history of Bantu Education, little has been written specifically about gender or girls' experiences. As Meghan Healy-Clancy highlights, this can be attributed to two main reasons. First, research on Bantu Education (like so much of radical South African history) has predominantly focused on the prevailing issues of race and class, rather than gender. And second, since the Soweto Uprisings of 1976, scholarship has largely been concentrated on student politics, where again race and class have been seen as more central factors in explaining student protests than gender, and in which girls' participation has been obscured by history's focus on leadership and those who were tried and prosecuted.[3] The small body of historiography that does touch on gender, including the works of Glaser, Morrell, Moletsane, Healy-Clancy, and Elaine Unterhalter, reveals that schools were ambiguous spaces for African girls under apartheid.[4] On paper, girls' schooling opportunities expanded under

---

[3]   Healy-Clancy, *A World of Their Own*, 7; Pohlandt-McCormick, *Doing Violence to Memory*, E-book, paragraph 632.

[4]   Glaser, *Bo-Tsotsi*; Robert Morrell, 'Corporal Punishment and Masculinity in South African Schools,' *Men and Masculinities* 4:2 (2001): 140–157; Morrell and Moletsane, 'Inequality and Fear,' 224–242; Healy-Clancy, *A World of Their Own*; Elaine Unterhalter, 'The Impact of Apartheid on Women's Education in South Africa,' *Review of African Political Economy* 48: 17 (1990): 66–75; Elaine Unterhalter,

Bantu Education; increasingly over the apartheid period, more African girls were attending and staying in school. While in 1960 they constituted only 27 per cent of African students in higher secondary education, by 1985 they outnumbered boys at 54.5 per cent of the total.[5] Some female students clearly found schools to be empowering spaces. As one student from Inanda Seminary, a private boarding school for African girls, recounted to Healy-Clancy, 'leaving Inanda you could almost feel you could conquer the world and do everything and anything that you wanted to do.' Her interviewees spoke of this empowerment in gendered terms, stating that education helped them to shed feelings of gendered inferiority.[6]

However, the 'feminisation' of schooling in apartheid South Africa occurred within 'a profoundly anti-feminist historical context', as Healy-Clancy argues, and girls' increased access to education did not lead to an increase in gender equality.[7] Morrell and Moletsane highlight how the racial inequalities of Bantu Education produced deeply uneven gender relations in schools. During apartheid, girls were disadvantaged and endangered within school walls. Both labour and education in schools were sexually divided; girls were given fewer opportunities to take math and science and were expected to do all the classroom cleaning. Schools were thus spaces that tended to reproduce rather than challenge patriarchal township gender ideologies. Moreover, schools did not offer girls complete protection from the violence they were subjected to in the home or streets. Rather, many were sites of gender violence. From the 1970s, the threat of rape against school girls increasingly moved from streets into schools themselves, as not only gangsters but male students too were reportedly engaging in rape. Sexual violence perpetrated by teachers and male students tended to go unreported and unpunished and was often not considered 'rape' by those who committed it or experienced it. In a 1998 survey of 1500 young people in Soweto, one third of women responded that they had

---

'Remembering and Forgetting: Constructions of Education Gender Reform in Autobiography and Policy Texts of the South African Transition,' *History of Education* 29:5 (2000): 457–472; Mark Hunter, 'The Bond of Education Gender, the Value of Children, and the Making of Umlazi Township in 1960s South Africa,' *The Journal of African History* 55:3 (2014): 467–490.

5   While girls' access to secondary schooling greatly increased from 1960, it is important to acknowledge that the vast majority of black women under apartheid did not complete primary, let alone secondary, schooling. In 1980, only 37.8 per cent of African girls aged fifteen to nineteen were attending secondary school. Unterhalter, 'The Impact of Apartheid on Women's Education in South Africa,' 70–71.

6   Healy-Clancy, *A World of Their Own*, 179.

7   *Ibid.*

personally experienced sexual violence at school.[8] During the political upheav-
als of the 1980s many Soweto schools became warzones – sites of violent
conflict between students, teachers, gangs and security forces. Such violence at
times played out along gendered lines and bred violent masculinities amongst
many male students. Within the struggle, student activists included amongst
their demands a call for the end of abuse of female students. However, there
was rarely any specific attention given to bettering the conditions of women's
education as distinct from the general focus on ending repressive conditions
in schools as part of the wider liberation struggle.[9]

Becoming a Female Comrade

It is difficult to know exactly how many girls and young women in South
Africa joined the township uprisings or became committed activists during
their high school years. Given the oppressive nature of the apartheid state,
there was little incentive for these organisations to keep detailed lists of their
membership. Interviewees estimate that girls made up somewhere between 10
and 30 per cent of active COSAS membership before the organisation was
banned in mid-1985. These recollections corroborate the findings of Seekings and Charles Carter, who in their research in Tumahole and Alexandra
similarly found that girls represented between a quarter and a half of student
or youth congress membership in the early years of the township uprisings.[10]

What is more challenging to discern is what percentage of school-age girls
were engaged in the struggle in a committed, sustained way. Most female
interviewees report that they were one of only very few girls at their individual
schools who joined, but these recollections of their extraordinary involvement
are likely shaped by interviewees' desire to claim historical agency. While
many girls may have initially been drawn to marches, rallies, and COSAS
meetings, becoming a dedicated member of COSAS involved a much more
dangerous commitment that scared many students away. Consequently, many
more people identified themselves as 'comrades' during the 1980s than were
actually active, long-term members of student and youth organisations. Several interviewees lamented that while some of their fellow female students
were initially attracted to politics for social reasons, they soon stopped attending meetings. It is likely that committed, politically active girls would have
compromised only a small minority of teenage girls in the townships. This

---

[8]   Morrell and Moletsane, 'Inequality and Fear,' 228–237.
[9]   Unterhalter, 'Impact of Apartheid on Women's Education,' 74.
[10] Seekings, 'Gender Ideology and Township Politics,' 81; Carter, 'We are the Pro-
      gressives,' 215.

is not to say that most girls and young women passively accepted apartheid rule or their subordinate status in society. Many likely rebelled against both traditional gender norms and the state in a myriad of quiet, subtle ways. But female comrades' committed participation in the liberation struggle would have been unconventional, requiring a substantial challenge to hegemonic gender norms and placing these girls in significant danger. On a wider scale, any child – male or female – who committed themselves to politics during these years was undertaking a serious risk that offered little personal material reward. We must thus ask which girls were drawn to the struggle, how they became involved, and why.

In previous literature on the comrades, scholars have sought to disaggregate young activists according to their class, level of education, race, and organisational affiliation, countering portrayals of the 'youth' as a homogenous group.[11] The same efforts must be made with female comrades to understand the specific conditions which led some, but certainly not all, young women to join the liberation struggle. Firstly, female comrades in Soweto predominantly came from the middle economic strata of township society; most were neither destitute shack dwellers nor members of the African middle class who often sent their children away from the politically volatile townships to schools such as Inanda Seminary. They also tended to be younger than male comrades, usually aged eighteen or younger and still at secondary school when they joined. These two trends make sense given that both more economically disadvantaged girls and older female youth would have had greater constraints placed on their time by the need to work or look after children. Furthermore, schools provided girls with an access to politics that was not available in the home or in many non-unionised work places.

Despite the previous literature's focus on class, educational level, and employment status when explaining comrade membership, these structural factors were rarely prominent in comrades' own understandings of who joined the struggle and why. Women themselves placed much more emphasis on more subjective characteristics and insisted that it took a girl who was particularly curious, tenacious, and already active in the school or community to join the liberation struggle. In highlighting these particular elements of their personalities, and linking them to their political mobilisation, these women challenge the frequent claims made by male comrades that girls were too quiet or shy to engage in political meetings or were too frivolous to be interested in political discussions. Many stressed their prior engagement in extracurricular activities,

---

[11] Seekings, *Heroes or Villains*, xiv–xv; 15; Naidoo, 'The Politics of Youth Resistance,' 145; Sitas, 'The Making of the "Comrades" Movement in Natal,' 633–637.

whether these were debating clubs, athletics, choirs, or church groups. Social networks formed by youth clubs and churches were central to mobilising young men into the struggle, and this was certainly the case for young women too.[12] Furthermore, showing commitment to such activities helped young women prove to their fellow comrades that they could become dedicated activists, female comrades claimed. Crediting her recruitment to her disposition and active lifestyle, a comrade from Jabavu described, 'Prior to that [joining her school's SRC] I was playing soccer, I was playing netball…I was also doing modern dance…I also leading a debate team at school. And so these guys [male comrades] thought, you know, we can work with this one.'[13] Female interviewees also stressed the importance of being a 'talkative' girl. Vicky, who participated in the Diepkloof COSAS branch during the mid-1980s, described her childhood self as mischievous and loquacious, 'this naughty little girl' who loved to debate and became curious about politics early in life. While several male comrades recounted that female comrades tended to be quiet in meetings and had to be pushed to voice their opinions, Vicky proclaimed, 'I was the talkative one!' She recalled that her male comrades often had to tell her 'time out' to stop her talking, 'Because I was going on and on.'[14] Likewise, another woman explained how and why she was recruited to COSAS: 'At school, they knew me, that I talk too much, all the time, every time I have something to say.'[15] Compared to other girls, interviewees explained, they tended to be curious and to question events around them.

How Girls Joined

Some female comrades' political curiosity was first sparked in the home. While girls were typically shielded from politics by their parents, this was not necessarily the case for those whose family members were already involved in the struggle. Shirley from Orlando West recalled that her sister's boyfriend was a comrade who held political discussions with his friends in her garage. Although she did not understand what they were talking about, she would often listen, and when given the opportunity to find out more about the struggle through the student movement at school, she eagerly joined.[16] Beatrice's political interest was also first sparked at home by her mother, who as a nurse treated patients who had been abused while detained for political

---

[12] Bozzoli, *Theatres of Struggle*, 99.

[13] Interview with Thabisile, Johannesburg, 25 May 2015.

[14] Interview with Vicky, Diepkloof, 14 May 2014.

[15] Interview with Penelope, Jabavu, 12 June 2015.

[16] Interview with Shirley, Orlando West, 3 May 2014.

reasons. After being formally recruited by a male friend at school, Beatrice went on to recruit her female cousin and best friend into the student movement as well.[17]

But for the most part, Soweto's female comrades first became formally involved in politics at school – even those who had prior knowledge of or connections to the struggle through their families or friends. Many happened to attend schools known for being particularly politicised at the time, such as Bopasenatla in Diepkloof and Morris Isaacson in Jabavu. In explaining student mobilisation in South Africa in the 1970s and 1980s, Harold Wolpe argues that schools were a 'protected space' where students could discuss politics and congregate away from the reaches of the repressive state.[18] While this argument has since been criticised for underestimating the authoritarian nature of schools under Bantu Education, Glaser contends that schools still provided a space in which inquisitive people from similar backgrounds and with similar grievances were brought together and could engage in more subtle forms of resistance, informal discussion, and debate:

> In spite of a mostly cautious teaching staff and pervasive inspectorate, the high school as an institution was uniquely suited to politicization. Teenagers were drawn together in large numbers for several hours of the day; they had time to talk, they circulated books and ideas, they had easily accessible venues to meet in, they had debating clubs to hone their public speaking skills.[19]

Despite the violence and discrimination girls were subject to in Soweto's schools, these spaces were their main site of politicisation. Girls tended to be exposed to political debate and liberation organisations at school rather than in Soweto's more public, masculine spaces such as streets or soccer fields. This makes sense given that schools were the one space outside the home, and perhaps the church, where girls were collectively present in large numbers alongside boys. By the mid-1980s, African girls were more present in township schools than ever before and tended to spend more time in school than boys. Schools provided girls with a more protected and more socially acceptable place than the streets where they could meet with others their same age who shared their grievances, inquisitiveness, or frustrations.

---

[17] Interview with Beatrice, Pimville, 23 May 2015.

[18] Nozipho J. Diseko, 'The Origins and Development of the South African Student's Movement (SASM): 1968–1976,' *Journal of Southern African Studies* 18:1 (1992): 45.

[19] Glaser, 'Youth and Generation in South African History,' 128. See also Clive Glaser, '"We must infiltrate the Tsotsis": School Politics and Youth Gangs in Soweto, 1968–1976,' *Journal of Southern African Studies* 24:2 (1998): 302.

Almost all female comrades' official entry into politics began when they were elected to student representative councils (SRCs). From its onset, COSAS campaigned for the replacement of secondary schools' despised prefect system with SRCs – which the Department of Education and Training (DET) reluctantly allowed in 1984. SRCs were not explicitly connected to the liberation movement; their purpose was to represent students to the faculty and to ensure students had essential supplies such as stationary and uniforms. However, COSAS largely co-opted SRCs and used them as recruiting grounds – an affiliation the DET did not accept.[20] In some of Soweto's secondary schools, particular efforts were made to ensure that each class had one male and one female SRC member, which greatly facilitated girls' recruitment into the struggle. Girls elected as SRC reps saw joining COSAS as the next logical step in their roles as student leaders. As Nonkululeko from Diepkloof described, 'by the time we entered [secondary] school we never had that mind that I'm going to be a member of COSAS or something. I just went to school. But at the time they elect you to be a member of an SRC, obviously you have to participate, to be a member of COSAS.'[21]

For most female interviewees, their recruitment into the struggle was not marked by a single event or motivation but happened 'little by little'; many first joined SRCs and campaigned against problems specific to schools, such as the continued use of corporal punishment and the lack of school supplies.[22] As they were introduced to existing COSAS members, they were then taught that these educational struggles were inseparable from larger, community issues and nationwide calls for an end to apartheid. Some eventually took on leadership roles as secretaries, treasurers, and branch presidents. The campaigns they engaged in at school differed little from those of male comrades and were largely centred on the daily inequalities they faced under Bantu Education: poor school infrastructure, school fees, age caps on secondary schooling, unaffordable uniforms and examination fees, and too few black teachers. Many participated in school boycotts aimed at addressing these various issues. Female comrades also worked to recruit other girls at school. Lucy, a COSAS leader from Diepkloof, described how there were still very few girls engaged in the struggle at school, as most were too afraid of police harassment or unwilling to defy their parents' authority.[23] But by demonstrating to their fellow female students the inadequacies and inequalities of

---

[20]   Clive Glaser, 'Learning Amidst the Turmoil,' 426.
[21]   Group interview with female comrades from Diepkloof, Diepkloof, 27 June 2015.
[22]   *Ibid.*
[23]   Interview with Lucy, Fleurhof, 7 April 2014.

their education compared to white students, many female comrades were successful in persuading more girls to join COSAS or SOSCO.

Female comrades' life histories contained few descriptive details of their day-to-day lives as student activists. When asked about their political activities at school, many responded with simple lists of issues they sought to address without much detail, and very few punctuated their descriptions with anecdotes of particular moments from their pasts. Where women's recollections did become more vibrant was in describing more confrontational activities partaken in as student activists. Shirley, a comrade from Orlando West, recalled her involvement in the 'Pass one, pass all' campaign, in which comrades insisted that they be passed to the next standard based on their grades earlier in the year without having to write exams due to the disruption caused to education by the state of emergency. On the day of matric examinations, Shirley and her fellow comrades discovered that there were some students in White City, Jabavu, defying the comrades' exam boycott and sitting for their exams. Shirley excitedly and proudly recalled how the comrades attacked the students with *sjamboks* and tried to burn their exam papers. Similarly, Phumzile, a female comrade from Diepkloof, described how she was tasked with recruiting more female students at school. When asked if persuading students to join was difficult, she responded, 'It was very, very difficult. Sometimes we were forced for them to join us by force. And then we said – we were having our own language – "join the force"…So we used to force them to join us, to go to the police stations and ask police to release our comrades.'[24]

Where female comrades' narratives of their activism in school were the most dynamic was when they recalled instances of personal agency and defiance, and particularly those in which they challenged the expectations of feminine behaviour or patriarchal nature of student culture. Nomsa explained how her school's principal was particularly stubborn to student calls to abolish corporal punishment. She narrated how she and another female student went up to the principal and declared, 'Principal, this corporal punishment is being abolished. We want to do away with it.' They explained to each teacher in the school, 'there are many mechanisms of punishment whereby at least that punishment is going to build a child rather than the corporal punishment.' Although their efforts were not successful in stopping the use of corporal punishment in their school entirely, Nomsa recalled with pride, 'eventually, myself and Thembi, there was no teacher that was touching us because of that.'[25]

---

[24] Interview with Phumzile, Johannesburg, 17 April 2015.
[25] Interview with Nomsa, Diepkloof Extension, 19 April 2014.

'I wanted a better life': Why Girls Joined

Within the existing historiography, there is very little understanding of why girls and young women participated in student or youth politics over the course of apartheid history. Official investigations into the 1976 Soweto Uprisings noted the involvement of female students, but without inquiring into their motivations or actions.[26] Helena Pohlandt-McCormick notes how because of history's focus on those in leadership or those who are traditionally heard in sources, female students' involvement in the uprisings has largely been obscured from history, and not explored in the same analytical detail as male students'.[27] Interviews with Soweto's 1980s female students offer new insights into why girls joined the struggle, and what they remember today as their main motivations for becoming politically active. Most female comrades were not initially drawn to COSAS out of a deep political or moral commitment to the anti-apartheid cause. Rather, they were largely ignorant of ideology when they first joined SRCs and were initially more concerned with 'bread and butter' issues affecting students. Like their male comrades, they resented being corporally punished for not wearing the uniforms their parents could not afford, sitting in dilapidated, overcrowded classrooms without windows, or not having the books they needed to study and pass their exams. Many explained such things simply; they knew they were being treated unfairly and wanted to do something about it. As Beatrice explained, 'I got interested [in politics] because I could feel I was not happy the way I was treated at school, and the education that I was getting.'[28] It was only after joining COSAS and engaging with older students in leadership positions that they linked these daily issues to the wider system of apartheid.

The exact details of their formal entry into political organisations are hazy in female comrades' recollections; many cannot remember exactly how or why they attended their first COSAS meeting. Female interviewees repeatedly stressed how they were not forcibly recruited into the struggle. As Ntsiki from Diepkloof explained, COSAS was 'not like a church, it's not like somebody will recruit you. But the situation of that time will make you jump, voluntarily...I don't remember us feeling forced.'[29] When specifically asked why they joined COSAS, many female comrades provided what at first appeared to be vague and idealistic reasons. One female comrade from Diepkloof responded, 'because I wanted a better life... I was joining the struggle because of my heart

[26]   Glaser, *Bo-Tsotsi*, 172.
[27]   Pohlandt-McCormick, *Doing Violence to Memory*, e-book paragraph 632.
[28]   Interview with Beatrice, Pimville, 23 May 2015.
[29]   Interview with Ntsiki, Diepkloof, 5 April 2015.

and commitment that I was having, and the...way we were treated when we were growing up.'[30] Similarly, Ntebaleng, also from Diepkloof, remarked, 'I wanted to join COSAS because of the way I saw things were...I wanted to bring more improvement so that our children and our grandchildren must get a better education, better future.'[31] Narrating her decision with similar broad, ambitious motivations, Ntsiki from Diepkloof recalled, 'We were young, the blood was boiling, and we wanted change... We just want to liberate our country, we want to go to exile, we want Mandela to be free. That was in our head, nothing else.'[32]

But simultaneously, both male and female comrades recalled that they were initially drawn to COSAS for more superficial reasons. Comrades were known for singing and marching in the streets, often performing a popular protest dance/march known as the *toyi-toyi*. Joining this exhilarating, militarised youth subculture provided students with feelings of enjoyment, pride, and belonging, as previous historians exploring male comrades have highlighted.[33] But these feelings were shared by male and female students alike. Explaining her mobilisation as a simple process, one female comrade recalled, 'I just love seeing people like, they're singing their song...and then I go there [and join].'[34] Speaking about the first political rally she attended as a teenager, another female comrade described, 'It was nice, people were singing revolutionary songs...that's what I enjoyed.' She described how she was also enthralled by the presence of journalists and photographers at this rally and felt a sense of affirmation and pride at being there alongside them: 'There were these people who were taking videos, taking photos and things. And being young, I didn't know what that was. For my side, I was just happy that I will appear on newspaper...If you appear on the *Soweto News*, the local newspaper, you were like, a big thing.'[35] Even the aesthetic style of the comrades was appealing. One male informant spoke admiringly of the way comrades would wear their ties around their foreheads and tuck their trousers into their socks.[36]

Toyi-toying, attending rallies, and even wearing the right type of clothing may appear to be superficial motivations for joining the struggle, ways in which young people blended politics with play in the particularly heightened political contexts of the townships. Yet such activities provided both male

[30] Interview with Thobile, Diepkloof, 12 April 2014.
[31] Interview with Ntebaleng, Diepkloof, 15 April 2014.
[32] Interview with Ntsiki, Diepkloof, 5 April 2015.
[33] Seekings, *Heroes and Villains*, 63–64.
[34] Interview with Rethabile, Diepkloof, 1 May 2014.
[35] Interview with Stompie, Naturena, 29 May 2015.
[36] Interview with Sello, Diepkloof, 14 May 2014.

and female youth with an important sense of camaraderie and adventure that fuelled their participation in the struggle. In their own recollections of joining, female comrades do not focus on deep political discussions held at school or the specifics of how and when they participated in particular campaigns. Rather, their memories focus on the more emotional, subjective aspects of comradeship: on fighting against daily injustices they experienced, and on their new-found feelings of power, authority, and pride in their actions. As Bozzoli argues, oppression and poverty alone were not enough to explain the revolts of the 1980s in South Africa; 'township dwellers did not behave in ways which simply reflected the strategy of the liberation movements. Their actions and beliefs always emerged to some degree out of their own experiences and local systems of ideas, culture and social institutions.'[37] For South Africa's female comrades, their subordination, confinement to the home, and vulnerability to violence made up such 'experiences', and help to explain why they joined student organisations. The gendered dynamics of township life would have perhaps made such involvement even more exciting and adventurous for girls than for boys. Singing and protesting provided girls with a presence on township streets that their domestic-centred lives otherwise did not afford them. Engaging in such activities was not just a means of enjoyment, but also of challenging gender norms, escaping the confines of the home, and learning about the political culture so many of their parents had tried to shield them from since 1976. That becoming a comrade was more of a transgression from youthful norms for girls rather than boys in part explains why the struggle was male dominated, but also why female comrades recall their entry into the struggle with such palpable zeal. More so than men, they describe this period of their lives as one of excitement and awakening. Florence described her recruitment as 'eye opening' and a 'relief', as she could finally engage in the political debates that her parents sought to silence in their home.[38]

These emotional appeals of being a comrade, and interviewees' vague and idealistic understandings of why they first engaged in the liberation movement, can be better understood through what Elisabeth Jean Wood terms 'pleasure of agency'. Both male and female comrades experienced emotional benefits upon initially participating in the liberation movement, as they felt joy, camaraderie, excitement, and pride. As Wood describes of *compesinos* in El Salvador, such emotional benefits speak to the importance of the assertion of agency itself in joining protests or liberation movements. 'The key to the logic of insurgent collective action,' she writes, 'is the assertion of dignity and

---

[37]   Bozzoli, 'Why were the 1980s "Millenarian"?' 79–80.
[38]   Interview with Florence, Diepkloof, 8 May 2014.

defiance through the act of rebelling.'[39] In both male and female comrades' narratives, these feelings of pride and accomplishment are clearly expressed. As Sissy from Diepkloof explained, 'I'm proud of participating. I'm proud of risking my life and my family's life for this freedom.'[40] Her words corroborate Wood's research which found that her interviewees too expressed a distinct pleasure in their defiance of the state.

A New Political Girlhood

In much of the wider work on social movements there is an assumption that when girls or women join political struggles, they must do so out of feminist motivations or in pursuit of gendered causes. But in making this assumption, scholars often neglect to explore women's own motivations, which may or may not be gendered. In Bantu Education schools, both female and male students faced poor quality education, high matric failure rates, corporal punishment, and the prospect of future unemployment. Although female students faced particular barriers to becoming politically active, they nevertheless experienced and sought to address these grievances, much like male students. No female comrades recalled joining the student struggle out of any clear feminist consciousness or an explicit desire to promote women's rights. Many conversely insisted that they did not join the struggle out of a primary desire to contribute to women's liberation. Ntsiki explained how comrades 'don't care' about gender, they 'just want to see our country liberated.'[41] Likewise Bessie stated that the problems she saw at school effected all students, regardless of gender, and it was these issues that they wanted to fight against rather than gender ones.[42]

Yet these clear denials of gender motivations were often contradicted by interviewees themselves, who later gave details of how their experiences growing up as girls in the townships shaped their decisions to join the struggle. Both male and female students were frustrated by the lack of change in their lives by the mid-1980s and saw the student struggle as an opportunity to fight for a better, utopian future. But for female comrades many of these frustrations were gendered. As Jo Beall and her colleagues write of women's political action in South Africa more generally, 'while they may have political

---

[39] Elisabeth Jean Wood, 'The Emotional Benefits of Insurgency in El Salvador,' in Jeff Goodwin, James M. Jasper, and Francesca Polletta (eds), *Passionate Politics: Emotions and Social Movements* (Chicago: University of Chicago Press, 2001), 268.

[40] Interview with Sissy, Diepkloof, 17 April 2015.

[41] Interview with Ntsiki, Diepkloof, 5 April 2015.

[42] Interview with Bessie, Johannesburg, 25 April 2014.

interests in common with men, South African women, like South African men, do not fight these shared struggles as natural subjects, but as *gendered* beings.'[43] Morrell and Moletsane argue that schoolgirls during the late apartheid period were, 'angry, bitter, with limited self-esteem, victims of their male peers, teachers, and more generally the repressive apparatuses of apartheid.' Yet they contend that while dissatisfaction with racial injustices bred organised resistance against apartheid, anger over gender injustices did not lead to similar social action against gender inequality in schools.[44] However, with Soweto's female comrades we see how gendered and racial injustices were connected in motivating their political action, and how participating in student resistance against apartheid could be used as a means to address both types of discrimination. Through interviewee testimony, it becomes clear that female comrades were unsatisfied with the status quo of how young women were expected to behave in their wider society, and that participating in the student struggle offered them a means of challenging accepted feminine norms.

For Beatrice, a female COSAS leader from Pimville, joining the liberation movement became a way to rebel against gender inequalities in the home. She explained, 'You could see every woman...your work is in the kitchen...So we were fighting that we should be equal with men, because we only differ with parts. But basically whatever they can do, we can do it.'[45] Contrary to previous literature, which has argued that girls' household chores prevented them from joining the struggle, these women cite their burden of domestic work as a key motivating factor in their participation in township politics.[46] As a female comrade from Diepkloof stated, 'Women are the most oppressed people in this country...If you are a woman, even if you are a school child, at home they expect you to do the house chores. And when you didn't do those things you'd get punished.'[47]

In schools too, such discrimination was commonplace. Speaking about what motivated her to join her school's SRC, one female comrade described how only female students were expected to clean classrooms. If classrooms were left dirty, female students would be beaten with *sjamboks*. But Amahle protested: 'We don't clean the class with our breasts. Because everybody is making the class dirty, we should all clean. He [the teacher] was not beating the boys...The only difference between boys and girls is the breasts, otherwise

---

[43] Authors' emphasis. Beall et al., 'A Bit on the Side,' 33.

[44] Morrell and Moletsane, 'Inequality and Fear,' 230.

[45] Interview with Beatrice, Pimville, 23 May 2015.

[46] Beall et al., 'A Bit on the Side,' 30–56; Seekings, 'Gender Ideology and Township Politics.'

[47] Nonkululeko, in group interview with female comrades from Diepkloof, 27 June 2015.

we all have hands, we all have feet. Why can't they clean?'[48] Morrell and Molet-sane describe how for girls, 'corporal punishment is woven into a femininity that accepts the right of authority figures, especially men, to dominate and assert their power.'[49] Another female comrade recalled how corporal punish-ment was still used against female students, and recounts the embarrassment and insecurity this caused: 'Because some of us women, we were punished, and we were beaten on our behinds! Our behinds! Can you imagine when you had a skirt on and then the *sjambok* is like "floop!" The skirt flies up, and it wasn't nice for girls.'[50] While male and female comrades alike protested against the continued use of corporal punishment in schools, female students had particularly gendered reasons for doing so, as this enabled them to rebel against gendered divisions of labour in the school, and challenge expectations of girls' submissiveness in the face of male power.

Some female comrades were aware of gender imbalances in the struggle and demonstrated a desire to play a part in the political transitions occurring around them. As Vicky from Diepkloof stated, 'I couldn't stand waiting for guys to do things for us when we women can stand up.'[51] Similarly, Nomsa believed, 'we [women] also need to play a role…we mustn't isolate our-selves.'[52] A number of interviewees drew on the strong history of women's involvement in the struggle during such discussions. Nomsa continued, 'the women, if they are pushing forward, then things are happening.' Khosi, who participated in the Pimville branch of COSAS, recalled, 'It came to a point that we cannot allow men to run things for us. We should stand for our-selves. And, I just believed that if women stand…like we are so strong and firm. We are stronger than men.'[53]

Female comrades found that participating in the student struggle could bring positive changes to their lives generally less available to non-politicised girls and young women. First, it provided those who joined with a political edu-cation that certainly was not offered in Bantu Education schools. Most female interviewees admitted that when they joined the struggle, they were ignorant of the political intricacies of the liberation movement. Yet the comrades knew that as teenagers attempting to be leaders in their communities, education and knowledge were paramount to gaining legitimacy. All new recruits therefore underwent a rigorous process of political education. At least once a week, the

[48]   Interview with Amahle, Jabavu, 10 June 2015.
[49]   Morrell and Moletsane, 'Inequality and Fear,' p. 235.
[50]   Interview with Vicky, Diepkloof, 14 May 2014.
[51]   *Ibid.*
[52]   Interview with Nomsa, Diepkloof Extension, 19 April 2014.
[53]   Interview with Khosi, Orlando East, 1 May 2014.

comrades would hold education seminars known as *umrabulo*. In these seminars, girls would learn not only about their own country's struggle, but also about other liberation movements across Africa and Latin America. Through their ties to the ANC leadership, male comrades would access and disseminate a wide array of political literature, from the ANC's Freedom Charter to *Das Kapital* and *The Communist Manifesto*. Such education empowered girls within their communities and encouraged them to adopt political outlooks that expanded beyond the immediate confines of their townships.

For female students, politics also offered an alternative ideal of what a young woman should be like: contrary to the passive, home-centred girl that parents and wider societal structures imagined, a female comrade was strong, vocal, and active. In creating this new political girlhood, Soweto's female comrades looked to other women in the struggle for inspiration. While they admired a range of female activists, two South African women stood out in their testimonies: Winnie Madikizela-Mandela and Thandi Modise. Both of these women played particularly militant roles in the struggle, and defied gender norms in doing so. Winnie was a particularly powerful female figure in the 1980s, who presented an alternative version of political womanhood.[54] At a time when women's political involvement was constrained by a number of obstacles, Winnie appeared as a symbol of defiance against traditional gender norms. She was neither meek nor submissive, and refused to be controlled by any male activist involved in the struggle – even her own husband. One female comrade described that while she looked up to all the 'big mammas' in the struggle, Winnie was 'different than the others...she was so strong.' She recounts that seeing Winnie, and even Winnie's daughter Zindzi, play such powerful roles in the struggle made her realise that she could also contravene gender stereotypes and play an equivalent role.[55] Similarly, Thandi Modise was one of the youngest women to ever leave the country to receive military training in exile, having left South Africa during her matric year at the age of seventeen in 1976. She was also the first female combatant to be captured by the South African government and was imprisoned for eight years for sabotage.[56] She was cited as a role model by female comrades, and also as a useful tool by male comrades, who used Modise's symbolic importance in their efforts to convince young women that they were not alone as young women in the struggle.

---

[54] Emily Bridger, 'From "Mother of the Nation" to "Lady Macbeth": Winnie Mandela and Perceptions of Female Violence in South Africa, 1985–91,' *Gender & History* 27:2 (2015): 446–464.

[55] Interview with Vicky, Diepkloof, 14 May 2014.

[56] Cock, *War and Gender in South Africa*, 149–150.

Within their own generation, female comrades did not look up to beauty queens or girls on the cover of *Drum* but to their own fellow student activists who managed to rise into COSAS' leadership ranks. Those who continued to feel shy in meetings or meek compared to their male comrades looked to female comrades who exerted more confident personas for encouragement. An interviewee from Pimville spoke of the respect and admiration she had for the female students in leadership, and one comrade, Beatrice, in particular. She stated, 'I never told Beatrice that she's strong, but when I talk about her around people, I envy her. She knows, she knows where she wants to be.'[57] Even male comrades acknowledged the effect such female activists had on girls in Soweto. As one man described, 'I remember we had most in Soweto, a popular one, it was Bessie, you see?...Every woman wanted to become Bessie, you see? She was a role model. If I come with a woman from Pimville in a meeting, and Bessie starts talking, when we went out this woman would say, "I want to become that girl".'[58] Even Bessie herself recognised the effect she had on other young women in Soweto. She recounted that recruiting women was easy, because they looked up to her and the bravery she exhibited.[59] Zanele from Diepkloof discussed how girls who were raped at school had no one to turn to and were expected to silently accept their fate. Seeing this as a problem, she began to talk to girls who she knew had been abused and take their complaints to higher authorities. After speaking with one student about her experiences, Zanele found that others were suddenly coming forward telling of similar incidents that happened to them. 'I was a hero,' she stated.

The education and life experiences that female comrades gained through the struggle helped to counter the feelings of inequality instilled in them since childhood. In interviews, they recount being changed for the better because of their involvement, particularly when compared to those girls who chose not to join. In his research in Mozambique, Harry West similarly found that political activity broadened the horizons of young female combatants, giving them 'greater range of movement across both social and geographical landscapes.'[60] Female comrades in South Africa saw COSAS as an opportunity to gain greater autonomy and agency *as girls*. Some female comrades sought to share these feelings of empowerment with their friends and fellow schoolgirls. Beatrice, who worked as a woman's organiser in Soweto, described, 'I was

---

57 Interview with Khosi, Orlando East, 1 May 2014.
58 Interview with Max, Pimville, 17 May 2015.
59 Interview with Bessie, Johannesburg, 25 April 2014.
60 Harry G. West, 'Girls with Guns: Narrating the Experience of War of Frelimo's "Female Detachment",' *Anthropological Quarterly* 73:4 (2000): 187.

telling them about women, that we are supposed to be empowered, you know? We must understand you are being suppressed as women, we cannot voice our voices as women, we are suffering. We are being exploited.'[61]

Through joining the student struggle at school, female comrades thus constructed and performed an alternative, oppositional femininity which enabled them to step beyond normal girlhood experiences of powerlessness and insecurity. Their participation provided them with feelings of empowerment and self-importance, and earned them status and respect, particularly in the eyes of their male comrades. Research into young female participants in other liberation contexts or civil wars has similarly demonstrated how young women's experiences of exclusion, inequality and violence in peacetime can lead them to join political groups. In Sri Lanka, female Liberation Tigers of Tamil Eelam (LTTE) members became combatants as a means of breaking gender taboos and restrictions on their behaviour.[62] In Latin America too, young women who were angry about the multiple inequalities they faced daily saw joining liberation movements as an opportunity rather than an obligation.[63] Similarly, South Africa's female comrades saw the struggle as an opportunity to fight not only against poor education, increasing rents, and the apartheid state's coercive tactics, but also against gender discrimination in the home, school and public sphere. Despite COSAS' tenuous commitment to gender issues (as will be discussed in chapter four), its female members nevertheless gained a sense of self-importance and agency through their involvement in the student movement at a time when girls otherwise had little influence in society.

However, there a few important caveats that must be made here. First, no female comrades interviewed labelled themselves as 'feminists'; when I asked some explicitly about the term, they rejected it as a western ideology with little application to their lives.[64] Their actions and narratives demonstrate that they were conscious of and unsatisfied with their unequal position as young women in township societies. Yet despite their espousal of oppositional gender identities, labelling their political aspirations as 'feminist' would be an imposition not necessarily welcomed by these women themselves. Interviewees

---

[61] Interview with Beatrice, Pimville, 23 May 2015.

[62] Sumantra Bose, *States, Nations, Sovereignty: Sri Lanka, India and the Tamil Eelam Movement* (New Delhi: Sage Publications, 1994), 111.

[63] Karen Kampwirth, *Women and Guerrilla Movements: Nicaragua, El Salvador, Chiapas, Cuba* (University Park: The Pennsylvania State University Press, 2002), 9.

[64] This was something generally encouraged within South Africa's liberation movement. For a critique of how 'feminism' was defined and used by the movement see Beall et al., 'A Bit on the Side,' 32.

were aware of the patriarchal nature of township life often because of their own individual experiences as girls. They saw the struggle as a means through which they could address the inequalities they experienced daily, rather than a means to completely overthrow township gender ideologies. As they clearly state in interviews, they saw themselves as 'comrades' more than as girls or young women. Second, COSAS was also far from being a feminist organisation. Within the student movement, political freedom was always placed before female students' emancipation.

There are a number of ways to read the inconsistencies in female comrades' accounts between their lack of gender consciousness on the one hand and gendered motivations and inequalities on the other. In many ways these women's narratives reflect the official line taken by the ANC during apartheid, in which the liberation of the country and of African people as a whole was placed before the specific liberation of women. They may thus reflect women's desires to conform to ANC policy and not be seen as a divisive force within the movement. In a different way, we can interpret female comrades' gendered motivations for joining the struggle in part as post hoc statements influenced by post-apartheid gender-talk. While these women may not have been in an environment saturated with discussions of gender rights and equality as teenagers, they would have been at the time of their interviews as gender has consistently been a prominent topic of public debate in South Africa since the 2000s. These women may thus be re-analysing their pasts through the present and developing a new understanding of how their gender shaped their teenage lives. After speaking at length about women's history in the struggle and women's issues, Ntsiki – a Diepkloof-based comrade – revealed that 'then' in the 1980s she did not know about these things: 'I think it was the conditions there and then, because the understanding of the politics of the day then didn't say much about women per se. Ya, because we were still young, at school, and our political understanding wasn't that ripe.'[65] Overall, it appears that the feelings of empowerment female comrades gained through joining student organisations were brought not by their explicit campaigning for gender equality or a complete overthrow of societal gender relations, but by breaking gender taboos and expectations, and participating in political activism alongside men rather than separately from them.

---

[65] Interview with Ntsiki, Diepkloof, 5 April 2015.

Conclusion

It is important to emphasise that not all students and young people in South Africa's townships joined the liberation struggle, although academic focus on politicised over non-politicised youths may make it seem this way at times. This book is focused specifically on girls who joined COSAS or SOSCO as an entry point into the wider liberation struggle and has thus only explored the lives and choices of a minority of Soweto's female students. Further research is still needed on other girls in South African townships who developed different understandings of and responses to the overlapping racial and gendered inequalities that shaped their lives under apartheid. However, this focus allows us to challenge static representations of African schoolgirls as merely victims of violence and discrimination – representations which are constructed passively and ignore girls' own understandings of their lives. Through researching girls' survival strategies (both historical and contemporary), scholars can better understand the different means available for increasing girls' agency – particularly in places such as South Africa where girls continue to experience extremely high rates of violence in and out of schools.[66]

This chapter has demonstrated that secondary schools were pivotal sites of girls' politicisation during apartheid, despite the dangers and discriminations girls faced within their walls. It was in schools where girls were able to gain access to political education, meet and socialise with already-politicised students, and address some of the most immediate problems they faced as young people under the late apartheid state. Moreover, schools and girls' experiences of education often provided the incentive for girls to seek out comrades and political groups in the first place. Expectations placed on girls that they clean classrooms, tolerate corporal punishment by male teachers, and not speak out against sexual abuse perpetrated by both staff and students were often key motivating factors in their decisions to join student organisations as a first step towards becoming committed participants in the wider liberation struggle. Soweto's female comrades did not join COSAS out of a deep ideological commitment to the struggle, nor out of a desire to completely overhaul township gender structures. Rather, they found that through their involvement in the student movement they could simultaneously address the multiple and overlapping injustices they faced on a daily basis on account of their race, age, and gender. Through this participation they gained feelings of joy, purpose, and empowerment – feelings shared by their male comrades too.

[66]   Bhana, 'Girls are not free,' 352–358.

Yet in understanding what drew female students in particular to political activism, we must acknowledge the gendered benefits of this 'pleasure of agency'. For female comrades were not only rebelling against the state or seemingly apathetic parents, but also against gender norms of patriarchal township society; they not only repudiated the injustices they experienced as students, but also the particular vulnerabilities they experienced being female students at a time when schools were both unequal and often violent spaces for girls. Through their involvement in COSAS, and later in the wider liberation movement, female comrades constructed a new, political girlhood, centred on empowerment and defiance rather than obedience and submissiveness. As this book will demonstrate, this empowerment was fragile, and repeatedly threatened as girls became more heavily involved in the liberation struggle. However, these women today present the moment in which they first joined COSAS as one in which they felt a new sense of optimism and hope in their capacity to better their lives in lasting and multiple ways.

3

The Home: Negotiating Family, Girlhood, and Politics

Growing up in Diepkloof, Soweto, Zanele lived with her grandparents – a strict couple who, like most township parents, expected their granddaughter to cook and clean most evenings after school. But after joining her school's SRC, Zanele found that she was often busy in meetings until six or seven o'clock in the evening, leaving little time for her domestic work. As she became increasingly involved in the struggle, her household chores became more and more of an impediment. 'It was a little bit difficult,' she explained, 'because sometimes you want to go somewhere to attend maybe the meetings. But you know that at home you must go and prepare the fire. You must go and put the pot for supper.' She continued:

> And then when you go there, maybe you are preparing the fire. Then you hear next door, they loud telling that, there's police who are coming! Then you have to leave all those things, and the pots are going to [laughs] be ruined. You know, it was so difficult. Maybe it was easy for men but for us it was difficult because I got beaten everyday by my grandmother. I didn't finish to do this [cooking, cleaning]…I was beaten, maybe in a week, thrice.

Once the police became aware of her political activities, Zanele's home life was complicated further. 'Because I wasn't allowed to go inside the house,' she explained. 'When I go inside the house, you'll hear my grandfather and grandmother, "Ai, ai, ai! You are going to bring the Boers here!" All those things, you know?' Yet Zanele's relationship with her guardians was not a simple one of disapproval and chastisement. As a supportive gesture to her granddaughter's new political lifestyle, Zanele's grandmother would prepare food and leave it outside the house to make sure that Zanele was fed, even though she could no longer sleep at home. While Zanele at times expressed her joy in rebelling against parental pressures, she also spoke openly about the personal difficulties her politicisation caused: 'It was so painful, because I missed them. I want to see them, you know? I want to change my clothes. But I wasn't allowed.

Because immediately when I take that food and go outside, you'd hear that the police were at my place. So it wasn't safe for me to go home.'[1]

This chapter explores how becoming a female comrade affected girls' lives at home and shifted their relationships with their parents, families, friends, and neighbours, providing insight into the social worlds of activists beyond the struggle. Simultaneously, it asks how girls' identities as daughters, caretakers, domestic labourers, and mothers shaped the roles they took on as activists. In doing so it contends that the home was not a marginalised space removed from the main sites of student and youth activism during the township uprisings. Previous studies of the comrades have tended to overlook how activism was lived and experienced in the more private spaces of the home, instead limiting their analysis to the highly masculinised spaces of township streets. As Angela McRobbie and Jenny Garber argue, it is exactly this focus on masculine, public, and confrontational spaces within subcultures that has come to dominate public and academic conceptions of youth activity. But this focus renders girls and young women's participation in youth cultures invisible or incomprehensible.[2] In focusing on the home, this chapter dismantles the false boundary between private and public spheres in South Africa's townships during the liberation struggle. It contends, as Helen Bradford does, that 'unless the personal is perceived as political – and unless the (predominantly female) sphere of the family is articulated to the (predominantly male) domain of political economy – black resistance cannot be adequately understood.'[3] Understanding African girls' political lives requires a rethinking of activism spaces in South African townships, away from the overtly public towards more informal and diffuse spaces in which the liberation movement was carried out on a day-to-day basis.

For female comrades, the home was inextricably linked to political activism. In many ways, female comrades joined the struggle to escape or challenge the home-centred lives expected of girls in 1980s Soweto. In doing so, they abandoned their household duties, rebelled against parental authority, and contravened ideals of the 'good' girl who remained in the home outside of school hours. To an extent, these efforts to construct a new political girlhood were successful: female comrades no longer felt inferior or submissive within their families; they took on new roles in their communities; forged new friendships and family ties with their comrades; and found a greater sense of purpose beyond the home. However, these girls – even as activists – could not

---

[1]   Interview with Zanele, Diepkloof, 12 April 2014.
[2]   Angela McRobbie and Jenny Garber, 'Girls and Subcultures,' in Stuart Hall and Tony Jefferson (eds), *Resistance through Rituals: Youth Subcultures in Post-war Britain* (London: Routledge, 2003), 209.
[3]   Bradford, 'We are now the men,' 293.

escape the gendered and generational power dynamics of the home that had driven so many of them to the struggle in the first place. Township gender ideologies and girls' roles within the home shaped their activist commitments and the nature of their participation in the liberation movement in ways that were both empowering and restricting. Their central role within the home enabled them to politicise the domestic space by using the relative safety of the home to hold covert political meetings, recruit new activists, or draw their parents into the struggle. The caregiving roles they played within their own households also led them to take on wider social roles within the liberation movement, providing care and support (and sometimes parental chastisement) to struggling members of their communities.

But the gendered power dynamics of the home also produced multiple complications and obstacles for female comrades. Because of their deviance from girlhood norms, they were often stigmatised by their friends and parents. Their politicisation brought new hardships and dangers directly into their homes, jeopardising their families' safety and wellbeing. The conflicts sparked between them and their parents could also lead to new emotional hardships for female comrades, who today still speak of the pain of being a disappointing daughter in the 1980s. Nevertheless, female comrades developed complex strategies in their attempts to manage parental concern, strategies which allowed them to simultaneously challenge and negotiate the gendered expectations placed on them by older family members. By studying these strategies and the restrictions placed on girls' activism by their families, we can see the burden of emotional labour that female comrades bore, and better understand girls' less visible or less obvious presence as comrades in the 1980s.

The Home

As Linda McDowell writes, the 'home' 'must be one of the most loaded words in the English language.'[4] Often, it brings to mind connotations of privacy, safety, a nuclear family, and a single, specific geographical place. Yet this is often not the case in South African townships, both historically and today. First, the homes of African families were rarely private spaces during apartheid; instead, they were subject to constant surveillance and the threat of intrusion in the forms of pass raids, forced removals, and midnight visits from security police.[5] For these reasons, they were also not necessarily safe spaces. Particularly for women and girls, the home was rarely a refuge or haven but instead a space of

---

[4]   Linda McDowell, *Gender, Identity and Place: Understanding Feminist Geographies* (Cambridge: Polity Press, 1999), 71.

[5]   Bonnin, 'Claiming Spaces,' 303.

domestic and sexual violence, perpetrated by husbands, fathers, and other male relatives. Third, the majority of township families do not resemble the Western, nuclear model, but instead are often multi-generational, female-headed, or led not by parents but by one's grandparents, aunts, or other relatives. And finally, Soweto's female comrades were often raised by a multitude of shifting relatives, moving between homes and locations throughout their teenage years. The 'home' in this chapter thus does not always refer to a set, singular place for each female comrade; for one interviewee, it may signify a range of houses in Soweto, including those of their parents, grandparents, neighbours, friends, and other family. This chapter explores girls and young women's lives and forms of activism within not just their own homes, but also those of other township residents.

Much of the work on the uprisings of the 1980s creates a false binary between the private and public spaces in South Africa's townships, and thus between men and women's roles in political activism and violence. While popular images of the comrades depict them as being openly engaged in the public sphere, protesting, *toyi-toying*, and confronting police in township streets, girls and women have largely been conveyed through stock depictions of concerned mothers and daughters, 'defenders of home and hearth', during these years.[6] These portrayals ignore the ways in which private and public spaces are inextricably connected, and the boundaries between them blurred and contested by political conflict. In her work on KwaZulu-Natal, Debby Bonnin demonstrates how the domestic space became a central site of political contestation during the 1980s, as children brought home the political identities they forged on the streets or at school, and as women were increasingly drawn into the struggle as their homes became subject to attacks from police or political rivals.[7] As she argues:

> Eliding the public and the political hinders one's recognition of the multiplicity of sites in which women engage in power struggles. Both private and public spaces are the site of collusion, oppositional politics and social movements. Both provide a space for the mounting of challenges against the state and its power, and against the dominant discourses of class, race and gender.[8]

For the study of female comrades, this separation between the public and private spheres not only makes girls' involvement in the struggle more difficult to see, but also isolates girls' politicisation and the wider liberation struggle from the gendered and generational power dynamics of the home. Previous

6   Sapire, 'Township Histories,' 191.
7   Bonnin, 'Claiming Spaces,' 303.
8   *Ibid.*, 304.

scholarship has contended that it was girls' confinement to the home that kept them from participating in the township uprisings.[9] However, as this book demonstrates, it was often the very inequalities girls experienced within the home – the burden of household labour they bore, their experiences of sexual violence, or their feelings of gendered inferiority – that motivated their initial involvement in the struggle. Unlike in other liberation contexts where activists or combatants left their home communities for the 'bush' or camps, in South Africa many of the comrades active in the township uprisings remained in their communities throughout their time as activists. Consequently, female comrades were not only comrades, but were simultaneously daughters, sisters, friends, and students. But the political roles they took on both inside and outside the home shifted their relationships with their parents, friends, and neighbours, and required them to abandon many of the norms and the few comforts typically enjoyed by children and youth in the townships.

Giving up Girlhood

'Normal' life was, to an extent, suspended for all of those living in South Africa's townships in the 1980s due to rolling school boycotts and the prevailing state of violence. Yet the normalcy that schooling, family life, and relationships could provide was further denied to those committed to politics from an early age. Many female comrades stopped regularly attending school not long after joining COSAS. While some stayed away from classes to avoid police detection, others were told not to come back by teachers or principals who feared the negative impact comrades would have on other students. Spending prolonged periods in detention forced many comrades to miss their exams, or to fail exams because of their repeated absence from classes. In the years leading up to the state of emergency, COSAS launched a campaign to boycott exams, and thus some students purposefully refused to sit their tests as a political statement. Consequently, the majority of interviewees never passed their matric.[10]

One particular consequence of political involvement was the forsaking of normal family life. Due to police harassment, many comrades stopped sleeping at home, instead spending their nights in various safe houses, seeing their family members less and less frequently. For many, detention inevitably

---

[9]   See Beall et al, 'A Bit on the Side'; Seekings, 'Gender Ideology and Township Politics.'
[10]   Comrades were not the only secondary students to not write exams during the 1980s. In November 1985, only 420 out of a total 6000 matric students in Soweto wrote matric exams due to boycotts. Glaser, 'Learning Amidst the Turmoil,' 426.

cut off their access to their parents for periods of six months or more. As Nomsa from Diepkloof explained, 'We have this fear that maybe somebody is looking for us...so you gonna spend maybe a few minutes maybe to pick up few clothes and then you go...that was the type of life we were living. We are no longer spending enough time at home.'[11] For female comrades who were as young as twelve when they joined the student movement, this consequence of their political involvement could be particularly difficult – as Zanele's account from the beginning of this chapter demonstrates. As she mentioned, sleeping away from home for prolonged periods also made it difficult for girls to maintain their hygiene. In interviews, they speak of the hardships of not being able to bathe or go home and collect clean clothes. Worried that the police were most likely to come looking for her at night, Lucy spent many nights at the age of sixteen sleeping in a car scrap yard, only going home occasionally in the mornings to wash.[12]

Conversely, politicisation also affected comrades' experiences of motherhood. Several interviewees had children as teenagers but decided to keep participating in the struggle, either leaving their babies with other family members or taking them along to meetings and marches.[13] These women's narratives were dominated by their political experiences rather than their experiences as mothers. It was not until over halfway through her interview that Vicky, speaking about her experiences in detention, suddenly stopped and said, 'By then I had a baby! Sorry, I forgot to tell you, I have a son that I got in 1983.'[14] In contradiction to stereotypical views of the centrality of motherhood to women's lives, Vicky's identity as a mother was superseded by her identity as a comrade.[15] The marginal position of motherhood in female comrades' self-constructions stands in contrast to the central role motherhood played in the public political identities assumed by older women involved in the liberation struggle.[16] This generational difference evidences the liminal

---

[11]   Interview with Nomsa, Diepkloof Extension, 19 April 2014.

[12]   Interview with Lucy, Fleurhof, 18 February 2016.

[13]   It is important to note, however, that it was not just female comrades who left their children in the care of older female relatives. As Rebekah Lee highlights, this was a common strategy used by unmarried mothers during these years. Lee, *African Women and Apartheid*, 69.

[14]   Interview with Vicky, Diepkloof, 14 May 2014.

[15]   This was something that was encouraged for young ANC mothers in exile. See Rachel Sandwell, '"Love I Cannot Begin to Explain": The Politics of Reproduction in the ANC in Exile, 1976–1990,' *Journal of Southern African Studies* 41:1 (2015): 63–81.

[16]   See Meghan Healy-Clancy, 'The Family Politics of the Federation of South African Women: A History of Public Motherhood in Women's Antiracist Activism,' *Signs* 42:4 (2017): 843–866.

position of female comrades who, despite being biological mothers, did not yet see themselves as social mothers or having achieved full adult status.

Being a comrade also changed girls' relationships with their friends, and greatly affected how they spent their teenage years and what their priorities were. I asked Bessie, a COSAS leader from Dlamini, if she had any sense of a normal teenage life. She responded:

> That's an interesting question. It was sort of normal then, because it was normal in the struggle, your life was the struggle. Sometimes we go out and party, but there was that element of consciousness that police might come any time...But we didn't enjoy our normal youth...But our youth, what we were supposed to be doing in a normal environment, we did it in the struggle. Our life was the struggle. When you woke up, the first thing you thought about was the organisation...Sometimes you would spend days away from home, but at home you were never the same.[17]

Speaking before the Truth and Reconciliation Commission (TRC), Sandra Adonis, a female comrade from the Western Cape who joined the struggle at the age of fifteen, stated, 'It is only now that I realise that I have, like, I do not know what it is to go to a bioscope on a Saturday afternoon or even to a disco, like many young people do today or maybe that time as well. I mean, I never had friends really.'[18] Thabisile, a comrade from Jabavu, similarly recalled how before she joined the struggle she, 'had many friends growing up, because I was playing soccer...But as I changed to become this young activist, I didn't have them because we couldn't relate on anything. They'll be speaking soccer, I'll be speaking struggle.'[19]

Female comrades had a particular reputation amongst some in their communities for being disruptive, dangerous, and dirty, and such stigmatisation made it difficult for them to maintain friendships with non-politicised girls. As comrades stopped sleeping at home, they were not always able to bathe or fetch a change of clothes before school. When Thabasile joined the struggle, her old friends ridiculed her and her fellow activists, saying 'you are with your comrades now...your dirty friends, they don't wash.'[20] Nonkululeko from Diepkloof recalled that other girls would call her a *vuilpop*, a term which she translated as, 'someone that is dirty, doesn't wash.'[21] Dlamini translates

---

[17]   Interview with Bessie, Johannesburg, 25 April 2014.

[18]   Sandra Adonis, TRC Youth Hearings, Athlone, 22 May 1997, <https://www.justice.gov.za/trc/special/children/adonis.htm> accessed 7 September 2014.

[19]   Interview with Thabisile, Johannesburg, 25 May 2015.

[20]   *Ibid.*

[21]   Interview with Nonkululeko, Diepkloof, 8 April 2014.

the Afrikaans term as 'dirty little scoundrel', a word reserved for young people considered uncouth by adults. '*Vuilpops* were the worst of the worst,' he explains. 'They were the kids who lived in a rubbish dump...were the kids who came from homes that were not quite up to the standards and expectations of the neighbourhood. So it's not difficult to see why *vuilpop* was the last thing you wanted to be.'[22] Because of their lack of hygiene and their involvement in forms of activism generally seen as masculine, female comrades were also deemed by some friends to be lacking in femininity. A woman from Jabavu described how she was stigmatised for being too masculine. When asked what other girls at school thought of her, she responded, '[that] I like guys' things, and I'm a rough girl.'[23] Khosi from Pimville was also labelled as deviant for lacking in traditional femininity. She remembers, 'We were like guys. That is why I'm saying people, when you're a lady comrade, some of them they look you with another eye.' She described that other girls in the community would question her gender and asked whether she was a girl or a boy. 'Actually,' she clarified, 'they say I'm more or less like a lesbian, who is most of the time participating with guys.'[24]

Several interviewees recounted how other parents would forbid their daughters from associating with them out of a fear that their gender transgressions would spread like a disease to their own children. As Sibongile described, 'I did have friends, but not when we started going this direction [becoming involved in the struggle]. Obviously, their parents told them no, this is not a good way, don't be involved with Sibongile and other things. And I lost most of my friends.' She explained how parents would stigmatise female comrades as a means of keeping their own daughters away from the struggle, telling their children, 'They will teach you wrong things and, what kind of girls are doing this? They never spend time with their families, they don't clean the house, they don't cook for their parents...They are not going to get married, they will make babies.'[25]

Female comrades were also stigmatised for their involvement in collective action and political violence. 'They were taking us as criminals,' Sibongile said of her schoolmates and teachers. 'The parents said they didn't want their children to associate with me, because of this. And then, they will call you names. Hey! What was this name they used to use? *Iphekula*. In Zulu, it's terrorist.'[26] Similarly, Nonkululeko from Diepkloof explained, 'Most of the time, when

[22] Dlamini, *Native Nostalgia*, 149.
[23] Interview with Amahle, Jabavu, 10 June 2015.
[24] Interview with Khosi, Orlando East, 1 May 2014.
[25] Interview with Sibongile, Johannesburg, 9 June 2015.
[26] *Ibid.*

you are a member of SRC or a member of COSAS, we were involved with boys mostly. The girls were afraid to be branded with us, because they thought maybe we are thugs or something.' Her fellow comrade, Lucy, interjected, 'By that time, they used to call us *abasayinyova* [people who chant *siyayinyova*, "we will destroy"] – the violent people – so that's why even the parents didn't want their kids to be involved with us!'[27] Nonkululeko replied, 'Even if in the street where you stay…the parents wouldn't like their kids to be friends with you, because they were afraid that you'll pour the spirit, and then their kids will change and become those *siyayinyovas*.'[28]

However, many female comrades refused to let their friends' perceptions of their political work bother them. A comrade from Diepkloof stated, 'You know, everywhere, people are talking. So they will say that because of maybe there are a lot of boys, there are a lot of men there, that's why you did go there. They did call us with names, but we didn't care.' She later asserted, 'They would swear at us. But it didn't make us to go back. Instead…they give us courage.'[29] Reciprocally, a few female comrades stigmatised other girls for their lack of political involvement or expressed their disappointment with their non-politicised friends and fellow students. When asked what she thought of girls at school who did not join the struggle, an activist from Jabavu replied, 'I thought they were stupid, because they don't want to fight for their country, and they enjoy the abusive life.'[30] Also speaking about non-politicised girls, Phumzile stated, 'I was thinking that they're afraid, they don't have this strength we are having, they don't have this belief that we are having.'[31] Such a critical perspective was not unique to Soweto, but was also espoused by female comrades elsewhere. 'DP', a young female activist from Alexandra, similarly criticised her cohort of young women for their frivolity during such a politicised time, for '[dressing] up especially to go to a meeting.'[32]

But within the struggle, girls found alternative forms of youth sociability within their political organisations. In her TRC testimony, student activist Sandra Adonis continued, 'My friends, my comrades was my comrades [sic]. Those were the only people that I could trust at that point in time.'[33] As Bessie

---

27   *Siyayinyova* can loosely be translated as 'we will destroy', and was a popular slogan chanted by militant youths in the 1980s during their marches or while attacking 'targets'. It came to be used by both local communities and state police as a term synonymous with 'comrades'.

28   Group interview with female comrades from Diepkloof, 27 June 2015.

29   Interview with Ntebaleng, Diepkloof, 15 April 2014.

30   Interview with Amahle, Jabavu, 10 June 2015.

31   Interview with Phumzile, Johannesburg, 17 April 2015.

32   Bozzoli, *Theatres of Struggle*, 105.

33   Sandra Adonis, TRC Youth Hearings, Athlone, 22 May 1997.

is quoted as saying above, 'But our youth, what we were supposed to be doing in a normal environment, we did it in the struggle. Our life was the struggle.'[34] Within COSAS, a new normalcy of teenage life emerged, in which *jolling* was replaced with *toyi-toying*, and one's biological family was replaced by one's comrades. The strength of the familial bonds between comrades were demonstrated by Lucy, whose parents sent her to live with relatives in rural KwaZulu-Natal in an attempt to protect her from the dangers of the struggle. Yet Lucy ran away from her biological family back to Soweto, stating, 'I was not going to run away from my other comrades, because we were like a family.'[35] Florence from Diepkloof likewise described, 'I felt more at home within the organisation than with my family. Because my family didn't know all the secrets that I had, that I was not happy with the status quo, with the things that were happening in South Africa.'[36]

Managing Family Relationships

Yet swapping one's biological family for one's new, political family was not a simple or painless task. In interviews, female comrades rarely expressed regret or a sense of loss at having abandoned the activities and friendships associated with 'modern' African girlhood at this time. Rather, in hindsight, they framed this period of their adolescence as a period of rebellion against the expectations placed on them by their age and gender, and of creating a new, political girlhood. However, when discussing their relationships with their parents or grandparents, and how these were affected by the struggle, they did not speak with such carefree, defiant attitudes. Instead, they spoke of the lasting emotional stress of upsetting their parents, the difficulties of balancing political work and parental expectations, and the emotional labour of trying to maintain family harmony during the township uprisings.

Many parents initially responded negatively to their daughters' politicisation. Having a comrade in the family could bring significant new hardships and dangers into the home for parents, grandparents, and siblings.[37] When police raided houses looking for young activists, it was not uncommon for them to destroy property or beat family members in the process. When Nomsa, a female comrade from Diepkloof, was first elected to her school's SRC, she had little understanding of the political consequences. But her grandmother immediately quashed her excitement when Nomsa told her the news, responding,

---

[34] Interview with Bessie, Johannesburg, 25 April 2014.
[35] Interview with Lucy, Fleurhof, 7 April 2014.
[36] Interview with Florence, Diepkloof, 3 March 2015.
[37] See Motsemme, 'The Mute Always Speak,' 924.

'As from today you're going to sleep in the kitchen. Because when the police, when they come looking for you, they must just get you in the nearest place because they're going to wake up all of us in this house, and we are not interested in that.'[38] Nomsa's grandmother's fears were realised by the parents of many other female comrades. For Vicky, a female comrade from Diepkloof, her political activities brought the dangers of the state right into her bedroom, arguably the most private of spaces, which she shared with her three sisters. She described how the police came to her house in the night looking for her after an informer had divulged her identity. They entered the bedroom and pulled the blankets off each of the girls in turn, before bringing the informer himself into the bedroom to identify Vicky.[39] Multiple women spoke of their parents' efforts to hide them in such circumstances, ushering their daughters into wardrobes, under beds, or over backyard fences. But such efforts could lead to increased suffering for parents. Beatrice recalled how her aunt would hide her cousin, also a comrade, in a wardrobe covered with clothes when the police arrived, only to be beaten herself when the police could not find her daughter. Interestingly, in her narrative of this event Beatrice lays blame not with the police, but with her uncle, who refused to allow his activist daughter to sleep away from home to avoid arrest.[40] Police beat the mother, father, and siblings of another female comrade, Thobile, and also smashed many of her family's possessions.[41] Lucy's parents and siblings were also beaten by police before her parents' house was eventually burned – whether by the state or local rivals Lucy remains uncertain. Describing the effect it had on her family she recalled, 'So everybody in the family, my parents, my siblings, they were also scared that because of me we don't have a home now. My father had to start from scratch to try and build a house again.'[42]

Parents also expressed disappointment in learning about their daughters' involvement in politics. By becoming comrades, girls contravened a number of the norms of 'good' girlhood: they transgressed ideals of women's domesticity and place in the private sphere by abandoning chores, attending night meetings, and protesting in the streets; and they drew accusations of promiscuity due to their nights spent away from home and their close relationships with male comrades. Such disappointment can clearly be seen in this book's opening story about Vicky – the Diepkloof activist whose police officer father

[38]   Interview with Nomsa, Diepkloof Extension, 19 April 2014.
[39]   Interview with Vicky, Diepkloof, 14 May 2014.
[40]   Interview with Beatrice, Pimville, 23 May 2015.
[41]   Interview with Thobile, Diepkloof, 12 April 2014.
[42]   Interview with Lucy, Fleurhof, 7 April 2014.

chastised and beat her when he discovered she was a comrade.[43] Parents also objected to their daughters' involvement in the struggle because of the damage it would do to their reputation and future career prospects. When asked what her parents thought about her involvement in the struggle a COSAS leader from Diepkloof responded,

> My parents said, 'You better forget about everything that you are doing.' Because they had a future, they've planned something for me…My mother said, 'You know, the way you are so patient, one day you'll be a nurse. I wish that you will be a nurse.' But when I was in the struggle, not attending school, running away from the police, my mother used to say, 'You know, you are playing with your future.'[44]

Sibongile's mother too was concerned about her daughter's prospects when she found out about her political involvement: 'What are you doing with these people? Where is your future? You're not going to get married,' she would say. I later asked why her mother believed her new identity as a comrade would prevent her from getting married. Sibongile responded, 'Who can marry a thug? Let me say that. Ya, they were taking us as thugs, so there's no man who can marry you [laughs].'[45] For Tandeka, a comrade from Orlando who already had a young child when she joined the struggle, her mother was concerned with both her future and her reputation. Given Tandeka had already delayed her matric year while she was pregnant, her mother was particularly angry when told by teachers that her daughter was skipping classes to attend political meetings. What made matters worse was that in these meetings, Tandeka seemed to be surrounded only by boys: 'My mother was so angry…she was saying, you know, you have a child and yet you are busy with these boys. You are just going to bring another child.'[46] Female comrades' parents often assumed their daughters were using politics as a pretence for promiscuous behaviour. Laughing, Lucy asked, 'If you are a parent, if your child doesn't sleep at home, what are you going to think?'[47]

To mitigate parental concern and stigmatisation, female comrades developed complex strategies that allowed them to still participate in the struggle whilst causing minimal disruption to their families' lives. An example of this can be seen in how women talked about the difficulties of balancing domestic labour with their new political commitments. Some women initially laughed

---

[43] Interview with Vicky, Diepkloof, 14 May 2014.
[44] Interview with Lucy, Fleurhof, 7 April 2014.
[45] Interview with Sibongile, Johannesburg, 9 June 2015
[46] Interview with Tandeka, Randburg, 25 April 2014.
[47] Interview with Lucy, Fleurhof, 7 April 2014.

when they spoke of how they simply disobeyed their parents and neglected their household duties once becoming activists. One female comrade, who stated that she would simply 'dodge housework and go to the meeting,' laughed when asked if this made her parents upset. 'I didn't care [laughs]. I did what made me happy.'[48] But most female comrades described this as a more difficult process. These women's narratives demonstrate just how complex a balancing act political activism was for girls in the 1980s, and how young women sought to maintain family harmony whilst simultaneously rebelling against patriarchal relations and expectations in the home. Many spoke of how they would stay up late at night or wake up especially early to complete their chores, leaving more time after school for political activities. Describing how she balanced domestic and political labour, Penelope from Jabavu explained, 'I did not want to get into trouble with my mother. So if I know I'm supposed to go to a meeting and I'll come back home late, I'll make sure in the morning when she leaves, I'll wake up and cook and clean the house.' But such strategies were often complicated by the impromptu nature of the struggle. Penelope continued, 'But sometimes, you were not aware that there'll be a meeting…some of the things were not planned. So you wouldn't know that you will not be able to go home early on that day. So when those incidents [happened], then when you get home you think, what am I going to say to this woman?'[49] Not completing household chores could lead to increased violence in the family, as Zanele's narrative from the opening of this chapter demonstrates.

Parents' or grandparents' disapproval of their daughters' political work at times caused significant pain or emotional stress for female comrades. Recollecting her grandmother's reaction, Florence stated, 'My Grandmum, she was so disappointed in me…When she learned that, when they were telling her that I'm this horrible, I'm the biggest terrorist that the local [police] office here in Soweto has ever seen, this woman is a very dangerous woman.' Her speech slowed and her narrative grew more disjointed as she continued, becoming noticeably upset:

> I could see her disappointment that after all, you know [sighs], but it's ok. I couldn't, you know, I tried all my adult life, I've always tried to…Because after that day, I could see that she was disappointed in me and that thing remained in me that if only I could get that removed. It was stuck in my head, you know, that someone is really, really disappointed in you.[50]

[48]   Interview with Amahle, Jabavu, 10 June 2015.
[49]   Interview with Penelope, Jabavu, 12 June 2015.
[50]   Interview with Florence, 8 May 2014.

Ntebaleng, another Diepkloof-based comrade, blamed herself for what she saw as a breakdown in her relationship with her grandparents whom she lived with as a child. In the late 1980s, they sent her away from Soweto to Pretoria to live with her mother who she hardly knew, in an effort to protect her from the police and remove her from the struggle. She described how at first she was very angry with her grandparents for this, but then later felt abandoned and cast off by them: 'I was like, they don't love me anymore. What did I do wrong? You know, I started blaming myself because of, maybe, I've joined the struggle.'[51] Lucy too felt guilty for the hardships her political involvement brought for her family. After her parents' home was burned, she felt her relationship with her father change: 'So that's when my father called me saying, "You see know what's happened? We have lost the family house, you don't have a house also, because of this struggle of yours."'[52]

To mitigate such emotional stress and family breakdown, several female comrades at first tried to hide their political commitments from their parents and lied about their whereabouts. One comrade told her parents she was attending reading groups rather than COSAS meetings after school. Another stated that her parents had no idea she was a comrade until the police came to their house looking for her. Amahle from Jabavu used to leave for weekend-long conferences with no bag or change of clothes so that her father would think she was just going to the shop down the street. After being chastised for always being with male comrades, Tandeka said she would hide anything to do with her political work from her mother.[53]

Some female comrades chose to completely defy their parents. After the burning of her home, Lucy's father tried to force her to stop participating in politics. But Lucy refused: 'Because I knew that there's a place I need to reach first…I told my father, I said, "Daddy, I've made a commitment that even if I die – I'm not pleased that the family house has been burned – but on my side, I'm not going to leave the struggle."'[54] But most girls chose a more delicate path between defiance and acquiescence, granting some concessions to their parents' wishes in the hope that, in the long run, this would ease their political participation. For Sibongile, her mother had no idea she was politically active until she had to collect her daughter from the local police station after she had been detained over a weekend. When her mother came to the station, she was furious. Having already lost her brother to the struggle and her son to illness,

[51] Interview with Ntebaleng, Diepkloof, 15 April 2014.
[52] Lucy, in Group Interview with Female Comrades from Diepkloof, 27 June 2015.
[53] Interview with Rethabile, Diepkloof, 1 May 2014; interview with Amahle, Jabavu, 10 June 2015; interview with Tandeka, Randburg, 25 April 2014.
[54] Lucy, in Group Interview with Female Comrades from Diepkloof, 27 June 2015.

she refused to lose Sibongile too, who by this point was her only child. 'No, you don't have to do this,' she told her daughter, 'You will die. These people are bad, they will shoot you…You must concentrate on your books.' At the time, Sibongile refused to listen, and became further involved in the struggle. But the next year she was detained again, and this time held in Diepkloof Prison for six months. Upon her release, she left Soweto to spend three months in Aliwal North in the Eastern Cape, over 600km away, at her mother's insistence. 'That was my mother's decision,' she explained. 'I said for once, let me respect her and go.' But even in the rural town of Aliwal North she tried to politicise other young people, and only three months later returned to the struggle in Soweto. Eventually, her mother accepted her involvement in the struggle, and even joined the Federation of Transvaal Women (FEDTRAW) and later the ANC Women's League (ANCWL) herself.[55]

Many other female comrades adopted similar paths that balanced defiance and compliance. Several spoke of their wishes to leave Soweto to join MK in exile, but only one female interviewee actually did. These women posited going into exile as the ultimate marker of political commitment, but one that would cause their families too much strain. Beatrice was about the leave the country when her mother found out and put pressure on her to stay. 'How can you do this to me?' She asked. 'You're my only daughter, you're my last born.' 'Eh, it was difficult for me,' Beatrice explained. 'So I had to stay.' While she continued her work within the township, and became involved in underground networks inside the country, she – like many other female comrades – chose not to join MK and thus not to transgress parental authority or expectations too much.[56]

For most parents too, their initial outrage or disappointment at their daughter's involvement in the struggle often dissipated once they realised that they were not going to completely abandon their political activities. Many engaged in small acts of support, ranging from the simple act of making sandwiches and leaving them in their yards for their daughters to swing by and collect, to allowing their daughters to hold meetings in their homes, to helping to hide their daughters from police. Others were eventually politicised by their daughters and joined FEDTRAW or civic organisations themselves.

Studying young women's complex negotiation of parental disappointment and contradictory efforts to defy parental authority and maintain family harmony helps to explain why their involvement in the struggle was often shorter in duration and thus less visible than male comrades'. Writing about teenage female activists in North America, Hava Rachel Gordon demonstrates how

---

[55] Interview with Sibongile, Johannesburg, 9 June 2015.
[56] Interview with Beatrice, Pimville, 23 May 2015.

'succumbing to parental constraint means that although a teenage girl might have a political consciousness and commitment to a cause, she may be unable to engage with others in public dialogue, dissent, and action.'[57] In South Africa, these struggles were not only faced by girls and young women in the 1980s, but also confronted female youth who participated in the 1976 Soweto Uprisings. This previous generation of young female activists encountered very similar problems in respect to clashes between their political and family lives: they were sent to live with relatives outside Soweto in attempts to stop their political involvement; they were begged by parents not to go into exile; and they failed to protect their private lives from the intrusion of the state. Pohlandt-McCormick writes of how this led female activists to face a difficult choice: to betray the struggle and stop participating or betray their families and keep going.[58]

According to Florence, male comrades did not face this same conundrum. 'For them to be politically aware,' she explained, 'to participate politically, it was something that they inherited from home, or it was something that they were encouraged, let me put it that way. Their parents were supportive. At home they [her parents] didn't know a thing that I was doing.'[59] The complex negotiations between parental expectations and political devotion that were so prevalent in women's accounts of the struggle were not so in men's narratives. Male comrades did speak of their parents' worries and attempts to dissuade them from political activism. However, these conflicts were mostly narrated nonchalantly by men, who did not speak of the same nuanced strategies or emotional labour involved in managing their relations with parents. In her work on teenage activists, Gordon similarly found that boys are more confident in confronting parental power and see parental authority as more manageable than girls.[60] Bongo, a male activist from Diepkloof, spoke remarkably casually about spending long periods of time not sleeping at home when the police were looking for him:

> Once we are involved, obviously that is when the life of being, not living with your parents starts now. Because you are now active and you are now wanted. You know that you are on the wanted list. Then you start distancing. That is when the life of being responsible for yourself starts, because now you have to not live at your place, sometimes you will see them [parents] once a month at your place and just pitch up, 'hey, what's happening?'

---

[57] Hava Rachel Gordon, 'Gendered Paths to Teenage Political Participation: Parental Power, Civic Mobility, and Youth Activism,' *Gender & Society* 22:1 (2008): 41.
[58] Pohlandt-McCormick, *Doing Violence to Memory*, E-book, location 419–432.
[59] Interview with Florence, Diepkloof, 8 May 2014.
[60] Gordon, 'Gendered Paths to Teenage Political Participation,' 42.

When asked what his parents thought of him not spending nights at home, he responded, 'Obviously all parents will be scared. But my parents were happy because I'm not living [as] a criminal, I was different from other people who lived criminal lives.'[61] Another male comrade recounted how his parents were particularly strict because they were Catholic. As a child, he was only allowed to go to school and come immediately home to study. But as a teenager, he joined a youth club within the Catholic Church which was 'a breeding ground for activists'. He posited defying his parents' concern as a simple matter once he'd developed a greater political awareness: 'Your parents can't get hold, they can't have that control. Because now you are able to have this kind of, different thinking.'[62] One male comrade explicitly acknowledged the differences in how young male and female activists dealt with parental pressures and expectations. Making specific reference to the nuanced strategies girls employed to deal with their parents, he stated:

> We always knew that women or female comrades had to be supported, because they had this extra burden that they were carrying – the expectation about them from society, and their parents. Not that we also did not have parental pressure at the time, but we, but for them it was much more coordinated and more complex.[63]

These men's narratives demonstrate how girls had different expectations and restrictions placed on them by parents, but also how girls took on a greater emotional burden in seeking to mitigate parental expectations, limit the disruption to family life, and maintain family harmony whilst still participating in the liberation movement.

Gendering Political Labour

However, the gender dynamics of the home did at times also play a more positive role in young women's activism, enabling them to take on particular forms of political labour. The home occupied a central place in female comrades' narratives of the township uprisings. In part, this can be explained by the fact that girls spent so much more time in the home than boys and young men; even once politically active, female comrades needed to manage parental expectations and fears for their safety and keep up with their domestic or caring duties. Yet they also emphasised that their time spent in the home was not separate from their time spent in the struggle. These young women

[61] Interview with Bongo, Diepkloof, 5 April 2015.
[62] Interview with 'Boy George', Pimville, 17 May 2015.
[63] Interview with Siphiwe, Pimville, 17 May 2015.

used the relative safety of the home to hold meetings, recruit more COSAS members, or hide sensitive documents and weapons. Bessie, a COSAS leader from Dlamini, described her home as 'like some head office of COSAS in Soweto,' while Beatrice spoke of using her house as a base for COSAS' Pimville branch.[64] Others used their time in the domestic sphere to talk to their mothers about politics, some successfully convincing their parents to join FEDTRAW or later the ANCWL. Lindiwe from Naledi described how she would gather girls from her neighbourhood in her house to try to recruit them to COSAS. As we sat in the very same house thirty years later, she recollected, 'You know, this room can tell a story! We would sit like we're having a tea party...and that's when we will discuss about the student politics.' Lindiwe used distinctly gendered strategies in her efforts to recruit other girls, as she organised a dance group and held rehearsals at her house. 'After dancing,' she explained, 'that's when we tell them about student politics and recruit them [laughs].'[65]

Lindiwe also mobilised the private space of her home for more dangerous political activities, including storing firearms. Pointing to a trunk in her parents' front room where we sat during our interview, she stated, 'I was one of the brave women who kept, you know [laughs] the AK-47s and the bombs. There's a trunk [points], it's still here. I kept them in there.'[66] Following my interview with Ntsiki, a female comrade from Diepkloof, her mother showed me the precise place on the couch where her father had once hidden a gun behind his back while police searched his home looking for Ntsiki.[67] She then took me around the house, pointing out the various wardrobes and under-bed spaces where Ntsiki had hid when the police came calling. These moments of reminiscence were narrated with particular excitement and obvious pride by former female comrades and their parents. In contrast to interviews with male comrades, the domestic space played a more active role in women's narratives, as they frequently gave tours of their houses to demonstrate where they concealed themselves or various documents or arms. This demonstrates how female comrades did not see their time at home as ordinary and mundane, or in stark contrast to seemingly more heroic activities in the public sphere. Rather, they transform the home in their narratives into a space inseparable from the wider liberation struggle, in which heroic deeds were performed.

[64] Interview with Bessie, Johannesburg, 25 April 2014; interview with Beatrice, Pimville, 23 May 2015.
[65] Interview with Lindiwe, Naledi, 18 June 2015.
[66] Ibid.
[67] Interview with Ntsiki, Diepkloof, 5 April 2015.

Despite rebelling against girlhood norms, female comrades' identities as young women, and their roles as daughters, carers, and domestic labourers in the home, thus shaped their activist commitments and the nature of their participation in the struggle. This was the case not only within their own homes, but also in their wider communities and in the homes or domestic situations of others in which the comrades intervened. While dominant narratives of youth politics in the 1980s tend to focus on street-based confrontations, the historiography also highlights the wider community-based issues that student and youth activists became involved in. Student activists' concerns at school about the provision of textbooks, cost of uniforms, and accessibility of education led them to help local families struggling to send their children to school by raising funds to cover school fees. Both male and female comrades also spoke about their efforts to better township spaces by cleaning the streets and creating new parks. They talked about cooperating with and acting alongside various UDF-aligned civic organisations, and participating in rent boycotts, street committees, and parent-teacher associations.[68]

When discussing these campaigns and actions they took part in, female comrades explicitly asserted that they performed the same tasks as boys and young men. However, within this wider community work there were specific roles that girls played, or tasks that they at least spoke about performing that men did not. Primarily, these involved girls and young women acting as social workers or dispute resolvers in their communities – roles which expanded and politicised much of the caretaking they were already performing in their own extended families. Although these roles were not linked to the explicit goals of the liberation struggle set out by the ANC, they were narrated by female comrades as an essential part of their political participation. As Jessica Taft argues, girls are more likely to engage in activism through such everyday practices rather than through formal political structures or hierarchical organisations.[69] The gendering of these tasks in part explains why girls' political involvement is often missed by observers, because it takes forms not immediately recognised as political.

Regardless of their young age, female comrades in Soweto intervened in family disputes or households where children were not receiving adequate care. Discussing the social work role that she played in Diepkloof, Zanele recalled, 'If maybe you've got a problem from home, yes, I was attending you and taking the issues to the upper structures. And then we go with them to home to sort

[68] See Hyslop, 'School Student Movements,' 192–193; Shaun Johnson, 'Soldiers of Luthuli.'

[69] Jessica K. Taft, 'The Political Lives of Girls,' *Sociology Compass* 8:3 (2014): 263.

out that problem.'[70] She explained how these types of issues were one of the primary concerns of the women's structures set up within COSAS, which were spaces where female comrades could address issues pertinent to them away from their male peers. Within these groups, female comrades would identify families that were struggling to buy enough food and seek out donations from the rest of the community to help. Vicky, another Diepkloof-based comrade, spoke of playing a similar role and told a story about when she confronted a mother who had abandoned her children to stay with another man. She then asked her other comrades for support, and together they convinced the woman to return home to her children.[71] Both Vicky and Zanele also talked about convincing children who had dropped out of school to return or helping those families who could not afford to feed their children.

Other female comrades took on roles in what they described as 'community development', which included addressing issues such as teenage pregnancy, drug and alcohol abuse, and problems with gangs, at times through more confrontational means.[72] Ntebaleng was involved in her local street committee in Diepkloof. Describing the purpose of these organisations, she explained, 'In those old days, our grandfathers and our fathers used to beat our mothers, abuse them. So we would get them. And the uncles maybe, or neighbour who rapes someone, we will go there…maybe in the rape case we would go there and take you and *sjambok* you.' Later, justifying such actions, she continued, 'I mean, why are you supposed to rape? Why must you beat the woman? She can never *klap* you, can never slap you back…So a real man doesn't beat a woman. Never.'[73] Female comrades also intervened in similar cases at school, contesting the normalisation of violence against women and girls. Amahle, a comrade from Jabavu, explained how she and her fellow comrades intervened when a male student was being physically abusive to his girlfriend and not letting her attend school: 'There was a time when we went to fetch another guy, our schoolmate, on our way to school. It's like, he didn't want her to come to school. And then he *klap* her, so we went to fetch him. Why does he deny her her right for education? While we were beating him up at school, the police

---

[70]   Interview with Zanele, Diepkloof, 12 April 2014.

[71]   Interview with Vicky, Diepkloof, 14 May 2014.

[72]   In these efforts we can see a clear connection with Black Consciousness activists from the previous decades and their insistence that community development was a key form of 'protest'. Yet Soweto's comrades did not explicitly link their actions in this field to any inspiration from earlier generations of activism. Meghan Healy-Clancy, 'The Everyday Politics of being a Student in South Africa: A History,' *History Compass* 15:3 (2017): 7.

[73]   Interview with Ntebaleng, Diepkloof, 15 April 2014.

came, here at Morris [Isaacson].'[74] In some cases action was taken against girls who were promoting a version of girlhood antithetical to what female comrades stood for. Phumzile, a Diepkloof-based activist, would confront students found drinking in *shebeens* during school hours, sometimes forcibly removing them. Again, this was an action specifically undertaken by young women's groups within COSAS without male comrades' involvement, Phumzile explained: 'We will do it on our own…we were taking girls out of our taverns, girls out of *shebeens*, girls out of like, the corners. You know, there were these girls who used to smoke *dagga*, smoke cigarettes, not going to school. We used to do that – take them back to school.' She also spoke of how she used to confront local girls involved in relationships with gangsters or the police: 'we used to go to them and, you know, beat them, harass them, chase them away from school, because they are telling police or gangsters to kill us,' she explained.[75]

Female comrades narrated these forms of community and household activism together with the more overtly or obviously political roles they took on as young activists, making no clear separation between the two. These broader, more 'everyday' forms of political action undertaken by the comrades can tell us much about their wider dreams of a utopian future, and their efforts to forge a new moral community through their involvement in the struggle. Bozzoli demonstrates how the comrades held romanticised, millenarian visions of post-apartheid society in which 'there would, the youth believed, be no crime, decay or alcohol, no oppression, no suffering.'[76] Exploring female comrades' engagement in community issues demonstrates that girls and young women shared this moral vision of the future, but also that this vision had certain gendered aspects for them. In this idealised future, particular forms of girls' deviance were not going to be acceptable, such as their teenage drinking, smoking, or hanging around in 'corners'. Yet simultaneously, there would be more protections in place for girls, mothers, and families. Girls would no longer be raped or abused at school, wives would no longer be beaten by their husbands, and mothers would not have to struggle to provide for their children. The centrality of these social work narratives to female comrades' stories highlights how integral creating this future was for them as young student activists.

Through playing such roles, some female comrades came to be role models not just to their fellow activists, but to some in their communities more broadly, despite possessing and exhibiting qualities that contravened feminine norms. When asked if the other girls in her school looked up to her, Zanele

[74] Interview with Amahle, Jabavu, 10 June 2015.
[75] Interview with Phumzile, Johannesburg, 17 April 2015.
[76] Bozzoli, 'Why were the 1980s "millenarian"?' 80.

responded, 'Yes. You know, if somebody trusts you to bring their difficulties to you, maybe to share something with you, I think you were something.' She continued, 'Because they would rather come to me and talk than their parents…And then they'll come back and say thank you.'[77] Campbell argues that the two primary obstacles to young women's political activity in the 1980s were women's own reluctance to see themselves as powerful social agents, and men's unwillingness to take women's political activity seriously.[78] Yet as Zanele's reflections demonstrate, female COSAS members seem to understand the importance of their actions, and upon reflection thirty years later, have come to see themselves as central actors in their communities despite their young age at the time. Speaking about her own community involvement, another Diepkloof comrade commented, 'I think a leader is born, leadership is within you.' Reflecting on the help she extended to those in need within Soweto, she recalled, 'I become fulfilled. It makes me happy. Because if somebody is coming crying, then I must help them. When the person is coming and give me feedback and they are smiling, I become fulfilled.'[79]

In her work on the autobiographies of male struggle leaders, Unterhalter argues that the work of political struggle and nation building is central to men's constructions of a particular 'heroic masculinity' performed during the liberation struggle. These men's focus on more public, formal political work leads to a separation between the public and private, and male and female spheres, in much of their writing.[80] But what female comrades' narratives of their political labour tells us is about the importance of this more caring, community-based labour to constructions of heroic *femininity*. Although female comrades so often conform their narratives to masculine comrade norms – emphasising their bravery, autonomy, and action in the streets – here we are offered insight into the feminised labour performed by female comrades.

And more broadly too, girls' involvement in these community initiatives tells us about the gendered division of labour, or at least gendered differences in memory and perception, within the student movement. Female comrades spoke much more about this emotional labour and care work than male comrades, and more about how the liberation struggle intersected with the everyday lives they continued to live as daughters, sisters and mothers within the home. This can be read in two ways. First, the lack of such stories from male comrades

[77] Interview with Zanele, Diepkloof, 12 April 2014.
[78] Campbell, 'Identity and Gender in a Changing Society,' 333.
[79] Interview with Ntsiki, Diepkloof, 5 April 2015.
[80] Elaine Unterhalter, 'The Work of the Nation: Heroic Masculinity in South African Autobiographical Writing of the Anti-Apartheid Struggle,' *The European Journal of Development Research* 12:2 (2000): 157–178.

suggests that female comrades carried the burden of caregiving and emotional labour within their communities, demonstrating how girls' gendered roles in the home shaped their identities and experiences as activists. In her work on young female activists in North and South America, Taft found that girls may be socialised to be more concerned for their communities than boys, and thus be more likely to participate in these forms of politicised social work.[81] She also argues strongly for a re-theorisation of youth 'politics' to include these more informal and diffuse spaces and activities in order to see girls' activism, which is so often missed by perspectives that focus only on formal political structures or more confrontational political activities. Exploring female comrades' activism within the home and in their wider communities not only helps to make the involvement of girls and young women in the struggle more visible, but also complicates ideas of 'heroic masculinity' and expands conceptions of activism beyond the usual focus on street politics or more organised forms of struggle. A second, alternative reading could be that we as researchers miss men's experiences of emotional labour and care work because they do not readily bring up such work in interviews, either because they are uncomfortable discussing seemingly 'unmanly' labour, or because they did not see such work as integral to the liberation struggle in the ways that female comrades did. If male comrades did participate in these social work or caring activities to the same extent, this was not apparent in their own narratives.

Conclusion

As feminist geographical research demonstrates, the private and public spheres are not distinct spaces, but ones that are explicitly interconnected. Furthermore, there is rarely a neat boundary between the home and other community spaces. This was particularly the case in apartheid South Africa, where the state regularly intruded in to Africans' homes, but also where social and family life tended to be more communal and not necessarily based around a single nuclear family. For Soweto's female comrades, the home was inextricable from the struggle. The inequalities they experienced within the home pushed many of them to seek out student organisations in the first place, and much of their political action was motivated by a desire to construct a new political girlhood in opposition to their previous, home-centred and subservient lives. Once they became committed activists, they did not formally leave their homes and abandon their families. Yes, many stopped sleeping at home for extended periods of time and constructed new 'families'

---

[81]   Taft, 'The Political Lives of Girls,' 264.

amongst their comrades; but their relationships within the home and the gendered dynamics of the domestic space continued to impact their lives and actions as comrades. Using their position within the home to their advantage, many female comrades further politicised their parents' houses, either by bringing comrades into them or drawing their parents out into the struggle. Girls also drew upon their gendered experiences of caregiving to take on the positions of community workers and dispute resolvers in their neighbourhoods. In these ways, we can see how girls politicised their domestic and gendered duties to take on new, empowering roles in the broader liberation struggle. However, the gendered dynamics of the home that drew girls into the struggle simultaneously produced obstacles that required female comrades to carry a great emotional burden, as alongside their activist commitments they needed to balance parental expectations and deflect stigmatisation from their families, friends, and neighbours.

This chapter has established the reciprocal relationship between the home and political activism during the township uprisings. In their own narratives, female comrades challenge any clear separations between the private and public spheres in 1980s Soweto. They include discussions of the home and their struggles with their parents and friends within their broader narratives of their political activities as comrades. This highlights two broader points. First, by focusing on activism through everyday practices and more diffuse spaces, we can better understand girls' political work, and expand ideas of activism in 1980s South Africa beyond the usual forms of street politics and organised struggle. We can see how wider caring and supportive roles played within township communities were very much seen as political work by female comrades. Further, girls also saw their emotional labour of managing parental concern as part of their activism; they perceive these burdens they bore and hurdles they had to cross as key markers of their dedication to the liberation struggle. Second, female comrades' understanding of what constituted political activism provides a window into constructions of 'heroic femininity' during these years. As Unterhalter argues, the home and domestic life is often something 'left behind' by South Africa's male struggle heroes. As Mandela himself recounts in his autobiography, 'a man involved in the struggle was a man without a home life.'[82] Srila Roy also argues that in living a heroic life, revolutionaries must leave behind the 'ordinary' sphere of women and domesticity. Yet female activists live heroic lives while still

---

[82] Unterhalter, 'The Work of the Nation'; Nelson Mandela, *Long Walk to Freedom* (Boston; London: Little, Brown & Co, 1994).

'performing the everyday labour of care and feminised domesticity.'[83] For them, heroic action does not only involve engaging in street battles or openly confronting the apartheid state. It also includes rebelling against, or at times simply managing and negotiating, gender dynamics within the home, and balancing the demands of being an activist with the expectations of being a young woman and good daughter.

[83]   Srila Roy, 'The Everyday Life of the Revolution: Gender, Violence and Memory,' *South Asia Research* 27:2 (2007): 188.

4

The Meeting: Contesting Gender and Creating a Movement

Bessie became engaged in student politics as a young teenager in Dlamini, Soweto. Of all the women interviewed for this book she was the first to join COSAS in 1982 at the age of sixteen. During her initial years in the organisation she was often the only young woman present at COSAS meetings, but this soon changed as she focused much of her efforts on recruiting more female students to the struggle. This helped propel her into a leadership role in the organisation, first on the Soweto executive and then in the regional executive of COSAS. Bessie understood that there were certain societal factors that tended to hold girls back from the struggle. Women were expected to remain in the home, cooking, cleaning, and raising families, whereas the more challenging domains of politics and war were ascribed to men, she explained. 'Our struggle was seen like a man's domain, you know?' But Bessie insisted that she never witnessed such attitudes affecting female comrades in COSAS. Personally, she never experienced derision or disrespect from the young male activists she worked alongside. 'They were so wonderful,' she said of her male comrades. 'I never had any problems…I was respected, highly respected.' She shunned the idea of organising separately as women, believing that she personally could grow more as an activist by participating alongside male comrades. 'I felt I grew faster, I grew much stronger engaging directly with men,' she explained.

Bessie's account of being respected and treated as an equal by her male comrades jars with the previous historiography on young activists during these years, which describes comrade culture as deeply masculinist and disparaging towards young women.[1] This chapter seeks to understand such contradictions and asks how young male and female activists related to one another at a time when township society was highly patriarchal, and during a period when young men increasingly asserted their masculinity through

---

[1] Seekings, 'Gender Ideology and Township Politics'; Campbell, 'Identity and Gender in a Changing Society'; Sitas, 'The Making of the "Comrades" Movement in Natal'.

participating in the struggle. It explores both the gender relations that developed within the student and youth movement and how women remember these relations today, asking important questions about their overwhelmingly positive narratives.

Unlike the others in this book, this chapter does not address a single or concrete space or place, but rather a conceptual one: the 'meeting' – where young activists discussed ideology, shared dreams for the future, and planned their actions. Student activists' meetings took place across numerous township locations: empty classrooms, parents' homes, parks, and churches. But when former comrades talk about their meetings, the dominant narrative they present is one of a lack of space, of confusion and contestation over which spaces were safe, and the complex strategies developed to make sure that COSAS meetings could not be traced by police or informers to any definable space or place. But despite lacking a set, physical corporeality, COSAS meetings were constructed by comrades as idealised spaces of political education, generational advancement, and ideological precocity.

Furthermore, both male and female comrades constructed the meeting as a romanticised, utopian space of gender equality, young women's empowerment, and fraternal 'brother-and-sister' relationships between activists, just as Bessie does. Regardless of the physical space meetings were held in, the conceptual space of the meeting was conceived of as separate from patriarchal township culture and its problems with gender inequality and sexual violence. Here, female comrades could overcome their feelings of inferiority and engage in political discussions on equal footing with young men. They insisted that they felt like respected equals in meetings, and never experienced derision, unwanted advances, or sexual abuse from their male comrades. Both men and women went as far as to insist that gender did not exist in these political spaces; those present were 'comrades' or 'youths' rather than boys and girls, and thus wider gender issues did not arise.

However, this construction masked the realities of how gender relations played out in meetings, and how wider township cultures and masculinities intruded into and shaped the student movement. Although comrades at first presented a uniform post-hoc account of gender equality, they often later contradicted this idealised narrative, with men demonstrating their discriminatory views and women acknowledging instances of their unequal treatment. Boys' generalised stereotyping of township girls as frivolous, ignorant, and weak affected how they treated female comrades, while girls' experiences of subordination in the home and school carried over into meetings, making them feel inferior to male comrades and thus less likely to speak out or engage in political discussions. In reality then, political meetings were often sites of discrimination and girls' exclusion and silencing. Moreover, they were not necessarily the safe spaces free from sexual coercion or violence that comrades initially painted them as.

This exploration of how gender relations were debated, challenged, or reinforced in student meetings exposes a discord between activists' public espousals of gender equality and the actual beliefs they held or actions they practised. It is essential to acknowledge that male comrades across South Africa or even within Soweto were not homogeneous in their views or actions when it came to their treatment of women. On paper, COSAS and other Congress-aligned youth organisations followed a policy of what interviewees describe as 'non-sexism' and made efforts to recruit female comrades into their ranks and to treat them as equals. Male comrades also sought to ban personal relationships between COSAS members to protect girls from unwanted male advances and to focus the attention of all comrades on the struggle. However, 'non-sexism' to comrades did not imply complete gender equality, but rather the erasure of gender as a salient category, and the assimilation of female comrades into male-dominated COSAS culture. COSAS's official policies aimed at combating gender discrimination were neither easily nor consistently implemented, as evidenced by girls' general exclusion from COSAS leadership, men's continued beliefs that girls were too frivolous and gossip-prone to be trusted as much as male activists, and cases where personal relationships did develop between comrades. Furthermore, COSAS's acknowledgement of gender issues and acceptance of female comrades did not necessarily affect a societal wide change in their attitudes towards women; while they granted equal status to some of their female comrades, they did so by treating them as honorary men rather than as emancipated women. Consequently, their gender ideologies were not permanently shifted, and their relationships with girls and young women outside political organisations remained largely unchanged.

This chapter speaks to wider debates within the history of South Africa's liberation struggle and contributes to recent discussions about the extent to which the movement was plagued by disrespect and abuse of its female members. This remains a contentious topic for both men and women involved in the struggle. The female comrades in this book are not alone as women who insist that gender discrimination and violence were negligible in their lives as activists. Several female former ANC and MK members who lived in exile have also rejected claims that sexual harassment or violence were common in ANC camps.[2] This chapter sheds new light on the issues of gender relations

---

[2]   Redi Tlhabi, *Khwezi* (Johannesburg: Jonathan Ball, 2017), 38; Carl Collison, 'Women freedom fighters tell of sexual abuse in camps,' *Mail & Guardian*, 27 October 2017.

and sexual abuse within the struggle, but also explores how former female activists themselves contribute to these debates and how they prefer to be remembered as agents rather than victims in this history.

Gender Ideologies and the Student Movement

In order to understand the complexities of gender relations within COSAS, one first needs to situate the organisation within wider township society and the longer history of political gender ideologies in South Africa. The 1980s were a period of great social, economic, and political upheaval, and thus also shifting gender ideologies. As with previous and subsequent decades, the 1980s were marked by high rates of domestic abuse and constructions of gender that granted men rights over women and their bodies. Yet this decade saw the emergence of, or heightened visibility of, specific forms of violence such as jackrolling that targeted young women in South Africa's townships and brutally ensured their continued subordination through fear and shame. Despite the rise of female-headed households and declining marriage rates over the 1970s and 1980s, women were still largely perceived as minors and secondary citizens in African societies, and violence was often used as a means of solidifying men's control over women.[3] As political confrontation in many townships increased during the 1980s, militarised masculinities grew more pronounced, fostering what some scholars refer to as a 'culture of violence' across private and public township spaces.[4] Political violence exaggerated existing gender ideologies which confined women to the roles of mother and protector of the home, and further sanctioned the use of violence against women for a variety of ends.

The militarised gender identities adopted by male comrades were not only influenced by wider cultures and structures of power in the townships, but also by those within the broader ANC-aligned liberation movement. Raymond Suttner contends that South Africa's liberation struggle was inextricably linked to the denial of African manhood. Yet assertions of manhood within the struggle were more multifaceted than previous historians have argued, as the masculinities espoused by ANC men were not monolithic.[5] Many (but not all) ANC leaders and cadres invoked a heroic masculinity that drew on past warrior culture. This militarist tradition 'entailed not only heroic acts

---

[3]   Meintjes, 'Political Violence and Gender,' 97.
[4]   *Ibid.*; See also Simpson 'Women and Children in Violent South African Townships.'
[5]   Raymond Suttner, *The ANC Underground in South Africa* (Johannesburg: Jacana Media, 2008), 111.

but also many cases of abuse and power over women.'[6] New debates around gender relations within the ANC were sparked following 1976 with the sharp increase in female cadres leaving the country to join MK. Women's heightened presence in MK during the 1970s and 1980s destabilised the organisation's masculine culture, and forced the ANC to recognise women's growing political presence. Oliver Tambo declared 1984 to be 'The Year of Women', and in his annual speech publicly called for women to participate equally in all levels of the struggle while arguing for the need to dismantle the 'triple oppression' black women faced on account of their race, class, and gender. However, the 1980s were not years of women's seamless integration into MK's ranks. Rather, the decade witnessed increased violence against women living in exile, with the ANC women's section writing in 1987 that cases of abuse had become common.[7] Attempts to deal with sexual violence in exile were largely unsuccessful as many perpetrators were in leadership positions, and there was generally little will or pressure to do so. While evidence of some of these abuses has since been revealed, much remains unspoken.[8]

As with the ANC and most of its aligned organisations, COSAS and SAYCO both adopted a socialist stance on women's oppression in which women's concerns were subordinated to, rather than addressed as part of, the wider struggle to achieve liberation. Until the concluding years of the struggle, the ANC largely believed that fighting specifically for women's rights was divisive, and that women's oppression would be naturally eliminated as part of the transition to a socialist democracy.[9] This was similar to the prevailing ideology held by Black Consciousness activists from the late 1960s to 1970s. Daniel Magaziner argues that Black Consciousness made a 'strategic choice' to put women's issues to the side out of fear of sowing any division or weakness in the movement.[10] For women within the movement gender identities were secondary; they were black first and women second. The extent to which Steve Biko promoted gender equality is still debated by historians, in part because of a central contradiction in how Black Consciousness supported women's participation while simultaneously remaining a sexist movement.[11] The movement's

---

[6]   *Ibid.*, 119.

[7]   Hassim, *Women's Organizations and Democracy in South Africa*, 85–96.

[8]   Tlhabi, *Khwezi*, 36–44.

[9]   Beall et al, 'A Bit on the Side,' 30–32; Gay W. Seidman, '"No Freedom without the Women": Mobilization and Gender in South Africa, 1970–1992,' *Signs* 18:2 (1993): 291–320.

[10] Daniel R. Magaziner, *The Law and the Prophets: Black Consciousness in South Africa, 1968–1977* (Athens: Ohio University Press, 2010), 34.

[11] Daniel R. Magaziner, 'Pieces of a (Wo)man: Feminism, Gender and Adulthood in Black Consciousness, 1968–1977,' *Journal of Southern African Studies* 37:1 (2011): 47.

leadership ultimately included a number of successful female activists – most notably Mamphele Ramphele and Deborah Matshoba. However, such women struggled to prove their worth to male activists and ultimately had to choose between two politicised gender identities: to either adopt masculine traits and become 'one of the boys'; or a more conservative female identity associated with motherhood and become 'an adjunct sufferer fighting for the liberation of the family, not herself.'[12] Reflecting on the movement, Ramphele later wrote that 'in general, sexist practices and division of labour along gender lines were never systematically challenged within Black Consciousness ranks.'[13]

The student and youth organisations of the 1980s adopted a similar position and consequently inherited this contradiction in how they encouraged young women's involvement without adopting a particularly progressive stance on gender. In 1989, SAYCO declared that it 'does not separate the struggle of the women from the broad national democratic revolution,' and stated that organising female youth was an urgent priority of the organisation.[14] In adhering to the ANC's stance on gender, COSAS and other Congress-aligned youth organisations followed an official policy of gender equality and declared themselves to be a 'non-sexist' organisation. As Kumi Naidoo writes of COSAS in Durban:

> In their rhetoric COSAS and other youth congresses supported an anti-sexist position...In practice this was difficult to implement. Nevertheless, the statement of intent was seen as a positive sign that the emancipation of women would be taken more seriously by resistance organisations. Although racist and sexist notions had permeated the minds of the youth to an appreciable extent there was hope that in future these would be overcome.[15]

Archival evidence demonstrates that student and youth organisations were cognisant of the gender imbalances in their societies and how women's subordination dissuaded many from joining the struggle. A COSAS document from 1984 highlights the burden of domestic work women and female children bore, stating how 'this makes it difficult for them to participate in our youth movements and student organisations and in activities meant to make our lives

---

12 *Ibid.*, 49.
13 Mamphela Ramphele, 'The Dynamics of Gender within Black Consciousness Organisations: A Personal View,' in Barney Pityana et al (eds), *Bounds of Possibility: The Legacy of Steve Biko and Black Consciousness* (Cape Town: David Philip, 1991), 219.
14 'Organising Women,' *Youth Focus*, July 1989, AL2425: K1, South African Youth Congress, SAHA.
15 Naidoo, 'The Politics of Youth Resistance,' 164.

meaningful.'[16] In an undated document, SAYCO too demonstrated its awareness of gender imbalances, writing, 'The society in which we live is a patriarchal
society. Men are regarded as the stronger sex and women as the weaker sex; and
women bow to this.'[17] Furthermore, COSAS records demonstrate that at least
prior to the 1985 state of emergency, the organisation dedicated some effort to
addressing gender issues in schools. In a list publishing its primary demands,
COSAS included the 'end to sexual abuse of female students/pupils be it by
a teacher or another student/pupil.'[18] The Soweto branch of the organisation
declared that 'pupils/students (girls) must be treated as human beings and not
as sexual objects,' and that 'no female student [should] be forced by any teacher
to fall in love with him.'[19] Male COSAS members also sought to protect girls
by banning womanising within the organisation – although the Soweto Youth
Congress (SOYCO) defined this as 'involvement in acts of concentrating on
women and neglecting important organisational work' rather than explicitly
engaging in multiple, casual sexual relationships.[20] Through such actions,
male student leadership hoped to recruit more girls and young women into
COSAS' ranks. While the organisation had always been male-dominated, its
female membership grew significantly following the decision made in 1982 to
limit COSAS membership to school-going youths only.

The Meeting as a Romanticised Space

In interviews, both male and female comrades constructed COSAS meetings
as a romanticised space, a haven separate from the rest of township society
and not plagued by the same social problems. Here, they were able to auton-
omously discuss ideas, ideologies, and strategies just amongst themselves.
Emphasising students' self-sufficiency, many former comrades discussed the
political education that would occur in meetings. Each week a particular comrade would be tasked with giving a presentation on a set topic, such as the
Freedom Charter, People's Education, or the history of the student struggle.
Those gathered would then discuss or *umrabulo*, sharing ideas and knowledge.
But more importantly for this book, these meetings were also constructed

---

[16] 'International Children's Day,' 1 June 1984, AD1790, Congress of South African
Students, HP.
[17] 'Women's Department,' undated, AL2423: B6.5, South African Youth Congress,
SAHA.
[18] 'Forward to Democratic SRCs,' 1984, AD1790, Congress of South African Students, Soweto Branch, HP.
[19] *Ibid.*
[20] 'Report of Discipline as Discussed in the Forum of the Soweto Youth Congress,' 23
February 1986, AL2425: B8, South African Youth Congress, SAHA.

as spaces free from gender discrimination, assault, or ill-intention; as spaces removed from the patriarchy and gendered power relations of wider township society. As Ntsiki from Diepkloof described, 'they [male comrades] don't make you feel that you are a woman. But the circumstances *outside* COSAS will make you feel that you are a woman.'[21]

In meetings, interviewees claimed, male and female comrades were seen as equals. One woman simply stated, 'the treatment was equal with men and women, we were all the same.'[22] Numerous women attested that there was very little gendered division of labour within the organisation, and that they never felt discriminated against by their male comrades and were never abused by them. Male comrades acknowledged that female members were a minority in the student movement, but that those who did participate were fully committed and brave activists who participated equally with and held their own amongst men. 'I remember,' said one male comrade, 'there's one belief that we used to operate on, to say, women can do what men are doing. So we wanted to instil that thing to say, there's no task that is meant for men and women cannot do…We discouraged the thing of discrimination.'[23] Similarly, another declared, 'our struggle was never discriminate…What I can do, any woman can do.'[24] A student leader from Diepkloof concurred, stating, 'we had that unity. And you would not see one of us maybe discriminating women comrades. We took them as leaders, we took them as comrades in arms.'[25]

Male comrades also spoke of the respect they had for young women who were brave enough to join the struggle despite the difficulties activism posed for girls. One male interviewee discussed his admiration for female comrades in leadership positions at length. His testimony was likely affected by the presence of such a female comrade, Florence, who was acting as a research assistant during his interview. When asked about women's role in the student movement, he responded, 'I'm scared of these ladies, that's why I'm mentioning her [Florence]. They are my elders. I need to respect them. I don't want to be careless with their history.' Concluding the interview, he stated, 'COSAS, ANC helped me to be a better man…to understand we are 50:50. Because my father used to say, "never be taught by a woman", eh! But I can listen to a woman…I'm what I am because of these ladies [points to Florence]…I'm a man because of them.'[26] Those few women who

[21] Interview with Ntsiki, Diepkloof, 5 April 2015.
[22] Interview with Nonkululeko, Diepkloof, 8 April 2014.
[23] Interview with Bongo, Diepkloof, 5 April 2015.
[24] Interview with Boy George, Pimville, 17 May 2015.
[25] Interview with Themba, Diepkloof, 6 April 2015.
[26] Interview with ATV, Diepkloof, 2 May 2015.

were elected to leadership positions in the student movement supported this narrative. When asked if she ever felt animosity from male comrades after she was elected to the Soweto executive, Bessie responded, 'I never, I never…I was respected, highly respected.'[27]

Both men and women also constructed political meetings as a space where girls could overcome their insecurities and feelings of inferiority through political education and careful nurturing by male comrades. While treating their female comrades as equals, young male activists nevertheless understood that girls faced particular obstacles in the struggle that they needed to address. Girls' double burden of fighting against apartheid and patriarchal gender norms was also acknowledged by the wider youth movement. Within both COSAS and SAYCO, women's forums or departments were established for 'sharpening the political outlook' of young women. SAYCO's women's department wrote of its aspiration to 'develop the self-consciousness of women and build self confidence in them.'[28] Exhibiting his awareness of the pressures politicised girls faced, Siphiwe from Pimville stated, 'We always knew that… female comrades had to be supported, because they had this extra burden that they were carrying – the expectation about them from society, and their parents.'[29] When female comrades could not attend meetings due to these pressures, their male comrades understood. Florence described,

> They treated me as an equal but at the same time they knew that I was a female and they treated me with…maybe with a golden glove…They would understand that I cannot participate in, let's say there has to be a meeting somewhere…and because I'm a female I can't go there because it's over the weekend or it's distant…They understood. And when they come back, they would get back to me and let me know…this is what happened. So they were not harsh in making me do things.[30]

Male comrades also recall that they understood the physical insecurity girls experienced in township streets, and would walk them to and from meetings, or call at their homes if they inexplicably missed a meeting. They sought to protect female comrades from the dangers posed by police and gangsters. Bessie, who described her male comrades as 'so wonderful' explained, 'as much as we saw ourselves as equals, they always took care of the lady comrades.' She continued, 'You know, we'd be chased, we would be trying to dive away from

27 Interview with Bessie, Johannesburg, 25 April 2014.
28 'Women's Department,' undated, AL2425: B6.5, South African Youth Congress, SAHA.
29 Interview with Siphiwe, Pimville, 17 May 2015.
30 Interview with Florence, Diepkloof, 3 March 2015.

bullets, they would always ensure that we were safe, we were there within the group.'[31] Florence recounted a similar experience: 'As we were running I felt that no man...I can't take this anymore...And this guy just came he said... "don't give up now"...Then he grabbed my hand and said 'come comrade, come!'...I knew that the guys were looking after me.'[32] Female comrades did not perceive such special treatment as antithetical to their equal status. As one clarified, they were protected 'not in that way of being spoiled' but 'in a good way'.[33] These recollections echo those of women who lived in ANC camps in exile, who were known as the 'flowers of the revolution' because of the protection they received from ANC men.[34]

Beyond offering them protection, male comrades also claimed that they sought to empower female comrades. Aware of how gendered socialisation tended to foster greater political understanding in boys than girls, they attempted to even this imbalance by educating female recruits in meetings. As Nomsa remembered, 'Male comrades, they were more advanced in understanding than us. But what was good...they were teaching us and we ended up having the common understanding.'[35] Zanele recounted how it was easy for her to talk to her male leaders if she did not understand a particular political concept, while another interviewee described, 'they were mentoring you, trying to teach you to be open to...these issues. They encouraged me a lot.'[36] Consequently, female comrades soon grew to feel more confident. As one remembered, 'We've become strong because of the male comrades who were teaching us struggle. If it was not [for] them, we wouldn't have made it at that time.'[37]

But when asked specifically about gender issues that arose during COSAS meetings, interviewees often denied the influence of gender altogether. Many adhered to the position adopted by the wider struggle: that women's liberation would come as a natural consequence of the transition to democracy. As Bessie explained, 'As much as we had organisations that were focusing specifically on women...we saw the struggle as a struggle for our society...we see our struggle as not separate from that of men.'[38] Several women admitted that although they are aware of gender issues now (many were involved in the ANCWL at the time of research), as students they were either ignorant or uninterested.

---

[31] Interview with Bessie, Johannesburg, 25 April 2014.
[32] Interview with Florence, Diepkloof, 8 May 2014.
[33] Interview with Khosi, Orlando East, 1 May 2014.
[34] Tlhabi, *Khwezi*, 38.
[35] Interview with Nomsa, Diepkloof Extension, 19 April 2014.
[36] Interviews with Zanele, Diepkloof, 12 April 2014; Thabisile, Johannesburg, 25 May 2015.
[37] Interview with Phumzile, Johannesburg, 17 April 2015.
[38] Interview with Bessie, Johannesburg, 25 April 2014.

One described, 'it was just liberation, we didn't even care about gender at that time.'[39] Ntiski, when asked if she was involved in any gender issues, replied no, 'at that time we were busy with *our* issues, because we were youth.'[40]

Here, Ntsiki employs the term 'youth' in a non-gendered way, implying that the identities of being a girl or woman and a 'youth' were oppositional, if not incompatible. Her use of a gender-neutral identity was common amongst female interviewees, who repeatedly reiterated that they were 'comrades' rather than women or girls, thus emphasising the salience of their generational rather than gendered identities. Florence too spoke of how she never saw herself as a woman, but rather as a comrade. She explained that COSAS was a 'non-sexist' organisation, which to comrades, rather than meaning a lack of prejudice on the basis of gender, was taken to mean a complete denial of gendered identities. She clarified, 'Then...it wasn't a gender issue...when it comes to gender politically at school, it wasn't there.'[41] This insistence on the comrades having no gender, or no gender issues to address, was stressed by other interviewees too. As Lucy from Diepkloof explicitly stated, 'you have to be a comrade without your gender.'[42] Male comrades too negated the influence of gender in COSAS. As one recalled, 'With the female comrades, they were recruited like any other...Then, the gender issue wasn't on the table. But we had this natural treatment of equal treatment of comrades within our midst. We did not discriminate.'[43] While they understood that male and female comrades were biologically different, they refused to accept any socially-constructed gender differences: 'We were saying we are comrades...This female thing, male thing, we used to say no, it's just a biological thing. It should not affect our minds.'[44]

Meetings were thus constructed by interviewees as a space in which female comrades could escape being girls; a space where their gender did not automatically imply their subordination and inferiority. Because of the de-gendering of female comrades, all interviewees insisted that meetings were spaces where girls were safe from all forms of sexual violence, abuse, or coercion. At a time when almost every other township space – homes, schools, and streets – had become sites of girls' potential victimisation, COSAS meetings were a haven where girls could be free from sexual advances of any kind, interviewees claimed. The state's surveillance of the comrades often meant that meetings

[39] Interview with Sissy, Diepkloof, 17 April 2015.
[40] Interview with Ntsiki, Diepkloof, 5 April 2015.
[41] Interview with Florence, Diepkloof, 8 May 2014.
[42] Interview with Lucy, Fleurhof, 7 April 2014.
[43] Interview with Themba, Diepkloof, 6 April 2015.
[44] Interview with Moses, Diepkloof, 19 April 2014.

had to take place late at night or in secluded corners of the township – situations which assumingly placed young women (who were numerically in the minority) in a potentially vulnerable position. Yet those interviewed insisted that no sexual advances took place. As the state of emergency intensified, many comrades stopped sleeping at home, instead sleeping together in various safe spaces around the township, including classrooms, neighbours' houses, and even junk yards, a practice they referred to as sleeping *emoyeni* or *amoya* – 'in the air'. Even in these instances, comrades explained, young women were respected and protected. Ntsiki described, 'And we will even sleep together, they won't do nothing! They won't harm us, they won't rape you, like – you know – the criminals. They were comrades, they were not like *comtsotsis*.'[45] Suggesting that male comrades suppressed any desires they may have had in such scenarios, Bessie stated, 'Now you go to that place [*amoya*]. It would be you and a number of male comrades...but they would ensure that they don't make any advances. Others, you could see that they were interested, and maybe you were also interested [laughs]. But then, fortunately, the comrades wouldn't act.'[46]

Men too supported this narrative. As a male comrade from Diepkloof described, 'We will sleep in the same bed but we will never have sex....She's one of my comrades.'[47] Again here, 'comrade' is used in a desexualised way to suggest that physical relationships between comrades were inconceivable at the time. Furthering this notion, almost all interviewees explained that their relationships with their comrades of the opposite sex were like those between 'brother and sister', and thus they never worried about being approached or victimised by boys and young men at meetings or when sleeping *emoyeni*. 'If you start a relationship it's like incest,' one man explained.[48] Nonkululeko and Ntebaleng, both female comrades from Diepkloof, gave very similar answers when asked if there were ever relationships between comrades, or if male comrades ever took advantage of female comrades. Nonkululeko proclaimed, 'We knew what we were doing. Even when we were sleeping there outside...we were like brothers and sisters. There's nothing more.'[49] Ntebaleng explained how comrades did not allow relationships to form between them: 'we didn't want to mix pleasure with politics. We were there as soldiers, so we are going to fight.' Speaking about her male comrades she stated, 'They protected us.

---

[45]   Dissident comrades, or criminals acting under the cloak of political activism. Interview with Ntsiki, Diepkloof, 5 April 2015.
[46]   Interview with Bessie, Johannesburg, 25 April 2014.
[47]   Interview with ATV, Diepkloof, 2 May 2015.
[48]   Interview with Bongo, Diepkloof, 5 April 2015.
[49]   Interview with Nonkululeko, Diepkloof, 8 April 2014.

They respected us. You know, we were like family…brothers and sisters.'[50] The spaces where comrades slept *emoyeni* were thus portrayed as refuges – not only from apartheid police and security forces but also from the gender relations that typically governed what happened when a young man and woman slept next to each other in the township.

The Meeting as a Space of Derision, Disrespect, and Abuse

Nevertheless, comrades' constructions of political meetings as safe, respectful spaces characterised by equality were frequently undermined by interviewees' own further discussions of how gender relations played out in practice. As Beall and her colleagues argue, 'gender-neutral policy is a myth,' and all men and women who participate in politics do so as gendered beings.[51] The student struggle was shaped by the prevailing gender norms within South Africa and the wider liberation struggle during the 1980s. It was a young man's world which may have tolerated, and at certain times encouraged, young women's participation, but predominantly on men's terms. It was male comrades who ran meetings, gave orders, assigned tasks, and largely controlled the organisation's gender ideology. Despite its public espousal of gender equality and non-sexism, the student movement – much like its parent organisation, the ANC – was marred by casual sexism and discrimination towards its female members. A closer examination of these various contradictions reveals a much more complicated picture of gender relations in political meetings than that first painted by interviewees.

First, men's narratives of how they did not see gender, and did not consider their female comrades to differ from themselves other than in their biology, were frequently undermined by their specific stereotyping of politicised girls and young women. This is not surprising given the wider research on the comrades, which has found that male youth involved in the struggle tended to be intensely masculine and often disparaging towards young women.[52] Despite at times celebrating the bravery of young women, male comrades also characterised them as frivolous, ignorant, and too gossip-prone to be serious political activists. Speaking about women's groups formed within COSAS, Moses – a male comrade from Diepkloof – described how when meeting just amongst themselves, female comrades tended to get distracted by non-political issues. 'We faced a situation where female are now discussing not relevant issues,

50 Interview with Ntebaleng, Diepkloof, 15 April 2014.
51 Beall et al., 'A Bit on the Side,' 33.
52 Seekings, 'Gender Ideology and Township Politics'; Campbell, 'Identity and Gender in a Changing Society'; Sitas, 'The Making of the "Comrades" Movement in Natal'.

you see?' he explained. 'They will begin to say, "Hey, that male comrade is handsome!" Or such issues. And we thought no, no, no, we are losing focus. So around 1986 we said no, dissolve these women's committees.'[53] Such attitudes were clearly prevalent in the wider student/youth movement. As one of Marks' informants from Diepkloof told her in the early 1990s, 'Women are not concerned about involvement or their rights. They just want to study gossip. They are highly ignorant....Even when women do have a women's department in their organisations, they just talk about their boyfriends and then they fight there.'[54] Campbell's informants from Natal also painted girls as too frivolous for political activism. As one stated, 'Township women are much more preoccupied with township life than with the struggle...luxuries such as dancing and visiting the [shopping centre].'[55] Another of her informants described young women as 'silly, over-emotional, shallow and unreliable in times of crisis,' and therefore not suited to politics.[56]

A number of male interviewees also expressed a belief that female comrades were more likely to divulge sensitive information to police due to their lack of emotional strength. Both Bongo and Themba from Diepkloof stated that it was females, more than males, who caved under the pressure of police harassment or torture and agreed to become state informers.[57] In his research, Seekings found that male activists 'often explained the absence or exclusion of women with reference to the alleged inability of women to keep secrets, both in public and especially under interrogation by police,' though he declares this to be 'a very dubious assertion.'[58] There is evidence to suggest that such views were common amongst young men in the townships. 'Stompo', a thirteen-year-old male activist from Tumahole who commanded a militant group known as the 'under fourteens', explained to a journalist why girls were not involved in his organisation: 'You can't trust girls because they tell our secrets...they are not strong enough to be with us.'[59] In their research in Durban, Beall and her colleagues found it difficult to access the perspectives of politicised female youth, but one of their interviewees explained: 'Meetings are called by the SRC and only the boys are invited to those meetings. When you question why the girls are not there, the boys will say it's because the girls can't keep important information to themselves.'[60]

[53] Interview with Moses, Diepkloof, 19 April 2014.
[54] Marks, *Young Warriors*, 69.
[55] Campbell, 'Identity and Gender in a Changing Society,' 323.
[56] *Ibid.*, 322.
[57] Interview with Bongo, Diepkloof, 5 April 2015; Interview with Themba, Diepkloof, 6 April 2015.
[58] Seekings, *Heroes or Villains*, 83.
[59] *Sunday Tribune*, 18 October 1987.
[60] Beall et al., 'A Bit on the Side,' 44–45.

Second, comrades' denial of any gendered divisions of labour within COSAS and the equal treatment of men and women in meetings were also contradicted later in interviews. Both interviewee testimony and wider literature demonstrates that there were a number of clear gender divisions within student and youth organisations: very few women ever occupied leadership positions; women tended to have fewer connections to the ANC underground and were seldom recruited into underground military structures; and the duration of women's participation tended to be shorter than men's, as they often left the movement due to parental pressures, the need to support their children, or fear of police harassment. Many of these divisions were consequences of wider gender ideologies within the township at the time. Because girls were kept under closer parental surveillance than boys, and due to the pressures of domestic work, female comrades often had difficulty attending meetings or participating in actions occurring at night. However, one can assume that men's discriminatory gender ideologies were also at play in excluding female comrades from decision-making roles. A few women recalled that female comrades were often left out of meetings where strategic planning would take place and were thus only able to participate in more peripheral ways. As Ntsiki described, 'I will say maybe that was the part of a gap between female comrades [and male comrades]. We wouldn't know where the action was planned…We are not part of the planning…but we will be there, we will be part of support.'[61] Confirming men's stereotyping of girls as gossip-prone, a female comrade from Jabavu explained, 'Male comrades usually did the plans by themselves. Because they were worried of information going out. You know, most of the females…they talk anyhow anywhere. So they [men] would always have their own meetings, secret meetings, to plan whatever they wanted to plan.'[62] While male comrades spoke of their efforts to empower and educate female activists, it thus appears that they often side-lined girls from most pivotal discussions about ideology and strategy that occurred in COSAS meetings.

Meetings were thus not always the idyllic spaces of gender equality and female empowerment that interviewees initially constructed them as. Rather, they could be sites of girls' exclusion and silencing. While girls would attend meetings whenever they could, they rarely spoke out or voiced their opinions. When asked if girls were involved in COSAS at his school, Sello, a male activist from Diepkloof, responded, 'Yes! Yes! At my school specifically, yes, they were. You know, their participation mostly…was not that visible in terms of participation in meetings. Because as I understand some took this male

---

[61] Interview with Ntsiki, Diepkloof, 5 April 2015.
[62] Interview with Amahle, Jabavu, June 2015.

dominance, you know, felt this thing of student struggle, because mostly they were men, you know?'[63] Musa, a close comrade of Sello's, explained the situation in similar terms. He said that women rarely voiced their opinions during meetings, as they lacked the confidence to speak about political issues in front of men.[64] Female comrades also confirmed this. As a woman from Diepkloof explained, 'It was men who did the talking. And ladies, we were shy to ask questions or talk about something.'[65] Bessie, a female COSAS leader, admitted that 'just a few of us were vocal, but most women were not talking in meetings. They wouldn't.'[66] This was a situation common to much of South African liberation politics. Writing about women and political organisation in Durban, Beall and her colleagues described how while women participated in the struggle and helped manage some campaigns, they lacked the confidence to address large meetings, which were increasingly becoming the central space of disseminating ideas and consolidating campaigns.[67]

Female comrades' tendency to remain quiet in meetings is also a reflection of the gendered constraints that limited their political participation and made it difficult for them to engage in the more intellectual spheres of the struggle. Contributing to ideological discussion and debate required a significant time commitment from activists – time which female comrades had much less of due to their burden of household labour. When asked if she ever listened to Radio Freedom or read ANC literature such as *Sechaba*, Nonkululeko responded that while Makgane, a COSAS leader in Soweto, always instructed her to, she never really had the time for such activities.[68] After being recruited by male activists at her school, Thabisile was given literature to read. But, she stated, 'at times it was heavy stuff for me. I couldn't understand.' She later elaborated:

> It was material that I couldn't read, it was – the first one that I could remember, it was *Communist Manifesto*, which is [laughs] heavy material for me. I can't even – I just became bored...they'll give you material about African writers and understanding history of our African leaders...most of the material I would just look at and I couldn't comprehend.[69]

---

[63] Interview with Sello, Diepkloof, 14 May 2014.
[64] Interview with Musa, Diepkloof, 8 May 2014.
[65] Interview with Rethabile, Diepkloof, 1 May 2014.
[66] Interview with Bessie, 25 April 2014.
[67] Beall et al., 'A Bit on the Side,' 40.
[68] Nonkululeno, in group interview with female comrades from Diepkloof, Diepkloof, 27 June 2015.
[69] Interview with Thabisile, Johannesburg, 25 May 2015.

Wider township cultures of patriarchy and women's subordination therefore did intrude into COSAS meetings, despite interviewees' construction of these spaces as being immune from such issues. The inferiority complex instilled in girls remained in meetings, making female comrades lack the confidence to discuss political issues in front of their male comrades. Some female comrades stated that they were not taken seriously in meetings or did not feel as though they could voice their opinions to men. One man recounted how a female comrade once rebuked him for not taking her ideas into consideration during a meeting: 'If I was a male comrade,' she told him, 'you will agree with me.'[70] While women were strong activists in their own right, and tended to be particularly militant and vocal when acting within COSAS's women's forums, once they came together with men they lost much of their confidence. As Musa described, 'women can be strong when they are on their own. But when you then expose them to the bigger involvement where males are also involved, they tend to say, "OK fine, they are there, they can take the lead."'[71] Sello explicitly linked these tendencies to broader cultural norms in South Africa: 'African women, it is in our culture that people were taught, don't talk too much in front of men when you're a woman...they're still living in that South Africa that...men is the head, men will always lead...So I would think that because of that, you know, the cultural morals, it affected their participation.'[72]

It is also necessary to explore the common language both male and female comrades used in interviews with greater scrutiny. When talking about gender relations within COSAS, men and women alike, across almost every interview conducted, drew on the same discourse of comrades being like 'brothers and sisters'. Their responses were so similar that they seemed at times to be reading from a prepared script. This suggests that this narrative is not simply an impromptu recollection, but one that was actively promoted by COSAS during the mid-1980s, and one that was internalised and since maintained by comrades in the decades since. Furthermore, it is a narrative espoused by women across multiple contexts who similarly participated in political activism or conflict alongside men. In El Salvador, both women and men who fought for the Farabundo Marti National Liberation Front (FMLN) provided almost identical stories about how they would sleep next to each other in camps but 'nothing would happen' because they were 'like brothers and

---

[70] Interview with Patrick, Diepkloof, 12 May 2014.
[71] Interview with Musa, Diepkloof, 8 May 2014.
[72] Interview with Sello, Diepkloof, 14 May 2014.

sisters'.[73] Amongst participants in Ethiopia's Tifray People's Liberation Front (TPLF) and the *Maquis* in Algeria, men and women likewise presented uniform accounts of brotherly and sisterly relations between activists of different sexes.[74] This further indicates that such fraternal language is commonly used by left-wing liberation groups to neutralise the threat of potential sexual harassment, or to create a veneer of gender equality within organisations that do little in practice to challenge existing gender orders.[75]

Governing Intimacy

Furthermore, comrades' narratives of political meetings as safe spaces for girls, in which female comrades did not have to fight against or attempt to ward off sexual advances, were also challenged. Much of the previous research on youth activism during these years presents political meetings in the exact opposite way, as sites of violence and sexual coercion for girls. In rural areas such as the Lowveld, comrades promoted a pro-natal campaign to 'build soldiers' and replace fallen comrades by impregnating local girls. Girls were often dragged out of their homes and forced to attend comrade meetings or all-night vigils, during which they would be coerced into having unprotected sex. Peter Delius and Glaser argue that while some girls (like Soweto's female comrades) relished the new freedom of attending late-night meetings, others 'found that they had little option but to accede to the sexual demands of the comrades.'[76]

Evidence of such pro-natal strategies has not been found in Soweto. Nevertheless, interviewees made numerous comments that suggested male comrades were not always the respectful men they cast themselves as. While Soweto's COSAS branch banned womanising as part of its moral doctrine, this prohibition worked better in theory than in practice. Female comrades asserted that they did not fear or experience sexual abuse perpetrated by their male comrades. However, these avowals were contradicted by the very existence of women's forums within COSAS. In both student and youth

[73] Jocelyn Viterna, *Women in War: The Micro-processes of Mobilization in El Salvador* (Oxford: Oxford University Press, 2013), 153; 210–211.

[74] Angela Veale, *From Child Soldier to Ex-fighter: Female Fighters, Demobilisation and Reintegration in Ethiopia* (Pretoria: Institute for Security Studies, 2003), 31; Natalya Vince, *Our Fighting Sisters: Nation, Memory and Gender in Algeria, 1954–2012* (Manchester: Manchester University Press, 2015), 94.

[75] Viterna, *Women in War*, 211.

[76] Peter Delius and Clive Glaser, 'Sexual Socialisation in South Africa: A Historical Perspective,' *African Studies* 61:1 (2002): 49; Isak Niehaus, 'Towards a Dubious Liberation: Masculinity, Sexuality and Power in South African Lowveld Schools, 1953–1999,' *Journal of Southern African Studies* 26:3 (2000): 399.

organisations in the 1980s, women's forums were established for the purposes of recruiting more female comrades and addressing gender issues. SAYCO's women's department spoke directly of liberating women from their feelings of subordination. A document outlining its purpose explained:

> It is common knowledge that we have to liberate women from the inferiority complex which they have inherited over generations – for this to be possible we have to build a strong and solid forum for youth women to work their way up the political strata. Women are faced with a very difficult task, that of liberating themselves and liberating male counterparts from the myth that policies are for men because they are strong and thus can defend themselves verbally and physically.[77]

But included in this work of 'liberating women' was educating them in how to avoid sexual abuse as activists. Describing the necessity for such forums, Lucy – who was elected as the chairperson of SOSCO's women's structure – stated:

> There were some issues that were concerning female comrades because you can understand that in the struggle there were those who were taking advantage of the female comrades. So we were trying to protect one another in that situation because…there were those maybe who joined the struggle…to be involved with some of the females. So we were talking things like: let us not be abused by male comrades.[78]

Similarly, Sibongile, who was active in COSAS in Zola, indicated:

> We have the girls and women, sometimes males will take advantage of these girls. So my duty was just to guide them, how to be strict with their bodies and everything: don't allow everybody to touch you…If you are in a meeting and you don't want – unless you want – if you are not interested, he doesn't have a right to force himself to you.[79]

These forums thus epitomised the contradictions within comrades' recollections of gender relations in their organisations. Their very existence, and their mandate to help female comrades protect themselves against abuse by men (including activists), demonstrates that such abuse was, or at least was felt to be, commonplace in the student movement despite interviewees denying this. Furthermore, it suggests that the onus was placed on female activists themselves to find methods of avoiding abuse. Beatrice stated that

---

[77] 'Women's Department,' undated, AL2425: B6.5, South African Youth Congress, SAHA.
[78] Interview with Lucy, Fleurhof, 7 April 2014.
[79] Interview with Sibongile, Johannesburg, 9 June 2015.

some young men chose to join the organisation just to gain access to women: 'Even the comrades, they will be womanising [laughs]. They will just join this organisation because they see the ladies, they want to sleep with the ladies.'[80] Another comrade from Jabavu also admitted, 'Ya, it happened with some of the comrades...because some...had babies at an early age, and some of them, the guys will make them pregnant and even deny to be the fathers.'[81] Male interviewees too at times acceded that such abuse occurred – not when asked specifically about gender or female comrades, but rather when asked about discipline within the student movement. As one male comrade from Diepkloof explained, 'In the comrades, there are issues where they take women by force, just because I'm a comrade. And if you do these things you'll be disciplined.'[82]

If more violent or systematic forms of sexual abuse occurred within the student movement in Soweto, this was not discussed by interviewees. Combined with the lack of documentary evidence, this makes it very difficult to know how prevalent sexual violence was within COSAS. But interviewees did speak about broader attempts to police comrades' sexuality and monitor relationships within and outside the organisation, which speaks to a wider culture of sexual control within the movement. Such attempts were not unique to Soweto's comrades, but are common to a range of liberation movements in South Africa and elsewhere, in which sexuality is tightly controlled as a means of focusing combatants' attention on the cause at hand. In Mozambique, the Mozambique Liberation Front (FRELIMO) regulated the sexuality of both male and female guerrillas, prohibiting consensual sex between combatants.[83] In many cases, these efforts are made to minimise any distractions or contradictory loyalties within groups. In El Salvador, couples within the guerrillas were seen as 'unstable', while in Colombia's FARC, long-term emotional relationships were discouraged out of fears that they would compete with one's allegiance to the organisation.[84] Within South Africa, the ANC also had a history of regulating personal relationships. Marriages in ANC camps in Tanzania were allowed, but had to authorised

---

[80] Interview with Beatrice, Pimville, 23 May 2015.
[81] Interview with Amahle, Jabavu, 10 June 2015.
[82] Interview with ATV, Diepkloof, 2 May 2015.
[83] West, 'Girls with Guns,' 190.
[84] Kampwirth, *Women and Guerrilla Movements*, 78; Rahel Kunz and Ann-Kristin Sjoberg, 'Empowered or Oppressed? Female Combatants in the Colombian Guerrilla: The Case of the Revolutionary Armed Forces of Colombia – FARC,' Paper presented at the Annual Convention of the International Studies Association, New York, February 2009, 28–30.

by the Chief Representative of the ANC.[85] In general, cadres living in exile were encouraged to replace personal relationships with 'love for the people' or 'the ANC as family'.[86] Women's sexuality was perceived of as dangerous in exile, as the ANC posited casual sex and pregnancy as representing poor commitment to political work. It was believed that those lacking self-control over their bodies 'may be difficult to trust in revolutionary missions.'[87]

In Soweto, COSAS leaders initially banned relationships between male and female members. Perhaps in response to conceptions of physical relationships as distracting or threatening to the liberation movement, female comrades often insisted that they were too disciplined as activists to have been interested in pursuing relationships anyway. For Pumzile, having such discipline was a key marker of her political commitment. She stated, 'There are some comrades who were involved with some other female comrades…but I was very strict.'[88] Additionally, female comrades wanted to avoid becoming pregnant in order to mitigate community stigma and prove to their parents that their political work was not merely a guise for promiscuity. As Lucy explained, 'We were trying by all means to…avoid that kind of situation because even to our parents, when that thing happened, obviously then we are not there for the struggle, we are there for men.'[89] In emphasising their self-control and focus on the struggle, many interviewees recounted that they did not have time for such frivolous activities. As one woman stated, 'the concentration of us, it was more on the enemy than on the relationships.'[90]

Male comrades insisted that the ban placed on relationships was essential to keeping activists focused on the struggle, maintaining discipline, and avoiding any additional dangers or state detection. A number of male interviewees expressed that having a girlfriend within the student movement would have put their safety in jeopardy. This fear was predicated on the belief that girls were more likely to divulge information under the pressures of interrogation and torture. As one comrade stated, 'No, I didn't have any girlfriends inside politics. Because if you had a girlfriend…if Boers arrest you, they will pressure her, then she will confess.'[91] Similarly, Paul explained 'I was scared of women!…Because there was this thinking of, the apartheid

85 Arianna Lissoni and Maria Suriano, 'Married to the ANC: Tanzanian Women's Entanglement in South Africa's Liberation Struggle,' *Journal of Southern African Studies* 40:1 (2014): 134.
86 Suttner, *The ANC Underground*, 4.
87 Sandwell, 'Love I Cannot Begin to Explain,' 74–75.
88 Interview with Phumzile, Johannesburg, 17 April 2015.
89 Interview with Lucy, Fleurhof, 7 April 2014.
90 Interview with Nomsa, Diepkloof Extension, 19 April 2014.
91 Interview with ATV, Diepkloof, 2 May 2015.

system will use women to get male comrades.'[92] One interviewee provided a more discriminatory explanation for why girls could not be trusted:

> You will find a situation where if this female is in love with this male, and then there's information that is sensitive. So if these people have a dispute…the other one can even go to the enemy, just to punish this one, forgetting now that it's affecting the whole organisation, the entire struggle becomes affected.[93]

Romantic connections were also assumed to cause in-fighting within the student movement. One male comrade from Diepkloof described, 'If you started to have a relationship with our member, that thing will make our working relationship not good because you'll start not being on good terms with this woman.'[94] Similarly, Moses recalled, 'we were not encouraging that because, you see, if there is any dispute [between the couple] it means you can lose both of these comrades because, especially females…will have this shy thing of coming to the meetings because Moses has done this to her.'[95] Women too expressed that if they entered into a relationship with a male comrade that did not last, they might feel uncomfortable attending meetings afterwards. Lucy explained:

> Even as female comrades, when we are having our meetings, we used to tell ourselves, 'don't have any feelings for your male comrades'…because it's very embarrassing when…a female comrade is pregnant by a male comrade. Even in the meetings, how are they going to look at her? The other one will feel shy to participate and all that because they're having a relationship.[96]

Yet male comrades also claimed that the ban on romantic relationships within COSAS was for female activists' own benefit. They were hesitant to engage in personal relationships with their comrades, knowing that these relationships would likely be unequal and not monogamous. While they did not seem to be concerned with subjecting girls outside of their organisations to such treatment, doing so to female comrades would violate COSAS' disciplinary code and espousal of gender equality. As Makgane described, 'We were scared to fall in love with our activists, because the discipline at the time was quite strict in terms of…not taking advantage of them…treating them as equals.'[97] Similarly, Bongo from Diepkloof explained how comrades

---

[92] Interview with Paul, Diepkloof, 2 May 2015.
[93] Interview with Moses, Diepkloof, 19 April 2014.
[94] Interview with Bongo, Diepkloof, 5 April 2015.
[95] Interview with Moses, Diepkloof, 19 April 2014.
[96] Interview with Lucy, Fleurhof, 7 April 2014.
[97] Interview with Makgane, Sandton, 17 April 2014.

wanted to protect and not abuse '*our* women', so rather dated women from outside the student movement. Bongo also spoke about male tendencies to date more than one woman at a time:

> Remember, we South Africans, maybe we don't live like other people. Like whites, I understand with whites once you have a relationship, that person becomes your husband. So South African men don't live by that.... You will have a relationship with other girlfriends, many girlfriends. So we thought that we discouraged that [dating female comrades] as an abuse.[98]

Bongo took dating a comrade much more seriously than dating a girl from the community. If activists did decide to pursue relationships within the organisation, he stated, 'you must tell us that you are prepared to commit.... because we won't accept you tomorrow to have another girlfriend outside the movement.' Such statements reflect the special status that female comrades held, and how other young, non-politicised women at the time were generally treated with less respect. Female comrades too were aware that if they entered personal relationships with their male comrades, they may not be treated well. Through SOSCO's women's forum, Lucy encouraged her fellow female comrades not to become involved with male activists, stating, 'We must...not be involved with them because if we can be involved with one of them, you'll end up having more than three relationships because all of them, they might take advantage of you.'[99]

While activists' sexual or romantic behaviour was controlled within the movement, young men were still free to pursue relationships outside of the organisation. Unlike members of most other liberation movements, Soweto's comrades remained within their communities during their time as activists – other than the few who left to join MK. They thus had regular access to women outside their organisations. However, female COSAS members were not necessarily allowed the same privileges when it came to dating outside the organisation. As scholarship on liberation movements demonstrates, controls that are meant to regulate both male and female guerrillas' sexuality often include a number of elements that specifically discriminate against women. Within the South African struggle in exile, female students in Tanzania who went out with local men were sometimes attacked by male students. While men in exile often engaged in long-term relationships with women outside the ANC, women were not accorded the same freedoms. Young women in

---

[98]   Interview with Bongo, Diepkloof, 5 April 2015.
[99]   Interview with Lucy, Fleurhof, 7 April 2014.

exile who dated members of the Pan Africanist Congress (PAC) were seen as ill-disciplined, and some were even corporally punished.[100]

Musa admitted that male comrades were often jealous when women dated men outside the organisation and would interrogate female comrades about their partners.[101] Sometimes, they would persuade girls to abandon these relationships by convincing them that their boyfriends were criminals or could be potential informers. As Bessie explained, 'We were discouraged from having a relationship with somebody who's not a part of the struggle because...it would put you at risk.' Yet this policy was not applied to men; Bessie continued, 'though our male comrades would have relationships outside [the organisation].'[102] For some female comrades this exertion of control over their relationships continues today, as their former male comrades continue to stipulate who they can or cannot date. Sissy, a former youth activist from Diepkloof, explained,

> And they are still protective. I can't have a boyfriend. Look at me! I'm old as it is but they will tell me that they don't trust this [guy]...So even now I'm not having a boyfriend, I'm not married, I don't have kids [laughs]. It's not a joke...They are like my brothers...When they see me with a man, they change faces. They say, 'don't trust these people! Some of them are probably still working for SB [Special Branch]'.[103]

Thus, the rhetoric of male comrades being like 'brothers' served two key functions: not only did it serve to deny the possibility of sexual abuse between comrades, but also justified male comrades' control over female comrades' sexuality under the role of protective 'brotherhood'.

'Behind Closed Doors': Gender Relations in Theory, Practice, and Memory

How then should we understand the various inconsistencies of comrades' accounts of gender relations, and reconcile their construction of student meetings as utopian, egalitarian spaces, yet also sites of gender discrimination and control? How were female comrades treated by their male counterparts, and how should we interpret their narratives of these relationships in the present? In

---

[100] Hassim, *Women's Organizations and Democracy in South Africa*, 91. For more on ANC men's relationship with Tanzanian women see Lissoni and Suriano, 'Married to the ANC.'

[101] Interview with Musa, Diepkloof, 8 May 2014.

[102] Interview with Bessie, Johannesburg, 25 April 2014.

[103] Interview with Sissy, Diepkloof, 17 April 2015.

many ways, these contradictions reflect a trend common to multiple liberation movements: a discord between theory and practice, or between public discourse and private realities, when it comes to gender equality. Natalya Vince argues that in Algeria, members of the National Liberation Front (FLN) were 'a long way off' promoting or believing in the public discourse which the nationalist movement maintained about the new Algerian woman.'[104] In her work on student activists in Italy's 1968 protests, Rebecca Clifford likewise discovered that within the student movement, 'the gulf between the theory and practice of liberation could be huge' – particularly when it came to gender relations, as the male leaders who supported the sexual revolution had little intention of relinquishing their own power over women. This discord between public discourse and private practice led to the feminist Italian slogan of *compagni in piazza, fascisti a letto* or 'Comrades in the piazza, but fascists in bed.'[105] Similar disjunctions can also be found in South Africa's broader struggle. Both Ramphele and Magaziner highlight the contradictions in Black Consciousness' gender ideologies, and how even Biko was simultaneously sexist and supporting of women's participation.[106] In Natal, Campbell also found that 'even the most dedicated and highly politicised male comrades show a conspicuous failure to integrate their political ideals with their personal lives' as there is often 'a wide gulf between [one's] political understanding of relationships on the one hand, and [their] personal socialisation and lived reality on the other hand.'[107]

In 1980s Soweto, student and youth organisations were committed to a certain level of gender equality on paper, whether out of their socialist alignment, a desire to recruit more girls into the struggle, or a genuine desire to protect girls from abuse and help empower them through politics. We need to take both women and men's accounts of this commitment seriously and acknowledge that male comrades were not homogenous in how they treated female comrades, and that COSAS may have been less discriminatory *within* its ranks than previously assumed. There was genuine comradeship between its male and female members, which has transformed into lasting friendships between many of these men and women in the present. It appears that most female comrades were given a special status and were often supported and treated with kindness by their male counterparts. In her work on Latin

[104] Vince, *Our Fighting Sisters*, 88.
[105] Rebecca Clifford, 'Emotions and Gender in Oral History: Narrating Italy's 1968,' *Modern Italy* 17:2 (2012): 217.
[106] Ramphele, 'The Dynamics of Gender within Black Consciousness Organisations,' 219; Magaziner, 'Pieces of a (Wo)man,' 47.
[107] Catherine Campbell, 'The Township Family and Women's Struggles,' *Agenda* 6 (1990): 15.

America, Luisa Maria Dietrich Ortega argues that masculinities espoused by male insurgents are not monolithic and can include 'repertoires of tenderness' alongside expectations of military prowess, bravery, and aggression.[108] We can see such 'repertoires' in the various supportive gestures that male comrades made to young female activists, and their genuine concerns for their safety and well-being.

However, this does not mean that COSAS as a whole was characterised by gender equality or adhered to feminist principles. Just as Ramphele states of Black Consciousness, 'there was an interesting disjuncture between the genuine comradeship one experienced within the movement, and the sexism which reared its head at many levels.'[109] This was a young man's world which at times tolerated, and in some circumstances encouraged, young women's participation. But female comrades participated largely on men's terms. It was predominantly male comrades who organised meetings, made plans, and gave orders. As the next chapter will demonstrate further, young women's membership amongst the comrades was in part predicated on the erasure of their feminine identities and sexualities. When Lucy stated that 'to be a comrade you have to be without your gender' she thus may have been referring specifically to female comrades, who had to assimilate to masculine comrade culture to be taken seriously as activists. This was the same tactic chosen by female activists a decade earlier within the Black Consciousness Movement (BCM) – to become 'one of the boys' in order to avoid being discriminated against as a woman.[110] As West writes about young female combatants in Mozambique, 'these statements reflect not so much the profession of gender equity...as the desexualisation of guerrillas, particularly female guerrillas.'[111] This desexualisation served a number of important functions. By relinquishing their femininity, female comrades gained status and respect as activists, and protected themselves from potential abuse or unwanted advances. Adopting desexualised identities also legitimised their close relationships with their male comrades, facilitating the male-female bonding that South Africa's comrades recall so fondly in their recollections. Their use of fraternal discourse and insistence that relationships between comrades of the opposite sex were like those between 'brother and sister'

[108] Luisa Maria Dietrich Ortega, 'Looking Beyong Violent Militarized Masculinities: Guerrilla Gender Regimes in Latin America,' *International Feminist Journal of Politics* 14:4 (2012): 491.

[109] Ramphele, 'The Dynamics of Gender within Black Consciousness Organisations,' 219.

[110] Ramphele, 'The Dynamics of Gender within Black Consciousness Organisations'; Magaziner, 'Pieces of a (Wo)man'.

[111] West, 'Girls with Guns,' 190.

served to make these relationships more publicly palatable.[112] Yet by insisting that female comrades were 'comrades' rather than girls or young women, interviewees were not transforming gender relations but making them invisible.[113] The de-gendering of female comrades thus worked to veil gender hierarchies within the organisation rather than address them.

Interviewees' narratives of the special protections given to female comrades also speak to the assumed fragility of these young women, and the wider gender inequalities that put them in need of protection. As Tlhabi argues, seeing female combatants in South Africa as 'flowers of the revolution' implies their fragility and tenderness, and further essentialises them based on their gender. 'Despite its good intentions,' she writes, 'casting women soldiers as flowers reflects, directly, the ideological construction of gendered roles, with masculinity being strong and brave, and existing for the sole purpose of protecting femininity, which is fragile and pure, like a flower.'[114] While Soweto's female comrades appreciated the respect given to them and their bodies by male comrades and COSAS' 'non-sexist' policy, neither they nor their male counterparts questioned the wider need for such rules or protections in the first place.

Furthermore, male comrades' respect towards female comrades certainly did not extend to all girls and young women in their communities. Young male activists made a clear divide between the actions and beliefs they practised *within* their organisations and how they perceived and treated girls *outside* of student or youth groups. This was most evident in their discussions of personal or sexual relationships. While male comrades may have been willing to respect their fellow female activists, they were less willing to abandon their power when it came to their relationships with young women in general. The 'special status' granted to female comrades helps to explain why their involvement in the struggle did not lead to any wider transformation of gender roles in their communities. In nationalist struggles girls and women are often accorded equal or greater status as part of the liberation effort, either due to the practical necessities of armed struggle or out of commitment to leftist ideology. Yet these concessions made to women are rarely carried over into peacetime,

---

[112] Vince, *Our Fighting Sisters*, 94–97.

[113] See Victoria Bernal, 'From Warriors to Wives: Contradictions of Liberation and Development in Eritrea,' *Northeast African Studies* 8:3 (2001): 135; Mayfair Mei-Hui Yang, 'From Gender Erasure to Gender Difference: State Feminism, Consumer Sexuality, and Women's Public Sphere in China,' in M. Yang (ed), *Spaces of their Own: Women's Public Sphere in Transnational China* (Minneapolis: University of Minnesota Press, 1999), 44–45.

[114] Tlhabi, *Khwezi*, 39.

and seldom cause a long-term, societal-wide shift in gender relations. In his work on the comrades in Alexandra, Carter acknowledges the important roles a select few young women played within militant youth groups. However, he found that young men's acceptance of female comrades was not demonstrative of their egalitarian beliefs but was rather a 'revolutionary favour' granted to young women by men who remained 'die-hard chauvinists'.[115]

There was also a clear discord between what male comrades preached in public, and what they may have practised in private. Through a conversation with Makgane, it became evident that these men did not necessarily believe in the gender ideologies they preached. Makgane recounted that when he is alone with his former male comrades, they often revert to using gender stereotypes and sexist language. 'Sometimes when we are one-to-one with the comrade, before he makes a gender insensitive statement, he will look around to check that there's no audience,' he explained. 'And because I'm a male comrade, he'll think it's acceptable, to be insensitive about gender… They think it's just a common secret between men.' Makgane explained further how such comrades will 'comply in public' or 'pretend' to adhere to a socialist position of women's oppression, 'but in the private space where they are by themselves, they will…just become…reactionary or gender insensitive in their language or in the analysis of an issue.' He warned me that some of his male comrades may put on a progressive front when speaking with me, assuming that as a Western female academic this would be what I wanted to hear. Speaking about a particular comrade, he explained, 'He'll rather be on his best behaviour. He'll talk like a progressive, like all of them do. But then when I'm one-to-one with him…'[116] Concluding this discussion, Makgane stated, 'We all pretend to be progressive and good,' but meanwhile 'things that people say happen in the private space are shocking…Even comrades… pretend that it's okay behind closed doors.'[117]

This private/public discord in the 1980s has direct parallels with contemporary South Africa. Although the 1996 constitution enshrines women's rights, many women have experienced little improvement in their actual lives or seen little change in their relations with men since the end of apartheid. As Helen Moffett writes, 'the tension between validating women's rights to full citizenship and political participation without revising their social subordination has created a new variation on the disjuncture between the private and the public

---

[115] Carter, 'Comrades and Community,' 270.
[116] *Ibid.*
[117] Interview with Makgane, Sandton, 17 April 2014.

realms typical of capitalist patriarchal systems.'[118] Moffett provides an anecdote illustrating this that is very reminiscent of Makgane's conversation with me quoted above. She discusses a senior male member of government who saw no incongruity between his enthusiastic, public endorsement of women's involvement in politics, and his firm belief that within his own home, he was the master, once stating that 'democracy stops at my front door.'[119] While spaces in the public sphere such as politics and work have become pervaded with talk of 'women's empowerment', a 'completely different set of rules' governs the private sphere, argues Gqola.[120]

Why then do female comrades recall gender relations in such overwhelmingly positive terms when specifically asked about them? There are multiple reasons why these women might not want to focus on discrimination or abuse within their narratives. First, doing so could challenge their belonging to the 'comrades' as a group. This could further their erasure from dominant historical narratives and potentially isolate them from a group which they still belong to and derive meaning from in the present. Given that so many female comrades remain close friends with their former male comrades, and continue to work politically alongside them, it would be risky for them to disclose or focus on specific cases of inequality or abuse they experienced at these men's hands. Discussing rape or discrimination within the struggle would also challenge the ANC-sponsored narrative of the liberation movement as heroic and united. This narrative has long silenced divisive issues such as gender-based violence and instead focused on heroism as a means of preserving the ANC's predominance in the present. Discussing discrimination or sexual violence is seen as a threat to the solidarity of liberation movements and is thus often subject to 'wilful forgetting' by their female members.[121] But simultaneously, female interviewees themselves may prefer narratives that focus on their heroism rather than their oppression so that they can, for once, be seen as active agents rather than as passive victims.

An alternative answer could be that there is a discord between what these women perceived as equality or fair treatment, and what we (or I as a Western academic) understand by these terms. Given the violence and subordination

---

[118] Helen Moffett, "'These women, they force us to rape them": Rape as Narrative of Social Control in Post-Apartheid South Africa,' *Journal of Southern African Studies* 32:1 (2006): 142.

[119] *Ibid.*

[120] Puma Dineo Gqola, 'How the "cult of femininity" and violent masculinities support endemic gender based violence in contemporary South Africa,' *African Identities* 5:1 (2007): 116.

[121] Srila Roy, 'The Grey Zone: The "Ordinary" Violence of Extraordinary Times,' *Journal of the Royal Anthropological Institute*, 14:2 (2008): p. 317.

that girls and young women were often subject to in South African townships at this time, COSAS may have seemed like a safe haven in comparison. This is alluded to by Kgomotso Nkadimeng, one of the first executive members of COSAS at its founding in 1979, who explained:

> Very few girls were involved, you were criticized from all angles including from other girls. Of course within the cells themselves you were constantly undermined by your male comrades. But of course if one understands the social influences one can't really say one was undermined, we were all under the same influences, they all thought women were lower, women are weaker, therefore they need to be protected. Therefore I wouldn't really want to label them as oppressive as such; we were all influenced by the same environment.[122]

But we must also remember that these women did not join the liberation movement primarily as women or out of a desire to affect a nation-wide shift in gender relations. As chapter two demonstrated, their gendered concerns as activists grew out of and related to their individual and collective experiences as girls and young women in the township, not out of a wider feminist consciousness or desire to promote women's liberation. Their own gender ideologies were thus ambivalent and at times contradictory. While they challenged gender norms in their personal behaviour (and particularly in their use of political violence as the next chapter demonstrates), they did not necessarily advocate for women's broader emancipation or organise around gender issues directly.[123] While their struggle against apartheid was in many ways a gendered one, it was not explicitly a feminist cause.

Conclusion

It is challenging to believe that, in a patriarchal society and during a time of militarised and hardened gender ideologies, student and youth organisations of the 1980s would have provided unique spaces of gender equality and respect. Yet the contradictions within and between comrades' accounts of gender relations in the student movement make drawing any definitive conclusions about the level of equality granted to female comrades difficult. Based on the overwhelming narrative of camaraderie and respect presented by both male and female activists from Soweto, one cannot argue that all comrades espoused a

---

[122] Kgomotso Nkadimeng in Nokuthula Mazibuko, *Spring Offensive* (Limpopo: Timbila Publishing, 2006), 17–18.
[123] Lesie Hadfield makes the same argument about young women involved in Black Consciousness community programmes. See Hadfield, *Liberation and Development*, 60.

masculinity that was disparaging towards women. Female comrades' narratives challenge existing depictions of 'struggle masculinity' and highlight the multiplicity of masculinities espoused by young activists, including the 'repertoires of tenderness' they often showed towards young female activists. COSAS leadership strove to follow an official policy of non-sexism and made significant efforts to incorporate more young women into its ranks. Yet this official policy was neither smoothly nor uniformly implemented and COSAS, like the ANC itself, remained marred by casual sexism and discrimination towards its female members. Furthermore, the conceptualisation of the meeting as a safe, egalitarian space may silence memories of more violent forms of control, coercion, or abuse from female comrades' narratives. Male comrades attest that they were aware of the patriarchal nature of township society and of the gender imbalances in the struggle and sought to empower female activists as a means of rectifying inequality. Yet such awareness was not enough for them to challenge patriarchal norms on a societal level, or to grant the same amount of respect to non-politicised girls as they did to their female comrades. Their attempts to eradicate sexual abuse by teachers in schools, recruit young women and empower them as political activists, and protect female comrades from abuse may have appeared egalitarian, but in the end did little to challenge the existing gender order. This is something common to insurgent groups, which often construct new gender regimes within their ranks to accommodate or encourage the participation of young women. However, such gender regimes are almost always temporary, and rarely affect change to gender relations beyond the membership of insurgent groups.[124]

Bringing these contradictions and inconsistencies to the fore and reading them alongside similar disjunctions found in both South Africa's wider liberation struggle and nationalist movements elsewhere, reveals multiple difficulties faced by COSAS: of being a leftist liberation group operating in a patriarchal society; of competing masculinities and the heterogeneous make-up of activists; and of maintaining public discourses of respect and equality behind closed doors. Such contradictions also help to explain why female comrades' involvement in the liberation movement did not affect a lasting, societal-wide shift in gender ideologies. This detailed exploration of gender relations in student organisations helps us to better understand the complex debates surrounding gender relations and women's liberation within the struggle, issues of sexual control and abuse, and how women choose to remember or narrate their time in liberation movements. It is imperative to analyse interviewees' memories for any reticence, silences, or revisions they may contain. More so than men,

---

[124] Ortega, 'Looking Beyond Violent Militarized Masculinities,' 503–504.

it is the women interviewed for this study who tend to consistently reflect positively on their past experiences as comrades. One must thus consider how their espousal of a gender-neutral and gender-equal discourse is tied to their identity construction and sense of selves, both in the past and the present. By highlighting memories in which their male comrades treated them with respect – rather than those where they experienced discrimination or derision – women emphasise their belonging to the comrade movement and insert themselves in to a male-dominated historical narrative from which they have been excluded. But this 'mythicisation' of these political spaces, as Roy argues, 'is sustained through the foreclosure of the gendered relations of power that structured it.'[125]

[125] Roy, 'The Everyday Life of the Revolution,' 197.

5

The Street: Gendering Collective Action and Political Violence

Born in Diepkloof, Soweto in 1969, Lucy first became involved in South Africa's liberation struggle through her school's SRC around the age of fourteen. As an SRC representative she campaigned against the poor quality of education in her school – Bopasenatla Secondary – and was soon encouraged to join COSAS by older, male student activists. Lucy was an excellent storyteller – a quality which led me to interview her several times over three years. In each of our meetings she discussed her childhood experiences of racialised inequality, her views on gender, and the strong relationships she forged with her male comrades. Yet almost an hour into our first interview I still had little sense of her day-to-day tasks and activities as a comrade. 'Can you tell me a bit more about some of your tasks?' I asked. 'Or what activities you participated in?' Lucy responded:

> We used to participate in all, in all of the tasks. There were boycotts…when we're boycotting the buses and all those things, we used to go there and [laughs] hit the buses, throw stones to hit the buses. When maybe we were boycotting the shops, like Pick n Pay and all those things, when [pauses], maybe you come out of the bus with grocery we used to take them and throw the groceries all over the place [laughs]. So we used to do the same things with the males.

After experiencing a number of attacks from police and security forces at school or in Soweto's streets, Lucy learned to walk around the township with her pockets full of stones so that she would always be ready to fight. 'They were so heavy,' she lamented, 'but we know we have to fight'. 'Sometimes,' she continued, 'we've got matches and all that. Then when they come and attack us, we have to attack back with petrol bombs.'[1]

Throughout our interviews, Lucy's description of her 'tasks' as a comrade repeatedly focused on confrontations in Soweto's streets such as those described above. She spoke candidly about throwing stones at police

[1]   Interview with Lucy, Fleurhof, 7 April 2014.

127

vehicles, making and using petrol bombs, and punishing suspected gangsters or informers. She repeatedly emphasised how her actions in the struggle were no different from those of her male comrades. Lucy's memories contrast starkly with depictions of township streets during the 1980s as deeply masculine spaces, 'clearly demarcated as the social territory of young men only.'[2] Yet Lucy's narrative is not anomalous. Street-based activism and confrontation occupied a central place in almost all female comrades' narratives. When asked generally about what kind of 'tasks' or 'actions' they were involved in within the liberation movement, most, like Lucy, responded with stories of their use of force, coercion, or violence against the state and its perceived allies in Soweto's streets. A select few were eventually recruited into more formal underground structures and received training in how to use hand grenades or AK-47s. Female comrades present their involvement in these forms of political violence as exciting and adventurous, telling stories about their pasts that are animated, detailed, and captivating. These intense moments of confrontation overshadow other memories of day-to-day life or more mundane forms of activism in their narratives. While female comrades were also involved in less confrontational activities, such as pamphleteering or various civic campaigns, such activities are absent or side-lined in their own narratives of the past.

From mid-1984 onwards, many South African townships witnessed widespread uprisings as the apartheid state failed to bring about meaningful reforms and increased its military presence in township streets. In response to the state's increasingly violent methods of repressing resistance, many activists – and particularly the youth now at the forefront of the struggle – developed new repertoires of political militancy. While the comrades' strategies drew on older forms of non-violent protest, such as boycotting, stayaways, and leafleting, they simultaneously developed new forms of violent confrontation. These included barricading township streets, using stones or petrol bombs against police and local councillors, attacking townships residents who defied declared boycotts, or punishing suspected informers, gangsters, or other community deviants. Much of this violence took place on township streets. Iconic images of the comrades bring to mind public displays of protest and power: surges of *toyi-toying* youths wearing UDF t-shirts; students and older residents processing alongside funeral caskets; and young people throwing stones at armoured vehicles. The streets were essential spaces of political power during the township uprisings: it was on street corners where young men gathered, shared information, and forged the social networks

[2]   Campbell, 'Identity and Gender in a Changing Society,' 125–126.

crucial for mass mobilisation; and from the mid-1980s onwards, comrades used the streets to theatrically perform their rebellion against apartheid, appropriating the state's political use of spatial ordering.[3]

But for adolescent girls, township streets had long been sites of masculine power, and spaces of their victimisation or exclusion. Since the mid-twentieth century, young unmarried women had enjoyed little freedom of movement in Soweto, as they were constantly at risk of being molested, harassed, or kidnapped by gangs.[4] In the 1980s, boys discouraged girls from 'loitering' on the streets during the day or leaving their homes at night to protect not only their physical safety but also their reputations as respectable girls.[5] Seekings argues that while young women were often prominent members of COSAS prior to 1984, girls were generally demobilised from liberation politics as the struggle shifted from the schools to the streets and grew increasingly violent. The insecurity and exclusion they experienced in township streets was exacerbated during these years, as 'violence bred exaggerated gender ideologies.'[6]

Yet in female comrades' narratives of the past, the streets were the primary space in which they engaged in the liberation struggle. These interviews tell us that female comrades were more involved in such actions than previously argued, and that girls and young women were not only victims of male-instigated violence or passive bystanders during these years. But they also reveal how important such actions were to female comrades, and the wider effects their involvement in political violence had, and continue to have, on their lives and sense of selves. Female comrades' engagement in political confrontation and violence represents their behaviour at its most transgressive: in Soweto's streets they defied dominant gender ideologies in their use of violence; appropriated masculine spaces; and even acted and dressed as men. Through such transgressions, female comrades demonstrated their strength and bravery, proved their capacity as comrades, and gained new feelings of freedom and power. From female comrades' recollections, we can see how the streets – despite being highly masculine spaces – offered girls opportunities to publicly challenge the power of both the apartheid state and dominant gender ideologies in new ways.

Nevertheless, it was no easy task for female comrades to perform these roles in public spaces which had for generations marked female bodies as targets of violence and disrespect. In redrawing the gendered geographies of

[3] Bozzoli, *Theatres of Struggle.*
[4] Glaser, 'Mark of Zorro,' 58.
[5] Campbell, 'Identity and Gender in a Changing Society,' 126.
[6] Seekings, 'Gender Ideology and Township Politics,' 82.

township streets, female comrades had to erase their femininity and assume the identities of gender-neutral soldiers or masculine comrades. They felt a constant need to prove that their actions were not limited by their sex, and consequently exchanged their skirts and blouses for trousers and trainers, and demonstrated their physical capacities by throwing heavy stones, outrunning police alongside their male comrades, and willingly engaging in various forms of political violence. In interviews thirty years later, there is still little room for these women to display much traditional femininity. In telling of their involvement in street confrontations, they present themselves as loyal, willing soldiers, emphasising their readiness for conflict and downplaying any moments of hesitation, weakness, remorse, or victimisation. By emphasising the active roles they played in street confrontations, and speaking so candidly about their personal involvement in political violence, they lay claim to these political activities which have long been seen as male-only pursuits, and challenge their absence from dominant historical narratives.

Township Streets and Political Violence

In Soweto, a new period of political violence began in January 1984 when the house of the township's new mayor, E. T. Tshabalala, was petrol bombed.[7] It was not until September of that year, however, that township masses became engaged in unrest across the country in the wake of uprisings in the Vaal triangle sparked by protests over high rents. Events in Soweto escalated further in 1985 following the commemoration of the 1976 uprisings in June and the subsequent declaration of a state of emergency in July. By mid-1985, media reports from white-owned newspapers presented the scene in Soweto as one of youth-dominated anarchy, 'a frenzy of looting and arson' with 'youths' on a 'rampage' commandeering buses, stoning vehicles, setting homes alight, and looting shops as police responded with birdshot, teargas, and mass detentions. Newspapers depicted scenes of hundreds of marching students attacking police vehicles, confronting policemen, and demanding the establishment of SRCs. Despite the banning of COSAS – which the state deemed responsible for much of the unrest – in August 1985, reports of students burning houses continued. In September, the Commissioner of Soweto Police admitted that despite its banning, COSAS was still active and disrupting education.[8]

---

[7]   Simpson, 'Umkhonto We Sizwe, We Are Waiting for You,' 160.
[8]   *Business Day*, 18 July 1985; *The Citizen*, 19 July 1985; *City Press*, 18 August 1985; *The Sowetan*, 3 September 1985.

Such media portrayals of youth violence were problematic. However, 'there *was* a strong relationship between political violence and township youth,' as Marks highlights.[9] Officially, COSAS was a non-violent organisation, and many of its strategies employed in township streets such as boycotts, stayaways, and protests can be seen as classic examples of non-violent political action. Yet the 1980s witnessed a blurring of violent and non-violent strategies, with the line between them not necessarily clear to either those in leadership positions or those on the ground.[10] Formerly non-violent strategies now relied on new forms of coercion to enforce community compliance, and new methods of attacking state forces and allies emerged in response to the state's escalating militarisation of the townships. Despite its historically complicated stance on the use of violence, the ANC also increasingly endorsed armed struggle in its rhetoric during these years, calling on the 'people' – rather than just MK agents – to bring about 'ungovernability' and 'people's war'.

According to comrades themselves, attacks against police and community members were not sporadic acts of retribution, but part of a wider 'programme of action' based on their interpretations of ANC instructions, passed down through Radio Freedom or publications such as *Sechaba*.[11] They drew a clear line between the legitimate, sanctioned forms of 'armed struggle' or 'action' they employed while distancing themselves from more ill-disciplined 'violence' committed by *comtsotsis*. When speaking about their involvement in political violence, both male and female comrades stressed how such attacks were sanctioned from above and were a means by which they could contribute to the liberation movement's wider goals. Yet on the ground this line was anything but clear, and the distinctions between political and criminal violence, or sanctioned and un-sanctioned forms of action, were messy and complex. Although the ANC had officially adopted armed struggle as one of its key strategies in the 1960s, its relationship to violence remained murky throughout the liberation struggle. Since the end of apartheid, the ANC has chosen to celebrate the 'heroic' military violence of its armed wing, MK, while distancing itself from the more irregular violence used by those within townships during the 1980s. Yet as Kim Wale demonstrates, the ANC relied on this violence;

---

[9]   Marks, *Young Warriors*, 87.
[10] Janet Cherry, 'The Intersection of Violent and Non-Violent Strategies in the South African Liberation Struggle,' in Hilary Sapire and Chris Saunders (eds), *Southern African Liberation Struggles: New Local, Regional and Global Perspectives* (Cape Town: UCT Press, 2012), 156; Rueedi, 'Patterns of Violence,' 399.
[11] For more on comrades and their relationship with the ANC see Simpson, 'Umkhonto we Sizwe, We are Waiting for You'; Rueedi, 'Patterns of Violence'; Bozzoli, 'Why were the 1980s "Millenarian"?'.

it was the grassroots military struggle that helped to re-popularise the ANC within South Africa and bring about ungovernability.[12] Throughout the 1980s the ANC consistently but euphemistically encouraged the comrades' use of violence – largely allowing young activists to pursue their own understandings of 'ungovernability'.

Student and youth organisations developed complex ways of dealing with the ethical murk of political violence. Many of the more explicitly violent forms of action employed by young activists – ranging from petrol bombing police houses to punishing suspected informers – were not undertaken under their identities as COSAS members but as wider township 'youth'. Planning for such action happened in more informal settings rather than official meetings, and strategically excluded leadership so as not to implicate COSAS itself.[13] 'Targets' – including police, councillors, and white-owned businesses – were loosely identified in meetings, but the specifics of who would be attacked, when, and how, were decided outside of meetings in discussions between just a few young activists. But simultaneously there were youths, generally classified as *comtsotsis*, who capitalised on the chaos of these years and engaged in violence for more personal or economic ends, going far beyond the confines of sanctioned violence approved by young activist leaders.

A further complicating factor in understanding political violence during these years is that township youth did not only target direct state agents or representatives. They also used coercion or violence to bring about social justice on a wider scale, targeting community residents who were deemed to be jeopardising the struggle or whose actions contravened the comrades' moral code. These included women caught buying groceries at white-owned shops during consumer boycotts; suspected informers and sell-outs; gangsters and criminals; and even wayward comrades. The comrades perceived gangsters, criminals, and other social deviants to be equal impediments to liberation as police and councillors were, and thus deemed them to be legitimate targets of political violence or 'discipline'.

The blurred boundaries between overt and covert operations, violent and non-violent strategies, and comrades and *comtsotsis*, all make any study of the township uprisings problematic. These difficulties are furthered by several methodological obstacles: the secrets, lies and over-embellishments contained within oral history narratives; the destruction of police records, and the unreliability of apartheid state records where they do exist; and the strict control

---

12 Kim Wale, 'Falling through the Cracks of South Africa's Liberation: Comrades' Counter-Memories of Squatter Resistance in the 1980s,' *Journal of Southern African Studies* 42:6 (2016): 1193–1206.

13 Marks, *Young Warriors*, 105–106.

the apartheid state had over domestic media outlets at this time. Due to these complications, political violence in the 1980s remains an understudied field in South African history. As Franziska Rueedi writes, 'To this day, there is a lack of information on the perceptions, experiences and strategies of those who engaged in violent protest during the final decade of apartheid.'[14] Yet listening to female comrades offers new perspectives on violence during this period. These women's narratives tend to move away from the euphemistically described 'actions' of the township uprisings spoken about by male political leaders. Their openness, and the emotions with which they recall their participation, provides new insight into why young people engaged in violence, how it felt to be a comrade, and how these now middle-aged adults contend with their past involvement in violence in the post-apartheid period.

Female Comrades and Political Violence in Soweto's Streets

When unrest over rent increases led to community violence against state agents in the Vaal Triangle in September 1984, Soweto initially remained relatively peaceful and, unlike in 1976, was not one of the townships at the forefront of renewed resistance against apartheid. Nevertheless, due to Soweto's volatile history, the state treated the township as if it were a key site of rebellion and cracked down on civic associations and student and youth groups – including COSAS and SOYCO. The declaration of the state of emergency on 21 July 1985 gave the police and army new powers to search homes and arrest and interrogate community members, radically altering the everyday life of Sowetans. The increased presence of troops and armoured vehicles in Soweto's streets was taken by many as a declaration of war.[15] Only 13-years-old at the time of the emergency, a female student at Morris Isaacson High School recalled, 'you see hippos all the time, you see policemen all the time, running after people, and you ask yourself, why is this happening?'[16]

As school students, female comrades were regular witnesses of state violence in Soweto. The increasing militarisation of the township from 1984 onwards affected students in particular, as schools became primary targets of security force patrols. Following the banning of COSAS in August 1985, students were often targeted indiscriminately, regardless of their level of political commitment. One Soweto student recalled, 'Police and soldiers were all over the schoolyard and, even if you have asked your teacher to go to the toilet

---

14 Rueedi, 'Patterns of Violence,' 400.
15 Philip Bonner and Lauren Segal, *Soweto: A History* (Cape Town: Maskew Miller Longman, 1998), 115–116.
16 Interview with Penelope, Jabavu, 12 June 2015.

during class hours, you can get beaten up because the soldiers didn't want to see you out of the class.'[17] Girls and young women were not immune from police surveillance and attacks. The archives of the Detainees Parents Support Committee (DPSC) reveal that several young girls were shot – either with rubber or real bullets – while on their way to school. Yet female students who joined the liberation movement recall that they were spurred on rather than deterred by the state's increased military presence. When discussing their initial involvement in low-level insurgency, such as confronting security force vehicles with stones or barricades, they posit such action as a warranted and defensive reaction to the state's intrusion into the townships. As Lucy commented, 'You'll find that you are sitting in the class, the police are shooting – they used to shoot even the kids that are walking around. The police are busy shooting them outside. We are sitting in the class. Who's going to fight for those students or the kids?'[18] The police's invasion of schools thus paradoxically drew comrades into the streets. Students such as Lucy saw few options other than defending themselves against state violence and perceived the militarisation of the township as a declaration of civil war. Speaking of a time she and her fellow comrades were confronted by police on their way to a COSAS meeting, Lucy explained:

> And we have to fight and protect ourselves. If they shoot, within us, those who have got something like guns and all that, they have to shoot back. Those who haven't got guns, they have to pick up – there were times when we used to go around with weapons, maybe jackets full of stones [laughs]…We were carrying stones all over, wherever we go…We used to fight a lot with police because if they shoot at us, to run away, obviously they are still going to shoot at you, even if you run away. You'd better do something just to protect us.[19]

Female COSAS members spoke of defensive violence as necessary and took up rudimentary arms to defend themselves as they moved around the township. A female comrade from Jabavu described, 'Sometimes when we had COSAS marches, we want to go outside of the [school] gate, police are there. We will just throw the stones at them, and then they will shoot at us.'[20]

But female comrades did more than just throw stones – which were not always the most effective tool for combatting the military might of the apartheid state. Rueedi highlights that petrol bombs were cheap, easy to make,

[17] Patrick Hlongwane, quoted in Bonner and Segal, *Soweto: A History*, 118.
[18] Group Interview with female comrades from Diepkloof, Diepkloof, 27 June 2015.
[19] Interview with Lucy, Fleurhof, 7 April 2014.
[20] Interview with Amahle, Jabavu, 10 June 2015.

and effective.[21] Interviewees narrated their escalation from using stones to petrol bombs as a necessary and natural development. As one Diepkloof woman explained, 'Eh, we are not having guns, we were using petrol bombs.' She justified, 'If they can shoot you, you are going to die. Because they were fighting with us…we had to fight back with them.'[22] Female comrades spoke of their use of petrol bombs with palpable enthusiasm. Laughing loudly, one explained, 'Petrol bombs, yes! We will mix sand and petrol and then we put matches. But you must make sure, it is hot, immediately you must throw it, so that it mustn't burn your hands!' Later, she excitedly recalled, 'Our blood was boiling. We will burn, we will target the cars of the state, we will burn! And the bottle stores, we will burn! Anything that belongs to the state we will just destroy.'[23] With similar fervour another woman spoke about her involvement in attacking a particular policeman: 'And we used to go to his house, break the windows, screaming, telling him to come out. "We are here! We want you! Come and arrest us! We want to kill you! We will burn your house!" and we would throw petrol bombs and we would fight.'[24]

Female comrades were forthcoming about their involvement in political violence enacted not only against state agents, but against fellow township residents too. The targets of such action included a wide range of community members who were seen to be transgressing the moral boundaries of the community and thus endangering the struggle. While community policing may not be seen as a form of political violence in many contexts, the lines between state agent and social deviant grew increasingly blurred in South Africa during the 1980s. Community policing initiatives during this time were in some respects a continuation of earlier forms of local discipline that emerged in the townships in the 1940s and 1950s. Yet comrades' efforts in the 1980s to punish deviants such as criminals and informers were framed under ANC calls for 'people's power,' and thus had a significant new political dimension. Punishing such deviants was thus justified under the wider campaign to dismantle government forces and seize control of policing, judicial, and administrative services in the townships.[25] The comrades saw gangsters, criminals, and other social deviants as equal impediments to liberation as police or councillors and thus deemed them to be legitimate targets of political violence.

---

[21] Rueedi, 'Patterns of Violence,' 405.
[22] Interview with Thobile, Diepkloof, 12 April 2014.
[23] Interview with Ntsiki, Diepkloof, 5 April 2015.
[24] Interview with Ntebaleng, Diepkloof, 15 April 2014.
[25] Lars Buur and Steffen Jensen, 'Introduction: Vigilantism and the Policing of Everyday Life in South Africa,' *African Studies* 63:2 (2004): 142–143.

Interviewees made little distinction between their confrontations with police and other community members, including both under their general descriptions of the actions they undertook within the struggle. The most common targets of such action against community members were those who defied the consumer boycott which had been launched in the Eastern Cape in January 1985 and then spread across the country, forbidding township residents from shopping at white-owned stores. While the boycott was not initiated by student activists, it was students and youth who became its primary enforcers, taking on the role of patrolling the townships for people with bags or goods from white-owned shops. It was through such enforcement that boycotts – long seen as an effective method of non-violent resistance – became associated with youth violence during the 1980s. At the time, stories proliferated of young comrades destroying groceries, or even forcing those who broke the boycott to drink bottles of cooking oil or laundry detergent. Many young people who engaged in such violence were not committed activists, but rather criminal youths who used the boycott as a means of robbing township residents of their purchases.

Nevertheless, almost all female comrades spoke about their involvement in enforcing the boycott – making this the most common form of confrontational political action engaged in by this group of young women. Even a female comrade from White City, Jabavu, who said she was rarely involved in violent confrontations, participated in destroying the groceries of township women caught with illicit goods, 'pouring fish oils and mealies on the floor'.[26] Some women engaged in more severe forms of punishment against those who broke the boycott. As a female comrade from Diepkloof explained, 'And if you've got that plastic bags, ah, we are going to deal with you!…We are going to take the plastics and break the things that is inside, because we said that we don't want that shop…Sometimes we take the *sjambok* and [claps] *sjambok* you.'[27]

Both male and female comrades posited such violence as necessary and communicative. One woman justified her use of force by stating, 'Most of us were in shops boycotts because if we are telling people that you mustn't go to town, we mean it! You mustn't go to town!' When asked if she ever felt remorseful about destroying people's groceries, she responded, 'No…I think I'm aggressive because we notify them first, that they can use other shops but that one is not treating our community in the way you want. Which means you are doing it purposely. That is why when we get you, we used to break all the bags.'[28] Enforcing boycotts was thus central to comrades' claims to authority in the community

[26]   Interview with Thabisile, Johannesburg, 25 May 2015.
[27]   Interview with Thobile, Diepkloof, 12 April 2014.
[28]   *Ibid.*

and was a performative means by which they could demonstrate the influence they held over older township residents. As another woman explained, 'Because I, we didn't want, we wanted people to, to not to do things that we don't want.'[29] In breaking the boycott, residents were demonstrating their defiance of the comrades' authority, and thus fell outside the comrades' demarcated community boundary. A Diepkloof woman described, 'If it's a consumer boycott, we make sure that everyone and everyone else knows that, OK, tomorrow is going to be a consumer boycott. And then whenever you go and buy…that means you don't want to fight with us. Now you are against us.'[30]

Members of the community who deviated further from the comrades' moral code faced harsher punishment. The two groups dealt with most severely by comrades were informers (often referred to by the term *izimpimpi*, meaning traitors or spies) and gangsters.[31] The most notorious gangsters in Soweto during the 1980s and 1990s were the *Makabasa*, a youth gang from Orlando that engaged in a heated, violent conflict with COSAS members in Diepkloof in the mid-1980s, and the Jackrollers, a term used more loosely in reference to gangsters who 'jackrolled' – a verb used to describe the increasingly common practice of public gang rape in Soweto in the late 1980s and early 1990s.[32] Both informers and gangsters were seen by the comrades as working against the liberation movement, and in many cases were severely beaten or killed. While male comrades rarely spoke about or only euphemistically acknowledged such incidents, female comrades spoke openly about their involvement in or support for meting out such punishment. Speaking of such violence as necessary and relatively unspectacular, one woman recounted, 'We knew that there were informers. And once we find out that you are an informer…we will hit you hard…I was involved with that, because it was part of the life that we now live.'[33] When asked more specifically how gangsters were dealt with, another female comrade recalled, 'Sometimes we burned them alive. Oh! We'd pour petrol, we'd put the tire (motions around her neck), we'd burn them alive.'[34]

[29] Interview with Vicky, Diepkloof, 14 May 2014.
[30] Interview with Nonkululeko, Diepkloof, 8 April 2014.
[31] For more on informers see Dlamini, *Askari*.
[32] For information on Makabasa see 'The Conflict between the AZAPO and the UDF – popular violence in the 1980s and 1990s,' *South African History Online*, September 2012, <http://www.sahistory.org.za/topic/war-between-azapo-and-udf-popular-violence-1980s-and-1990s> [accessed 14 June 2015]; for jackrolling see Mokwena, 'The Era of the Jackrollers'.
[33] In their discussions of punishing informers or gangsters, female comrades have been anonymised here. Interview with female COSAS member 1.
[34] Interview with female COSAS member 2.

Here, this woman refers to the 'necklace' – a form of punishment in which a tyre is placed around a person's neck, filled with petrol, and set alight. The necklace became an emblem of youth violence during the mid-1980s. Yet the exact agents of the necklace remain indistinct. While it is likely that some student and youth activists did participate in necklacings, officially political organisations distanced themselves from the practice, as it fuelled images of young comrades as anarchic and barbaric.[35] In July 1985, in one of the first widely reported necklacings in South Africa, a young woman named Maki Skosana was killed by a crowd at a funeral, suspected of being a police informant. Of the eleven eventually brought to trial for Skosana's death, five were female – with one being a fourteen-year-old girl. Seekings cites women's involvement in such extreme forms of violence as 'unusual'.[36] However, several female comrades spoke of their support for or involvement in punishing informers or gangsters, at times through the necklace. Talking about gangsters, a Diepkloof woman recalled, 'Ai, [they were] severely punished. We're going to use, oh! Tyres, yes, we're going to use that…sometimes we just beat them, badly.' I asked her if she and her fellow female comrades were specifically involved in such instances: 'Yes, you know [laughs], we will be involved. We'll be singing and adding, you know, taking part.'[37] Recollections such as this suggest that female comrades played more supportive roles during necklacings, either by singing or just being present. As one interviewee described in more detail, 'the men are the ones who light the light. Then if the women are there they will start singing and surrounding…when there's somebody burning there.'[38] What is particularly interesting here is that when they first mention necklacing, these women do not attempt to downplay their involvement in the killing of gangsters or informers. If anything, their initial use of imprecise language suggests they could have been *more* involved than they actually were. While generally speaking about such things openly, female comrades were also vague for the most part, very rarely providing any details of exactly who was necklaced in their areas and when, or what specific roles various comrades played. Given this, the personal involvement of female comrades in any specific necklacings remain indistinct and unknown.

---

[35] Bozzoli, *Theatres of Struggle*, 139. For more on necklacing see Joanna Ball, 'The Ritual of the Necklace,' March 1994, p.22, AG3245: L2, Centre for the Study of Violence and Reconciliation, HP; Riedwaan Moosage, 'The Impasse of Violence: Writing Necklacing into a History of the Liberation Struggle in South Africa' (Master's thesis, University of the Western Cape, 2010).

[36] Seekings, *Heroes or Villains*, 83.

[37] Interview with female COSAS member 4.

[38] Interview with female COSAS member 5.

Yet whether or not female comrades were actively involved in necklacings perhaps matters less than how forthcoming they are when narrating such events. One woman spoke particularly heatedly about informers, and stressed her own personal agency by repeatedly using 'I' rather than 'we' as other female comrades tended to do:

> Yoh! You know, I was the only person who, you know, I hate those people. I hate those people. Because we are fighting for everyone, even them. You see? They get paid to sell me. And me, I'm the person who was trying to fix things, for them! When they say there's an *impimpi* at this address, I was the first person to say 'let's go and attack'…And then, *I* was putting the tire to them…Ya, the tire, the necklace…And I wasn't satisfied if I don't see your eyes bursting. Really, really. Especially for the *impimpis*. I hate those people.[39]

Remarkably few women appeared to hide or lie about their involvement in necklacings. Only one woman displayed some reluctance in her narrative when I asked her to clarify what she meant when she said *izimpimpis* were 'dealt with': 'Yes, we did, but I, I can't say it because [laughs], I can't say it. We did have that at that certain time, where we know who's the *impimpi* and we've got a way that we discipline them, but I can't explain it to you.' She laughed and continued, 'At that time they say we are putting a tyre. Let me be honest with you.' 'The necklace?' I clarified. 'Ya, we are putting the necklace. We are putting them the necklace.'[40] Many female comrades spoke about necklacing in this way – using 'we' rather than 'I', even when asked about their own individual actions. This may be reflective of how communitarian, collective values often surpass notions of the 'self' in African communities.[41] But such narrative style may also be a means through which female comrades seek to collectively testify to their involvement in political violence. By speaking for a group rather than as individuals, these women claim a role for all female comrades in the most public and extreme form of violence used during the struggle, and cement women's assertions that they were not all marginalised during the township uprisings.

Underground Work

Despite their involvement in these various actions, young women were not equal participants in township collective action and political violence to young men during the 1980s. Female youth likely made up only a small minority

---

[39] Interview with female COSAS member 6.
[40] Interview with female COSAS member 7.
[41] Stephan F. Miescher, *Making Men in Ghana* (Bloomington: Indiana University Press, 2005), 15.

of the comrades engaged in such action, and they also were largely excluded from participating in missions planned not by young people themselves but by underground MK operatives working within the townships. In Soweto, as in many other townships, MK cadres formed increasing links with local youths from the mid-1980s onwards. As Oliver Tambo declared in January 1985, 'To move forward to victory with the greatest speed, we must pay particular attention this year to the task of building a strong underground presence of well-organised revolutionary cadres, drawn from the fighting masses and integrated among them.'[42] As the ANC spoke of the need to 'arm the masses', these operatives provided townships youth with crash courses in how to use hand grenades and AK-47s, and established paramilitary units within local communities.[43] While the exact relationship between COSAS/SOSCO and MK remains unclear, Gay Seidman argues that links between students and the ANC's armed wing were 'far stronger than activists or researchers generally acknowledged at the time.'[44] Many interviewees were aware of these ties, and drew a distinction between collective action organised by local COSAS branches and underground missions orchestrated by MK. One male comrade explained that the primary difference between the two was whether they attacked 'soft' or 'hard' targets: soft targets being local police and councillors, and buses or trucks symbolising white capital; and hard targets referring to Special Branch police or actual police stations, and armed local councillors.[45] Likewise, a female comrade clarified that while students would attack 'petty

[42] Oliver Tambo, 'Render South Africa Ungovernable,' *Sechaba*, p. 11, March 1985, AG2918:9.13.3, KAIROS, HP.

[43] Cherry, 'We were not afraid,' 154; Malose Langa and Gillian Eagle, 'The Intractability of Militarised Masculinity: A Case Study of Former Self-Defence Unit Members in the Kathorus Area, South Africa,' *South African Journal of Psychology* 38:1 (2008): 155.

[44] Gay Seidman, 'Guerrillas in Their Midst: Armed Struggle in the South African Anti-Apartheid Movement,' *Mobilization* 6:2 (2001): 119. Recent research has revealed that the relationship between COSAS and MK is much stronger, and dates back much further, than originally thought. Gregory Houston provides evidence of COSAS members being recruited into MK as early as 1981, and he and Bernard Magubande argue that COSAS was actually founded and formed by an ANC underground cell in 1979. However, these links were never publicly acknowledged in order to allow COSAS to operate legally and above ground. See Gregory Houston, 'The ANC's Internal Underground Political Work in the 1980s,' in SADET (eds), *The Road to Democracy in South Africa*, volume 4 part 1 (Pretoria: UNISA, 2010), 133–222; Gregory Houston and Bernard Magubane, 'The ANC Political Underground in the 1970s,' in SADET (eds), *The Road to Democracy in South Africa*, volume 2 (Pretoria: UNISA, 2007), 371–451.

[45] Interview with Musa, Diepkloof, 13 June 2015.

things' such as cars and shops, it was only those recruited into underground units who attacked 'deep things' such as specific police and councillors.[46] Yet such distinctions were not always clear. Another comrade explained that many of the actions students thought were coordinated by their own structures were actually based on instructions from MK operatives.[47] Much of this confusion is due to the secretive nature of the underground struggle. In Soweto, those students who were involved in the underground did not operate publicly as MK operatives within COSAS. Each underground unit tended to only consist of three to five people, and each member knew only their fellow members and their direct superior who provided them with instructions.[48] Consequently, few comrades were aware of who among their fellow activists were working underground, and what roles they played. This high level of secrecy, compounded by continued reluctance to share individual stories, makes it difficult to determine how many of Soweto's female comrades were recruited into the underground, and what roles they played.

Analysing evidence around these silences, it appears that female comrades were recruited into underground networks to a much lesser extent than males, particularly when it came to combat roles. Moses from Diepkloof explained that during mass actions, 'If you check in the forefront you will see males and females throwing stones and petrol bombs…But when it comes to the underground, few female comrades participated.'[49] Where women were involved, they tended to play 'softer' roles, as another comrade described, either as recruiters or arms smugglers.[50] Two female comrades spoke about working as MK recruiters. As discussed in chapter three, several women also transported arms, often storing them at their parents' houses. Young women's centrality to these roles did not go unappreciated by their male comrades. Patrick from Diepkloof emphasised, 'They were doing a very good job, especially in the underground movement, because other comrades, they will take their arms, give to the females…All of those females, were very, very key in our struggle.'[51] At times, having young women involved in these underground roles was particularly advantageous. Female comrades generally aroused less suspicion than males and were thus adept at performing certain tasks – particularly those involving subterfuge or surveillance. Drawing on assumptions of girls' passivity, female comrades performed purposefully exaggerated feminine identities

[46] Interview with Beatrice, Pimville, 23 May 2015.
[47] Interview with Patrick, Diepkloof, 12 May 2014.
[48] Interview with Musa, Diepkloof, 13 June 2015.
[49] Interview with Moses, Diepkloof, 19 April 2014.
[50] Interview with Makgane, Sandton, 17 April 2014.
[51] Interview with Patrick, Diepkloof, 12 May 2014.

to avoid arrest or detection. One woman recalled how she would be tasked with transporting tapes made by the ANC in exile. She described, 'The men, they will be suspected or whatever but because I'm the girl, and then in my boobs, I'm going to hide the cassettes. Then you're going to go there and pretend as if there's nothing that is happening.'[52] Other women would pretend to be pregnant to smuggle firearms into funerals, which were then used to salute fallen activists.[53] Talking about how she managed to hide her gun when travelling around the township, Sibongile from Jabavu explained, 'Sometimes, you just take it [a gun] like a baby, you just put it [motions around her back] and then take a blanket, so that people cannot see it.'[54]

A few female comrades did receive 'crash courses' from MK operatives in how to handle firearms including hand grenades and AK-47s. I asked one interviewee how such training made her feel. She stated, 'I was so happy, because during 80's I didn't know how to carry a gun. I was only carrying a petrol bomb, a Molotov.' But in the later 1980s, members of the underground trained her in how to use an AK-47, making her feel more empowered as an activist.[55] Another female comrade expressed her desire for military training: 'We were young, the blood was boiling, and we wanted change. And what was in our minds...we just wanted guns, guns in our hands. We just want to liberate our country.'[56] Later, she too was given a crash course: 'Then I learned a lot – Ok, this is Magnum, this is Makarov, this is AK-47, ya. That is why I ended up having a gun.' Thus, military training and the use of arms could provide young women with a 'sense of potency and agency' just as it could with young men.[57]

Despite enthusiastically recalling their training, no female interviewees spoke of the intended targets of their new weapons. The comrade cited above only spoke of using her gun to salute fallen comrades at political funerals, while another woman stated that while she was taught how to use a gun, this was only 'for safety sake [sic], not to attack.'[58] Other women more obviously silenced the exact nature of their training and involvement in the underground. One female comrade spoke of how she was given a 'crash course' in arms handling, but when asked what that training consisted of she laughed and responded, 'Um, a few things, I don't want to say about that.'[59] In a group

---

[52] Interview with Nomsa, Diepkloof Extension, 19 April 2014.
[53] Interview with Makgane, Sandton, 17 April 2014.
[54] Interview with Sibongile, Johannesburg, 9 June 2015.
[55] Interview with Phumzile, Johannesburg, 17 April 2015.
[56] Interview with Ntsiki, Diepkloof, 5 April 2015.
[57] Langa and Eagle, 'Intractability of Militarised Masculinity,' 155.
[58] Interview with Amahle, Jabavu, 10 June 2015.
[59] Interview with Sissy, Diepkloof, 17 April 2015.

interview, a number of women pointed out the comrade amongst them who had undergone the most rigorous military training, yet this woman declined to say anything about her experiences other than that it made her feel 'happy'.[60]

Girls and young women's relative lack of involvement in underground missions demonstrates the limits of their participation in the struggle. While female comrades were accepted or appreciated as participants in collective action that required significant numbers of youths, their recruitment into more formal military structures was not equally welcomed. One male comrade explained how men presumed that women were 'not ready' to be involved in the underground struggle because of their underdeveloped political consciousness. He stated, 'It was so dangerous and at the same time there was this fear from them. So to involve them, it was going to be dangerous for the entire operation…This fear, to fight it, the political conscious of that individual must be developed a little bit, so that she can fight this fear.' Later, he more frankly stated, 'They are not ready to carry such activities.'[61]

Only one female comrade interviewed ever left the country for MK's camps.[62] As discussed in chapter three, politicised girls and young women at times chose not to go into exile in deference to their parents' concerns and needs. But there is also some evidence to suggest that male comrades may have prevented those female comrades who wished to leave the country to join MK from doing so. Sissy and Florence both presented similar narratives: they were eager to join MK, but were told by their male leaders that their presence in Soweto was too important, and that the camps were already full.[63] Florence acknowledged the possible gender discrimination behind this decision, speaking vaguely about how there were 'blueprints' in the struggle and stating 'there's things that you cannot do because you are a woman.'

Struggle Femininity in Soweto's Streets

Engaging in political violence in Soweto's streets was no easy feat for female comrades: it made them more likely to be targeted by security forces, to be shot, or detained; exposed them to greater risk of attacks from gangsters or criminals as they spent more time moving around township streets; and involved the constant need to prove to their male comrades that they were not limited by the presumed weakness of their gender. So why then did

---

[60] Group interview with female comrades from Diepkloof, Diepkloof, 27 June 2015.
[61] Interview with Moses, Diepkloof, 19 April 2014.
[62] Interview with Bessie, Johannesburg, 25 April 2014.
[63] Interview with Sissy, Diepkloof, 17 April 2015; Interview with Florence, Diepkloof, 8 May 2014.

these young women choose to participate in street-based action and violence? In her research with Diepkloof youth, Marks identifies a number of central motivations or justifications for comrades' participation in political violence.[64] Many of the key themes she ascertains are also present in the recollections of the men and women interviewed for this research. In these ways, we can see that young men and women shared many similar motivations for engaging in collective action.

First, both female and male comrades saw themselves as responding to the calls made by the ANC in exile. Although they were neither under the direct control of the ANC nor motivated exclusively by a desire for non-racial democracy, students and youth nevertheless framed their actions as carrying out the ANC's commands, which were interpreted by listening to Radio Freedom or cassettes of Tambo's speeches, or by reading underground literature smuggled into the townships such as *Sechaba*. In explaining their actions, former comrades frequently made reference to a famous speech made by ANC president Oliver Tambo in January 1984, in which he called on the masses in South Africa to '[render] the enemy's instruments of authority unworkable' and '[create] conditions in which the country becomes increasingly ungovernable.'[65] A number of female comrades employed this exact rhetoric when explaining their actions. One female activist from Zola explained, 'Remember in 1985 the president Oliver Tambo initiated to make the country ungovernable. Whatever that he says we must accept.'[66] Another female comrade recalled,

> I think it was 1986 where they said, Oliver Tambo said, the Young Lions, they must roar. So it's where we started to roar. We have to burn the schools! We have to boycott the classes. We didn't write our exams. So, we have to make the world shake! And definitely it happened in that way, because there was no schooling actually. Everything, it was under our control.[67]

Soweto's male comrades employed remarkably similar discourse in explaining their involvement in violence against the state's organs of power. Voice, a comrade from Diepkloof, explained, 'And then everything in 1985 broke loose. And that's when the core student politics started really. We had instructions from the ANC in exile to implement all these programmes…to render the country ungovernable.'[68] Patrick – another Diepkloof-based activist – also

---

[64]   Marks, *Young Warriors*, 115–127.
[65]   Oliver Tambo, 'President's Message for 1984,' *Sechaba*, p. 4, March 1984, AG2918:9.13.3, KAIROS, HP.
[66]   Interview with Stompie, Naturena, 29 May 2015.
[67]   Interview with Nomsa, Diepkloof Extension, 19 April 2014.
[68]   Interview with Voice, Diepkloof, 9 April 2015.

referred specifically to Tambo's orders: 'Because the president of the ANC said we need to render South Africa ungovernable…We were very conscious to make sure that we implement those programmes.'[69]

Political violence was thus used by both young men and women to prove their capabilities as loyal and willing cadres of the ANC. Perhaps because gender stereotypes painted them as less capable soldiers, female comrades in particular were keen to stress how they would follow any orders they were given, without fear or hesitation. Speaking about destroying groceries during the consumer boycott, Nomsa explained, 'The community wouldn't like it, but it's the mission. We need to do it. We can't…you know if the instruction goes out, whether we are in favour of it or not we have to comply and do it.'[70] Male comrades too highlighted their ability to follow orders without question. Speaking about how the comrades followed calls from the ANC for the people to arm themselves, a Diepkloof activist stated, 'When it is called on us to act in a certain way, we really implemented it without questioning.'[71] On a similar note, his fellow comrade explained, 'Look, if a decision has been taken by a structure, I cannot change it. In fact, I'll have to implement it.'[72]

Female comrades also spoke of violence as a necessary defensive action in response to state violence. As Lucy's narrative from earlier in this chapter demonstrates, female comrades saw it as their duty to protect themselves, their fellow school students, and their communities. Multiple women presented a clear choice: either be the victim of state violence, or the agent of defensive violence. Simultaneously, they also saw violence as a means of demonstrating or increasing their authority as moral defenders and political leaders in the township. Their recollections of enforcing the consumer boycott illustrate this. As Thobile said, when comrades declared that township residents should not shop in town, 'we mean it!' She saw the punishment of those who broke the boycott as a necessary and justified means of communication and reprimand against those who defied the comrades' orders. Political violence for both male and female comrades was also used as a way to police and demarcate the moral boundaries of the community, drawing a clear line between those working towards the goals of the liberation movement and those thwarting them.

Yet previous studies of the comrades in the 1980s and early 1990s have also demonstrated the importance of male gender identities, and the need or desire to assert one's masculinity, as a central motivating factor behind young men's involvement in the liberation struggle, and particularly in political

[69]   Interview with Patrick, Diepkloof, 12 May 2014.
[70]   Interview with Nomsa, Diepkloof Extension, 19 April 2014.
[71]   Interview with Teboho, Orlando East, 6 April 2015.
[72]   Interview with Bongani, Johannesburg, 4 June 2015.

violence. At a time when increasing numbers of young people were attending secondary school but being met with decreasing job opportunities, being a comrade could offer a young man status and authority. Campbell argues that young men in Natal were facing a 'chronic loss of identity' in the 1980s, as changes in social reproduction meant that they were not automatically taking on the societal roles of husbands and fathers as they grew up. No longer able to demonstrate their masculinity through traditional markers, such young men turned to the struggle against apartheid. As Xaba writes, 'being a "comrade" endowed a young man with social respect and status within his community. Being referred to as a "young lion" and a "liberator" was an intoxicating and psychologically satiating accolade.'[73] Within comrade culture, masculinity and violence were closely linked, argues Campbell. Amongst the comrades she studied in Natal, 'violence was characterized as the prototypical male activity.'[74] If engaging in political violence in township streets was a key marker of young, successful masculinity during these years, what did violence mean for female comrades and their gender identities?

Female comrades' willingness to discuss their past involvement in political violence, and the enthusiastic ways in which they recall these activities, suggests that political violence was also central to their forging of new struggle femininities. Street-based action is so prominent in female comrades' narratives of the past because it was in Soweto's streets where these girls most publicly challenged both the apartheid state and township gender ideologies. Their stories of throwing stones or punishing gangsters are palpably nostalgic for the sense of joy these women felt in breaking gendered taboos and taking on new positions of power and authority in the townships as teenage girls. In her analysis of the Alexandra Rebellion of 1986, Bozzoli demonstrates how the inversion of apartheid's spatial control and the defiant repurposing of township spaces was central to the comrades' struggle during this period. Since spatial control is political, she asserts, 'resistance to political power may and perhaps should take a spatial form.'[75] She explores how (predominantly male) comrades transformed township streets, parks, schools, and other public spaces in Alex into sites where resistance was theatrically performed. But female comrades also politically appropriated township streets, not just to perform resistance to the state but also to publicly resist dominant gender ideologies that confined girls to the home and made them feel like vulnerable victims in public spaces. Through their participation in collective action in Soweto's streets, female comrades demonstrated their strength and bravery,

[73] Xaba, 'Masculinity and its Malcontents,' 109–110.
[74] Campbell, 'Learning to Kill,' 624.
[75] Bozzoli, *Theatres of Struggle*, 13–14.

proved their worth to the liberation movement, and challenged the exclusively masculine control of these spaces, defying gender norms and seeking to overcome their experiences of victimisation and inequality.

The streets offered girls and young women the chance to publicly demonstrate their capabilities as comrades, both to their male comrades and wider communities. These spaces became theatrical proving grounds for young women's strength, bravery, and defiance. As Campbell's interviews demonstrate, many male activists tended to see girls as ill-suited to political work; they were frivolous, unreliable, over-emotional, scared, and physically weak.[76] Young men in Soweto shared such perceptions, as one Diepkloof comrade described women as 'not energetic…they are not strong,' and consequently not suited to political violence.[77] But by engaging in political violence in Soweto's streets, female comrades performed the opposite of these stereotyped feminine characteristics, and in their narratives emphasise their bravery, strength, and willingness to use violence. In doing so, they highlight the equal roles they played in the liberation struggle alongside young men.

Engaging in 'tasks', as comrades often euphemistically referred to political violence, was also a way in which female activists could make up for their lack of engagement in meetings and intellectual debate. Given the constraints young women faced in fully participating in meetings, as discussed in the previous chapter, it may have been easier for them to pick up a stone and join a crowd than it was for them to read and share their opinions of the *Communist Manifesto*. As Lucy described, 'there are those that were in the struggle that, those who liked to read books and all that. And there were those who were just concentrating [on] what they were *doing* by that time.'[78] This distinction between reading and *doing*, or the intellectual and confrontational spheres of the struggle, was made by several interviewees. After explaining how young women rarely participated in meetings, a male comrade from Diepkloof explained, 'mostly we will see them during mmm, when we do certain action. We will see them emerging. But when we sit around in a meeting, they will silently listen.'[79] His close friend explained the situation in similar terms, stating that while women rarely voiced their opinions in meetings, 'in terms of action, women were all equally involved, let's put it that way.'[80] After admitting that women were rarely vocal in meet-

[76] Campbell, 'Identity and Gender in a Changing Society,' 322–323.
[77] Marks, *Young Warriors*, 105.
[78] Group interview with female comrades from Diepkloof, 27 June 2015.
[79] Interview with Sello, Diepkloof, 14 May 2014.
[80] Interview with Musa, Diepkloof, 8 May 2014.

ings, Bessie qualified that 'they would do whatever task they were given.'[81] Thus for female comrades, carrying out 'tasks' or participating in 'certain action' was a means by which they could prove their commitment to the struggle, despite their lack of active participation in meetings and ideological discussions.

Female comrades also use their narratives of engaging in political violence to distinguish themselves from other, non-politicised girls in the township and explicitly reject feminine norms. As a comrade from Pimville stated, 'Most of the women were scared, but I was not [laughs]…I was not even scared of the gun. I would hold it; it was easy for me.' In stating that even holding arms was 'easy' for her, she posits militarisation as natural, and not inherently contradictory to her gender. She continued, 'Because most of the time, [male comrades] know ladies, they are scared. They can't perform certain tasks. But with me, believe me, I could perform *any* task.'[82]

In these ways, female comrades also used violence as a social leveller; their involvement in attacking targets proved that they were not so different from their male counterparts. By becoming 'soldiers', they insisted, they shed the weakness or subordination associated with girlhood. As Penelope, a female comrade from Jabuvu, stated, 'We were like soldiers, there's not special treatment per say…It's once in a while that they [male comrades] would remember that amongst them there is a female comrade. Because then they look at you as a fellow comrade. If they are throwing stones, you must also throw a stone.'[83] After listing several campaigns she was involved in, including throwing stones at buses and destroying groceries during the consumer boycott, Lucy explained, 'so we used to do the same things with the males.'[84] Zanele described her desire to be given the same training as male comrades:

> Our heads were so hot, we didn't want to be left at the back…When you say, 'let's go and attack there,' we'll run fast! We'll run far! They'll [male comrades] say 'no ladies, please stay behind.' And we'll say 'no, we are going there! Why must we stay behind?' Because we were all fighting. If you throw a petrol bomb, I throw one too. If you mixed the petrol bomb there, I want to know, how did you mix it?[85]

[81] Interview with Bessie, Johannesburg, 25 April 2014.
[82] Interview with Beatrice, Pimville, 23 May 2015.
[83] Interview with Penelope, Jabavu, 12 June 2015.
[84] Interview with Lucy, Fleurhof, 7 April 2014.
[85] Interview with Zanele, Diepkloof, 12 April 2014.

Yet in seeking to demonstrate these capacities, female comrades needed to discard characteristics associated with femininity and adopt masculine traits and behaviours. Doing so allowed them to be accepted by young men as fully participating comrades, and to prove that their involvement in the struggle was not limited by their gender. As women from Diepkloof recalled in a group interview:

> Lucy: But as ladies, you know, our male comrades didn't take us as inferior. They used to treat us like males. Even what we wear – we used to wear *takkies* [trainers] and jeans and all that.
>
> Nonkululeko: Now and then! We wear trousers, we are like that. We only wear skirts when we go to church [laughs].
>
> Lucy: Ya, they were even saying we are tomboys or something...Because anything can happen – the police can chase us any time, we have to run away. So you can't run away with heels or those shoes. You must always [be] in *takkies* and all that. So it was a great experience for us.[86]

Demonstrating her rejection of feminine clothing, an activist from Pimville stated, 'I mean, you'd never hit a target wearing a skirt and not knowing how to run. When we jump those fences, if you are a sophisticated woman you won't be safe. You'd rather stay at home.'[87] This trend was not limited to Soweto. In Alexandra, 'DP', one of the few female comrades interviewed by Carter, also commonly wore trousers, which, as Bozzoli notes, was 'an uncommon form of dress for girls in those times.'[88] While DP joined every confrontation in Alexandra's Six-Day War in 1986, 'the girls in skirts... would get caught jumping over fences.'[89] One male comrade from Soweto confirmed the powerful effects of women's adoption of male clothing when speaking about a female comrade named Diana who was murdered by a gangster in the early 1990s: 'She was very much vocal...you will not find her wearing these skirts of women...[she] will wear a trouser and a t-shirt. She was militant in actual fact. At some point you will be afraid talking to her.' Later, he added, 'she was a very dangerous woman.'[90] Such women were idolised by younger female comrades. Also speaking about Diana, Phumzile from Diepkloof described, 'She was like a big man, she has these muscles,' explaining how even men were afraid to talk to her. 'That was a very, very,

---

[86] Group interview with female comrades from Diepkloof, Diepkloof, 27 June 2015.
[87] Interview with Khosi, Orlando East, 1 May 2014.
[88] Bozzoli, *Theatres of Struggle*, 105.
[89] Carter, 'Comrades and Community,' 270.
[90] Interview with Takazov, Diepkloof, 2 May 2015.

very brave lady.' Venerating her willingness to use force, she exclaimed, 'She used to do the consumer boycott like nobody's business!'[91]

These comrades were not the first female activists in South Africa to adopt masculine characteristics in order to succeed and prove their worth in a male-dominated political environment. During the heyday of Black Consciousness in the late 1960s and 1970s, women also felt the need to become 'one of the boys' and challenge gendered social conventions by being vocal, assertive, and defiant.[92] Speaking about her time in exile during the 1970s, Thandi Modise too recalled that female cadres had to constantly 'prove' they were not the weaker sex through engaging in the same physical activities as men.[93] This is a need that female combatants have felt beyond South Africa too. Given traditional assumptions of women's predisposition to peaceful behaviour and nurturing roles, women engaged in liberation movements or civil wars often are perceived to have to 'become like men'. As Chris Coulter writes of Sierra Leone, female fighters 'assume male roles and behaviour, and also outdo men, in order to fit our notion of how real combatants should be.'[94] Yet in doing so, female activists or combatants '[render] the male experience – and the male subject – normative,' rather than challenging dominant gender ideologies within their organisations. In analysing this, Magaziner asks an important question: did participating in a male-dominated political struggle offer South African women more than 'the right to act as surrogate men'?[95]

This is a challenging and complex question, but exploring one particular type of violence which female comrades in Soweto were involved in offers us a partial answer: the punishing of suspected rapists.[96] This case study demonstrates how female comrades' gender, despite their adoption of

---

[91]   Interview with Phumzile, Johannesburg, 17 April 2015.

[92]   Ramphele, 'The Dynamics of Gender within Black Consciousness Organisations,' 218. This need to 'become like men' was also reported by black female medical students and doctors during this period. See Vanessa Noble, 'Doctors Divided: Gender, Race and Class Anomalies in the Production of Black Medical Doctors in Apartheid South Africa, 1948–1994,' (PhD thesis, History and Women's Studies, University of Michigan, 2005), 260–304.

[93]   Thandi Modise and Robyn Curnow, 'Thandi Modise: A Woman in War,' *Agenda*, 43 (2000): 36.

[94]   Chris Coulter, 'Female Fighters in the Sierra Leone War: Challenging the Assumption?' *Feminist Review* 88 (2008): 63.

[95]   b. hooks, *Ain't I a Woman: Black Women and Feminism* (Boston: South End Press, 1981), 192, quoted in Magaziner, 'Pieces of a (Wo)man,' 48.

[96]   Emily Bridger, 'Soweto's Female Comrades: Gender, Youth and Violence in South Africa's Township Uprisings, 1984–1990,' *Journal of Southern African Studies* 44:4 (2018): 559–574.

masculine traits, remained salient in their experiences of collective action and political violence. As chapter one demonstrated, rape was pervasive in Soweto in the 1980s and early 1990s, and the fear of rape paralysed many young women and dictated where they could and could not go in the township. Once they became comrades, however, young women took a keen interest in challenging the most notorious perpetrators of sexual violence. The comrades as a group targeted known gangsters who were accused of attacking girls or young women in Soweto under their remit of purging the township of those who jeopardised the struggle or acted in ways contrary to the comrades' moral code. In such cases, perpetrators were often beaten in public in Soweto's streets. This punishment was typically unstructured, consisting of *sjamboking*, kicking, and assailing with stones. Both male and female comrades spoke about meting out justice against suspected rapists, but always within their wider discussions of the liberation movement – making no separation between this use of violence and their wider goals of making the township ungovernable and securing 'People's Power'.

Yet rapists were treated differently from other gangsters or informers punished by the comrades, as both men and women attested to the gendered nature of this punishment. As a female comrade from Diepkloof described, 'They [male comrades] used to put us as female comrades to go and hunt those rapists. We are the ones who are going to deal with them because what they've done, they've done to the females.' When asked how these rapists were dealt with, she laughed loudly and responded 'Yoh, it depends sometimes with the situation…but we used to beat them, give them a hiding.'[97] Even female comrades who were rarely engaged in political violence were involved in the punishing of rapists. A comrade from Jabavu who stated that she was afraid of police, not very brave, and rarely involved in militant activity, spoke of her engagement in this type of community policing: 'The gangsters were raping women, yes, we used to – because they will be saying, the boys will be saying, you should be in the forefront here because we are not raped, it's you who are raped. And so we'll be put in the forefront.'[98] Male comrades too stressed how this was a role that held particular importance for women. Explaining why female comrades were at the forefront of such punishment, another male activist explained, 'Because these rapes were happening to them…we felt, collectively, that they should be part of this. And these rapists, they must see that women are tired of being raped.'[99]

---

[97]   Interview with Lucy, Fleurhof, 7 April 2014.
[98]   Interview with Thabisile, Johannesburg, 25 May 2015.
[99]   Interview with Paul, Diepkloof, 14 February 2016.

When speaking about punishing perpetrators of sexual violence, female comrades spoke openly, in more specific detail, and more animatedly than at other points in their interviews. During a group interview with Diepkloof-based female comrades, two women laughed loudly and grew audibly excited when recalling this story:

> Lucy: You know…there was a guy, one of the good days, who raped a lady in zone 3 [Diepkloof]. We combine as females, and decided that, we don't want males to be involved. We are the ones who are going to deal with that man. We went there, and we caught that guy [laughs]. We gave him a hiding!
>
> Thobile: We used *sjamboks*, umbrellas!
>
> Lucy: Umbrellas!
>
> Thobile: We beat him hard!
>
> Lucy: So some of the problems, we wanted to solve it ourselves, not involving the males.[100]

These verbal displays of excitement and nostalgia suggest that punishing rapists was a particularly important way in which young women engaged in township confrontations. Women's stories of punishing rapists came up unexpectedly and without prompting in interviews, highlighting how essential such actions were to female comrades' overall understanding of the roles they played in the liberation struggle. How then should we answer Magaziner's question posed above: did engagement in political violence offer female activists anything more than being 'one of the boys'? In one sense we can understand female comrades' involvement in violence, and their emphasis on their strength and bravery, as a performance made to their male counterparts, a performance that proved their capabilities and allowed them to be accepted as full participants in the struggle. Yet this example of the gendered punishment of rapists demonstrates that female comrades could at times also use the wider political struggle for their own ends – in this case, to confront the injustices and victimisation they faced as young women growing up in Soweto and attempt to make the township a safer place for women.

Overall, engaging in street-based political violence and subverting the gendered geographies of township life brought Soweto's female comrades' feelings of agency, potency, and pride that are noticeably expressed in their interviews. Their laughter, excitement, and nostalgia are testament to how important these

---

[100] Group interview with female comrades from Diepkloof, Diepkloof, 27 June 2015.

moments of confrontation from female comrades' pasts are to their positive sense of themselves in the present. In the existing literature on male comrades, scholars generally agree that violence was used productively and purposefully by young activists in township streets to carve out social space, gain power, and assert masculinity. Yet it is clear from interview testimony that these feelings were not exclusive to male activists. Engaging in political protest and violence alongside male youth in such a public space not only enabled these young women to feel empowered, but to also perform that empowerment to their wider township communities.

But this public performance of authority or empowerment also had an important gender dimension. Whereas for men, street confrontations provided a means of asserting their masculinity, for female comrades these instances allowed them to, even if briefly, challenge and overcome their adolescent experiences of vulnerability and inequality. Across multiple regions, girls and young women have participated in political conflict for similar reasons. In Sri Lanka, female Tamil Eelam fighters took up arms as a means of breaking gendered taboos and engaging in behaviours usually prohibited for girls. By engaging in violence, they '[destroyed] the stultifying straitjacket of conformity and subservience traditionally imposed upon them by a rigidly and self-righteously patriarchal society.'[101] Similarly in Nicaragua, young women joined the Sandinista National Liberation Front (FSLN) in part to escape their tedious domestic duties and home-centred lives.[102] Soweto's female comrades' narratives of street confrontations imply that during these moments they felt free, powerful, and empowered – characteristics that contrast starkly with those they use to describe their pre-political childhoods.

South Africa's female comrades were eager to stress the empowering effects of their transgressive behaviour and participation in Soweto's streets. Being in the struggle made them different from other girls in the townships, they claimed; made them stronger, braver, and better equipped to resist victimisation. As Ntebaleng from Diepkloof stated, 'No man can touch me here on the street again. I know my rights…being in the struggle made me know my rights.'[103] By adopting more assertive feminine identities and directly engaging in carrying out 'justice' against gangsters, female comrades mitigated their feelings of physical insecurity in the townships. The empowering effects of comrade membership may have had an immediate effect on girls' susceptibility to sexual violence. Writing in 1989, SAYCO's then national organiser for women stated that politicised female youths were rarely victims of rape in

---

[101] Bose, *States, Nations, Sovereignty*, 111.
[102] Kampwirth, *Women and Guerrilla Movements*, 9.
[103] Interview with Ntebaleng, Diepkloof, 15 April 2014.

African communities, 'because the *tsotsis* or thugs are often scared of anything associated to or called a comrade.' She clarified, 'To my knowledge, no rape of a comrade has ever been reported – I don't say comrades haven't been raped, I'm merely emphasising the rarity of this occurrence.'[104] This comment should not be taken as an empirical statement that no female comrades were raped – such information is impossible to know given the silences that surround such topics. But it nevertheless reveals an important belief that comradeship helped to alleviate young women's vulnerability in the townships.

Memories of Political Violence: From Nostalgia to Reticence

However, female comrades' narratives of empowerment need to be examined carefully. First, while their participation in street-based action and political violence may have brought them individual feelings of agency and potency, they do not appear to have affected any societal-wide, lasting shift in gender roles. The extent of their empowerment and challenging of township gender ideologies should thus not be overstated. Second, these narratives may tell us as much about female comrades' positions in the present as they do about the past, and about how these women relate to dominant historical narratives of the 1980s.

What is particularly interesting here are the differences between men and women's accounts of political violence during these years. Women spoke much more openly about violence and their individual roles in various actions than men. Overall, they showed little to no hesitation in speaking about their personal use of stones, petrol bombs, and *sjamboks*, often incorporating these actions into their life histories without being asked specifically about them. This was most evident in their discussions of necklacings, in which they were remarkably forthcoming, especially given that they were speaking to a white foreigner and discussing a form of violence that the liberation movement has since tried to distance itself from. Here, some women even stressed their personal involvement – potentially exaggerating rather than downplaying their individual agency in these attacks.

Furthermore, they were often animated when recalling their involvement in political violence. Almost all female interviewees highlighted their enthusiasm for confrontations, describing their involvement in enforcing boycotts, using petrol bombs, or punishing gangsters as engaging and gratifying. In their discussions of political violence, they became noticeably passionate, as they laughed, spoke at a quicker pace, or punctuated their narratives with

---

[104] 'Organising Women,' *Youth Focus*, July 1989, AL2425: K1, South African Youth Congress, SAHA.

shrieks and shouts. A Jabavu-based activist laughed as she described beating a rapist as 'fun'. When I later asked her what she found most enjoyable about the struggle she replied, 'When they [police] were shooting at us, when we were fighting! [laughs loudly] We will scream! Then we will run!'[105] Recalling the time they were first taught how to construct and use petrol bombs, and group of women from Diepkloof exclaimed:

Nonkululeko: Yoh! I was so excited! I wanted to do it!

Lucy: Ya, it was exciting! It was exciting!

Thobile: Eh, we were very excited! Eh, it was very nice…Though it was so painful this thing, but we used to like it![106]

Similarly, another Diepkloof activist described how being trained in using firearms such as hand grenades and AK-47s made her 'so happy', and was a welcome development from her previously limited experience of only using petrol bombs.[107] Such emotional expressions seemed to convey women's deep pride in their past activist roles, and even a sense of nostalgia for the struggle – with one woman referring to a time when she and her fellow female comrades physically punished a gangster suspected of raping a local woman as 'one of the good days'.[108]

Female comrades' need to constantly prove their involvement in the more militant aspects of the struggle can be understood by looking more closely at the differing accounts male comrades provided of young women's roles during the township uprisings. Some men spoke admirably about women's bravery and strength and acknowledged their capabilities to engage in political violence. A male comrade named Sello explicitly stated that female comrades, 'were not just spectators. They were partakers to every action that we undertook… When we do this, they are here, they also do. If I throw a brick, this one will throw a brick, a female, you know? We are in this together.'[109] Some men also challenged notions of the struggle as monolithically masculine by admitting to their own physical or emotional limits when it came to engaging in collective action. Teboho, a dedicated COSAS member from Orlando East, was in many respects the exemplary militarised activists: after joining the struggle as a young teenager he left the country to join MK in exile and continued to

[105] Interview with Amahle, Jabavu, 10 June 2015.
[106] Group Interview with female comrades from Diepkloof, Diepkloof, 27 June 2015.
[107] Interview with Phumzile, Johannesburg, 17 April 2015.
[108] Lucy, from group interview with female comrades from Diepkloof, Diepkloof, 27 June 2015.
[109] Interview with Sello, Diepkloof, 14 May 2014.

work as a soldier after 1994 in the South African National Defence Force. In the following excerpt, in which Florence – who was present during the interview – interjects, he explained how he did not find his own militarisation an easy or natural process:

Teboho: You know (sighs), I've always been a person who's scared. What's that word?

Florence: A coward?

Teboho: Not a coward, no, a person who has always been afraid of confrontation, ya. But because now you are always facing confrontation, you no longer have a choice. You know at times, when they shoot at us from behind, my knees would be full of water, they would be shaking as I run. I would feel that I can fall at any given time. I had to run for my life. That's how scared I was of confrontation. But the situation really ultimately forces you. Either you surrender, submit, or fight. But submitting was not a choice for me.

EB: So, how did you feel the first time you had military training, the first time you learned how to use arms?

Teboho: It was scary! It was scary, but now I have a responsibility of making sure that I fight tooth and nails and I'll be given instructions to follow on a certain mission and I had to execute it without fail.[110]

Yet other men cast political violence as an exclusively masculine pursuit which came naturally to young men but was not suited to young women. Makgane stated that female comrades were rarely involved in attacking targets due to what he described as 'natural constraints and limitations in societal structures.' Such actions, he explained, were generally planned at night and forced comrades to sleep away from home. 'By its design and nature it's as if only men participate,' he explained. 'It's not conducive for a lot of comfort.' He continued, 'There will be a growing role for women in terms of them being, playing the softer part of the role. You know? So as they can continuously be there, as a feeder, or as a communications mechanism, between the comrades in detention or in hiding or in training.'[111] Men's refusal to see women as agents of political violence is not particular to this set of interviews. In her research with Diepkloof youth in the early 1990s, Marks similarly found that despite men's denials of young women's militancy, these women 'not only repudiated the notion of themselves as

[110] Interview with Teboho, Orlando East, 6 April 2015.
[111] Interview with Makgane, Sandton, 17 April 2014.

inherently more peace-loving than their male counterparts, but who wanted to be directly engaged in activities involving "hard violence".'[112] Nor are men's denials of women's agency specific to the final decade of apartheid. Pohlandt-McCormick describes how in men's accounts of the 1976 Soweto Uprisings, it appears as if young women were hardly involved. Unless specifically prompted, male interviewees rarely included the roles of female youth in their testimonies. However, Pohlandt-McCormick found that contrary to men's erasing of women's roles, 'girls were very much part of the uprising, their participation determined…more by their identity as students than by their gender.'[113] We can thus understand why female comrades emphasise, and perhaps even over-emphasise, their roles in political violence in an attempt to challenge their absence from history.

Conversely, men tended to speak vaguely and indirectly about their own involvement in violence. When discussing the township uprisings they spoke predominantly in the collective and relied almost entirely on euphemistic ANC discourse rather than narrating violence in their own words – providing little detail about how 'ungovernability' was achieved in practice. One man simply explained that 'when Oliver Tambo made the call that we should make the country ungovernable, COSAS, it was one of the key organisations that did that,' while another stated, 'Remember, there was a call to say, disarm the enemy and arm the people….all the calls by the ANC, we had to make them happen.'[114] In contrast to female interviewees, no male comrade spoke about witnessing, let alone participating in, a necklacing.

Yet men were not entirely reticent about their involvement in violence. Instead, they tended to keep obvious secrets – signalling to me through laughter, mumbles or facial expressions that their involvement went far beyond what they were willing to disclose. When asked if he could speak more about his personal role in the underground, Musa – a COSAS leader from Diepkloof – laughed loudly and responded, 'No [laughs], we made a pact with members of the unit that we are not talking about these things.'[115] Another Diepkloof comrade made it clear that he was expected to keep secrets. Speaking about a woman who was killed by the comrades for having intimate relations with a gangster, he paused and stated, 'I'm sorry, I'm telling a secret I was not supposed to tell you.' Later, when explaining how

---

[112] Marks, *Young Warriors*, 104.
[113] Pohlandt-McCormick, *Doing Violence to Memory*, E-book, paragraph 632–635.
[114] Interview with Paul, Diepkloof, 2 May 2015; Interview with Bongo, Diepkloof, 5 April 2015.
[115] Interview with Musa, Diepkloof, 13 June 2015.

informers were dealt with, he again declared, 'This is a secret, neh? I'm not supposed to tell you this thing because you are interviewing.'[116]

These differences in male and female comrades' narratives tell us a great deal about interviewees' own motives in agreeing to take part in oral history interviews, and the ways in which they relate their personal memories to dominant histories of the struggle. Both academic and more popular accounts of the 1980s depict the archetypal comrade as someone who was strong, brave, and steadfastly committed to the struggle. But this ideal is not gender neutral – it is masculine and has worked to exclude the involvement of female comrades from histories of the struggle over the past several decades. In seeking to have their political roles acknowledged, female comrades shape their narratives to conform to this exemplary image, making sure to emphasise their bravery, strength, and willingness to engage in violence. They thus tell of their involvement in violence as a 'currency of legitimacy', as a means of inserting themselves into a historical narrative from which they've been excluded.[117] By emphasising their possession of these traits linked with comrade masculinity, they distance themselves from the characteristics stereotypically assigned to girls at the time – fear, weakness, and vulnerability.

Male comrades on the other hand, with less of a need to prove their involvement, focus on distancing themselves from the unruly or ill-disciplined image of the *comtsotsi*. They provide just enough information to demonstrate that they were key actors during the 1980s, while still dissociating themselves from forms of violence potentially seen as unjustified. As Wale highlights, since the end of apartheid, the ANC have sought to disconnect the organisation from the more excessive forms of violence witnessed during the township uprisings, instead often blaming the comrades for such violence.[118] In their narratives, male comrades resist or push back against this blaming, portraying their involvement in political violence as thoroughly justified and sanctioned by the leadership. They also make sure to maintain the culture of secrecy encouraged amongst activists during the struggle. During apartheid, to tell of one's involvement in the liberation movement often meant to be killed or to be responsible for the killing of your comrades. In the post-apartheid period, this culture very much remains amongst male comrades, who tended to be in higher positions of leadership than female comrades and have closer ties to the ANC leadership in the present. Female comrades seem to be less bound to this culture of secrecy – in part

---

[116] Interview with ATV, Diepkloof, 2 May 2015.
[117] Stacey Hynd, 'Trauma, Violence, and Memory in African Child Soldier Memoirs,' *Culture, Psychiatry and Medicine* 45: 1 (2020): 86.
[118] Wale, 'Falling through the Cracks of South Africa's Liberation,' 1196.

because they are further removed from political leadership, but also because they cannot both keep silent about their past involvement in violence and have their roles as comrades publicly acknowledged.

The celebratory emotions expressed by female interviewees help them to create redemptive and productive narratives of their time as comrades, enabling them to hold on to their feelings of agency and potency in the present. Yet we must also ask what is excluded or silenced from these women's narratives of street-based action. By conforming their memories to images of the archetypal comrade, and emphasising their bravery and strength, female comrades leave little room for expressing vulnerability, fear, or remorse – emotions that could be taken as overtly feminine and thus challenging to their constructed gender identities. Only three women spoke openly about their reluctance to be involved in violence. Sibongile, a comrade from Zola, admitted that she was not involved in attacking targets because, 'for me it was not reasonable. I thought that maybe there's more important things to be done than taking from this truck.' However, she was not necessarily able to express such views during her time as an activist, fearing that she might be taken as disloyal or disobedient. 'But I was part of the struggle,' she explained, 'I couldn't say "don't do this".'[119] A Jabavu-based comrade named Penelope was offered a gun but chose not to use it. She explained, 'no, it's too heavy for my hands...I have that Christian background...But I just thought, this thing is too heavy, and it kills people...I just held a gun, I never used it.'[120] Thabisile, another female comrade from Jabavu, was the only woman to openly admit that she was too afraid of police to be in the forefront during collective action. 'I was not the brave, brave woman,' she explained. 'In some cases I will be there, but most of the time I will be at the back.'[121]

Female comrades were also hesitant to express any regret for their past actions. When they did share such feelings, they did so briefly, and often followed by renewed statements of their fearlessness or willingness to use force. Although rare, such recollections demonstrate that female comrades' memories of political violence are more complex than they at first seem, and that these women continue to grapple with the morality of their former actions in the present. While speaking about the necklacing of a gangster, one woman's tone quickly shifted from fast-paced and animated to laborious and reserved. 'You know,' she said, taking a deep breath and sighing, 'you look at the person dying in front of you, but there's nothing you can do because what he, that person, has done to other people is also painful. So, you tell yourself that...it's

---

[119] Interview with Sibongile, Johannesburg, 9 June 2015.
[120] Interview with Penelope, Jabavu, 12 June 2015.
[121] Interview with Thabisile, Johannesburg, 25 May 2015.

like 50:50, we are balancing.'[122] Another female activist, who spoke particularly unforgivingly about using the necklace against gangsters, admitted to the remorse she feels for attacking buses during a transportation boycott. 'It was wrong,' she repeated numerous times, 'It was wrong [because] when we were hitting [the buses], it was our parents inside, coming from work…The driver of that target, it was someone's parent…And they have children at home, and a wife.'[123] Such recollections are testament to the multiple and at times contradictory motivations these women have for telling their life histories, and the conflicting needs to both claim a central role in South Africa's past while not going too far in their narratives of violence that they come across as inhumane or unjustified in their actions.

Simultaneously, by focusing on the empowering effects of their involvement in the struggle, female comrades may be silencing the less empowering moments from their time as activists in Soweto's streets. Their narratives create a clear binary between a pre-political life marked by fear and vulnerability and a post-political life marked by their empowerment and strength. This binary helps to justify their decision to join the struggle – a decision that brought them considerable hardship including damaged family relationships, ongoing stigma, and for many, as the next chapter will demonstrate, detention and torture. Yet it is likely one that oversimplifies the day-to-day realities of being a comrade, and works to hide from view moments of fear, vulnerability, or discrimination.

Conclusion

In much scholarly literature, women's involvement in violence is either ignored, or portrayed through stereotyped tropes that grant women little agency. It is rarely acknowledged that, 'women, like men, sometimes see violence as the best means to their political ends.'[124] Both male and female comrades engaged in political violence and confrontational activism in Soweto's streets for numerous reasons: to contribute to the wider goals of the liberation movement and the ANC's call for 'ungovernability'; to demarcate new moral boundaries between community insiders and outsiders; and to address a range of racial and class inequalities. But, as Seekings argues, comrades' actions also 'provided spaces for a range of people to seek social affirmation, and even to enjoy themselves through collective action.' Yet such

---

[122] Again, interviewees have been anonymised here in their discussions of necklacing. Interview with female COSAS member 2.

[123] Interview with female COSAS member 6.

[124] Laura Sjoberg and Caron E. Gentry, *Mothers, Monsters, Whores: Women's Violence in Global Politics* (London: Zed Books, 2007), 4.

motivations applied predominantly to young men, he contends, as 'young women, by contrast, were largely marginalised.'[125]

Female comrades' narratives of their involvement in the more confrontational, public sphere of the liberation movement force us to question current understandings of gender and the struggle, and to re-evaluate much of the literature on youth and political violence in the 1980s. Regardless of the romanticised lens through which these women relate their pasts, female comrades were more involved in violent confrontations with state forces and community deviants in township streets than previously argued. In fact, for Soweto's female comrades represented here, it was precisely the increased militarisation of the townships that drew them deeper into the liberation movement, pulling them out of their schools and homes and into the streets in ways largely unprecedented for girls. Despite being masculine territory, the streets offered new opportunities to female comrades to rebel against the apartheid state, defy gender norms, and participate alongside their male comrades. The emotions with which these women recall their stone-throwing or petrol-bombing pasts reveals the seductive feelings of pride, camaraderie, and personal agency such actions could bring for young women as well as young men. Seeking to understand young men's empowerment through collective action during these years, scholars have focused on the masculinities espoused by the comrades, and argued that through activism and political violence young men could gain a sense of potency and agency, and publicly assert their masculinity and authority in a time and place where they had few other opportunities to do so. Yet we must also see the importance of gender in motivating girls and young women's actions during these years. For female comrades, engaging in collective action in Soweto's streets offered them a channel through which they could contest their inequality and victimisation, by both publicly challenging expected gender norms through their use of violence and appropriation of masculine space, and, in particular cases, of directly targeting some of those most responsible for their gendered physical insecurity in the township. Engaging in political protest alongside male youth helped them to feel a sense of equality with male comrades, while taking up arms against the state and its collaborators was a clear departure from the subservience and victimisation that typically marked African girlhood at this time. Furthermore, recalling their engagement in Soweto's streets in such forthright and enthusiastic ways offers these women a chance to challenge collective memory that has excluded girls' involvement from the history of the liberation movement.

---

[125] Seekings, *Heroes or Villains*, 97.

Yet the opportunities township streets could offer young women did not come without limitations and restrictions. To engage in collective action alongside male comrades, girls and young women needed to mask their femininity, and adopt the personas of hardened, brave young men who were willing to use violence and could perform any task asked of them. Although their gender could at times work to their advantage – particularly when performing surveillance or subterfuge – being a female comrade in Soweto's streets ultimately required one to not be female at all. While women today recall their gender transgressions and appropriation of masculine characteristics with enthusiasm, these narratives may mask the less empowering consequences of their involvement in street-based confrontations: the lasting stigma they face in their communities; their deeply gendered experiences of detention, interrogation and torture as discussed in the following chapter; and any push-back they may have experienced from male comrades or *comtsotsis* in Soweto's streets. As female comrades' involvement in the township uprisings has been continuously neglected from historical narratives, their own memories may have responded by stressing agency over victimisation and physical strength over weakness.

6

The Prison Cell: Gender, Trauma, and Resistance

Shortly after the declaration of a state of emergency in South Africa in July 1985, Florence, a female comrade from Diepkloof, was rounded up by police along with fourteen male comrades. Then aged seventeen, she was taken to 'Sun City', as Diepkloof prison was colloquially known, where she spent the next two weeks in solitary confinement, her isolation broken only by regular trips to Protea Police Station for interrogation. As a COSAS leader, she explained, she experienced particularly harsh abuse: 'you think of anything, they've done it to me.' During her interrogations police forced her to strip naked, placed a wet sack over her head, beat her, and made her perform strenuous exercises. Yet despite such violence, she cast her arrest and time spent in detention as a central marker of her political commitment. In our first interview in 2014, she presented detention as a terrible experience, but one that could be overcome through a focus on the goals of the struggle and steadfast commitment to the liberation movement. 'I told myself that even if I die, I'm happy,' she stated. 'Because I'd be dying for a cause.' She narrated her experiences in detention fluidly and assuredly, without being specifically asked to do so, and as we were wrapping up the interview she added, 'The only thing that I was praying for was to come out of that alive, so that I can tell a story one day. Luckily, thank you for coming today.'[1]

A year later, I arrived back in Florence's Diepkloof home for a second interview but found her demeanour as an interviewee to be remarkably different. She opened by saying that she was so nervous and anxious to speak to me again that she had not slept the night before. 'I feel so traumatised after talking about it,' she admitted. 'I realised that there are things that even though I want to remember... I cannot, because they can't come back to my mind... When you relive those moments, they bring up sort of anger in you and they open a chapter that you never knew you had.'[2]

[1] Interview with Florence, Diepkloof, 8 May 2014.
[2] Interview with Florence, Diepkloof, 3 March 2015.

The involvement of girls and young women in South Africa's liberation struggle during the 1980s did not go unnoticed by South Africa's security forces, and under the subsequent states of emergency declared between 1985 and 1990 many young female activists were detained without trial and held in prison or police cells for periods ranging from a few days to several months. Of the approximately 49,000 people detained in the country from 1985 to 1990, 12.2 per cent were known to be female, with one third of these being girls under eighteen years old.[3] According to these figures, at least 2000 girls under the age of eighteen were detained without trial during the emergency period. However, this is likely a very conservative estimate. Police were known to lie about detainees' ages to reduce official numbers of children in prisons, and detainees' gender is not always recorded in archival documents. Further-more, many young people detained only briefly, and quickly shifted between different police stations for interrogation, were never officially recorded as having been arrested.[4] Once detained, female comrades were often beaten, tortured, interrogated, and placed under immense pressure to become police informers. They also experienced particularly gendered forms of emotional and physical abuse: they were denied feminine hygiene products; taunted about their presumed sexual promiscuity; told they were merely 'pawns' in the male-dominated struggle; and had their bodies violated through strip searches, forced exercise, and electric shocks to their breasts. Female comrades who had joined the struggle in part to overcome the feelings of powerlessness they experienced as girls could not hide from the vulnerability they faced in apartheid's carceral spaces. Detention forced them to once again contend with feelings of weakness and helplessness, something that the apartheid state was keenly aware of and explicitly used to undermine young women's political identities. The struggle femininities they had created and performed as female comrades were thus threatened in detention, as they were separated from their male comrades, made to feel acutely aware of their gender difference, and forced to contend with the specific vulnerabilities that came with being young black women held at the will of older white men.

This chapter details such experiences but is also concerned with how former comrades narrate their time in detention, and how the trauma and pain they suf-fered is incorporated into their memoires of the past. While detailing their painful experiences of detention, female comrades refuse to portray themselves simply

---

3   Merrett, 'Detention without trial in South Africa'; National Medical and Dental Association, 'The Treatment of Detainees,' April 1987, AG2523: S4.1, DPSC, HP; 'Come bend those bars,' *The Star*, 21 February 1988, AG2523: M1.14.1, DPSC, HP.

4   Fiona Ross, *Bearing Witness: Women and the Truth and Reconciliation Commission in South Africa* (London: Pluto Press, 2003), 61.

as victims of the apartheid state. Instead, they create redemptive narratives of their time spent in detention, in which the trauma they experienced is ultimately overcome through their survival and the furthering of their commitment to the struggle. Their accounts thus focus on more than just brutality and ill-treatment, as many women also detailed their strategies of resistance, the political education they received, and the bonds of camaraderie they formed in prison.

Florence's initial narrative during our first interview epitomised this. Yet her later disclosure of the difficultly she still faces in speaking about her past is also exemplary of the fissures in these redemptive narratives, and the complexities of giving voice to trauma. Female comrades, in their attempts to both present themselves as empowered women and conform their personal narratives to collective memories of the struggle, face particular pressures to conceal their vulnerability and fragility in favour of heroic narratives that help to have their involvement in the struggle publicly acknowledged. In talking about their detention, female comrades attempt to create neat narratives of pain and redemption. But when examined closely, one can still see the lingering effects of trauma and the unresolved feelings of anger, hatred, or sorrow in female comrades' stories, visible through the stalls, silences, or stuttering in their narratives. Their at times confusing accounts of their detention, or their oscillation between agency and victimhood, reflect their continuing attempts to grapple with their pasts, and the competing needs they have in sharing such stories: to have their status as activists acknowledged; to find some sort of healing through telling; or to simply attach meaning or words to unspeakable and unsharable experiences.

The Prison Cell as a Gendered Space: Attacking Struggle Femininity

Even prior to the declaration of a state of emergency in July 1985, the apartheid government had begun to target young school-based activists through detention without trial. In 1982, previous security legislation was reformulated and extended under the Internal Security Act, which allowed the state to indefinitely detain anyone for interrogation purposes, keeping them in solitary confinement without access to family or lawyers (Section 29). Under Sections 28 and 50, it also allowed police officers to detain preventively for up to 180 days anyone they suspected might commit a crime . By the end of 1984, the majority of COSAS' Soweto leadership had already been rounded up and detained.[5] In June 1985 the state's efforts to deter youth activists escalated, and many of COSAS's rank-and-file members were held in police stations and prisons across the country. Those detained were often held in multiple sites within apartheid's carceral system, taken from police station, to prison, and back again as they were repeatedly interrogated and then sequestered with little knowledge of how long they would be held for. While detention did not target children alone, archival evidence suggests that during the first state of emergency from July 1985 to March 1986, 60 per cent of all detainees were under the age of twenty-five, and 25 per cent, or approximately 2000 detainees, were sixteen years old or younger.[6] As the government launched a second state of emergency in June 1986, the targeting of children and youths became more indiscriminate, with both politicised and non-politicised students taken in for interrogation. By late 1986, simply being young, black and living in a township could warrant not only detention, but also abuse and often torture.[7] Once in detention, children and youths had little connection with the outside world; for many, their families were never told of their imprisonment. Investigations into the conditions in police and prison cells revealed overcrowding, poor medical attention, and inadequate diets.[8]

Substantial evidence on the treatment of young people in detention was gathered by the Detainees Parents Support Committee (DPSC), an organisation founded in 1981 by the relatives and friends of detained activists and officially affiliated to the newly formed United Democratic Front (UDF) in 1983. The organisation was especially active during the successive states of emergency in the 1980s, when it too became a target of state repression; it was banned by the apartheid state in 1988 yet continued to operate underground until 1990. Much of the DPSC's work involved gathering information about detention through taking statements from recently released detainees and their family members. Their archives contain thousands of statements made by former detainees (their 'daybooks'), along with statistics, reports, and publications on the escalating use of detention. It is here where girls and young women involved in township struggles finally become visible in the archival record; many of those whose stories are recorded in these files attest to being

---

5   South African Institute of Race Relations, *Survey of Race Relations 1984* (Johannesburg, 1985), 763.

6   'Sixth Special Report on State of Emergency,' 30 April 1987, AG2523: F1.4.4, DPSC, HP.

7   'Daybooks: June 1987–October 1987,' AG2523: G4, DPSC, HP.

8   *Ibid.*

COSAS members or activists, or were accused of being 'stone-throwers' by guards and police and were later charged with public violence.[9]

Within these archives, it first appears as though young comrades largely experienced similar forms of physical abuse in detention regardless of their gender. Female detainees, just as their male counterparts, were often beaten at the time of their arrest, held for months without trial, interrogated, tortured, and pressured to become informers. In one case where four girls and three boys were detained together, all were reported to have suffered beatings and electric shocks.[10] Describing her initial arrival at a police station, a female comrade from Diepkloof described, 'They hit us on the hands, legs, knees, also on the head...They don't care whether we are a woman or a man. Sometimes they'd use their shoes, kicking at you...Eh, they were so cruel.'[11] Archival evidence reveals only small differences in the punitive tactics employed against female and male youths. Female detainees were slightly more likely to be kept in solitary confinement, experience verbal abuse, be threatened with violence, blindfolded, deprived of sleep, or threatened with prolonged interrogation.[12]

Yet statistics alone cannot paint a full picture of the gendered nature of detention. Oral histories reveal that apartheid's detention centres were distinctly gendered spaces for young female detainees, who despite suffering under similar conditions as young men experienced and remember their confinement in remarkably different ways.[13] Historically, women detainees in Africa have been seen as triple deviants in that they are black, criminal, and female. Besides contravening state laws, they have also contravened expected norms of 'good' female behaviour, and consequently often experience the

[9]   For the history of the DPSC see AG2523: A, DPSC, HP; for the daybooks see AG2523: G, DPSC, HP.

[10]   'Repression Trends in the Transvaal Area, June–September 1986,' AG2523: F1.3.7, DPSC, HP.

[11]   Interview with Thobile, Diepkloof, 12 April 2014.

[12]   Don Foster and Diane Sandler, 'A Study of Detention and Torture in South Africa: Preliminary Report,' Institute of Criminology, UCT, 1985, AG2523: S4.2, DPSC, HP.

[13]   Sheila Meintjes and Beth Goldblatt, 'Gender and the Truth and Reconciliation Commission,' submission to the Truth and Reconciliation Commission, May 1996, <https://www.justice.gov.za/trc/hrvtrans/submit/gender.htm> [accessed 10 August 2014]; Natacha Filippi makes the same argument in regard to women incarcerated in Pollsmoor Prison during apartheid. Natacha Filippi, 'Women's Protests: Gender, Imprisonment and Resistance in South Africa (Pollsmoor Prison, 1970s–90s),' Review of African Political Economy 43:149 (2016): 436–450.

toughest conditions of detention.[14] Women incarcerated or detained for their involvement in liberation struggles are also 'doubly dangerous' because 'they oppose the regime as well as defy tolerated female behaviour.'[15] In apartheid's carceral spaces, South African gender relations were played out and exaggerated, as gender became a central facet of the prison's power dynamic. As in South African society more broadly, African women occupied the lowest rung of prisoner hierarchy. As one female comrade stated, 'being a black female, that means you are right at the bottom.'[16] Apartheid security forces were aware of the gendered power dynamics at play in detention, and deliberately used these to their advantage when interrogating women. For Soweto's female comrades, detention directly challenged their espousal of struggle femininity and the feelings of empowerment that came with it. Female comrades' memories of detention are distinguished from those of their male counterparts in their emphasis on their physical vulnerability, feelings of isolation, and bodily concerns particular to women. Their narratives are testimonies to systematic state efforts to undermine their gendered political identities through both physical and psychological violence.

Overall, the treatment of young female detainees was designed to constantly remind these activists that they were vulnerable women rather than the strong, brave, and gender-less or masculinised soldiers they cast themselves as. The apartheid state managed this through a number of strategies. First, the conditions of detention placed an emphasis on female comrades' bodies, marking these as different from male bodies and encouraging women to feel shame or humiliation in not being able to attain standards associated with 'good' femininity.[17] When first describing their experiences of detention, many female comrades focused on the lack of hygiene and domestic necessities in police and prison cells. One problem particular to female detainees was menstruation; the DPSC daybooks contain numerous complaints about the lack of feminine hygiene products available in detention cells. Florence too spoke of how she was not given any sanitary pads but was able to obtain them discreetly from older female activists during exercise periods. Her narrative offers insight into why hygiene concerns were voiced so much more frequently

14 Dior Konate, 'Ultimate Exclusion: Imprisoned Women in Senegal,' in Florence Bernault (ed), *A History of Prison and Confinement in Africa* (Portsmouth: Heinemann, 2003), 155; 161.

15 Mary Jane Treacy, 'Double Binds: Latin American Women's Prison Memoirs,' *Hypatia* 11:4 (1996): 136.

16 Interview with Florence, Diepkloof, 3 March 2015.

17 This was a wider tactic used against adult women in detention too. See Ross, *Bearing Witness*, 63–65.

by female detainees: 'You know, with guys it's easy, they can just shower and they're done,' she explained, suggesting that while a lack of hygiene posed no threat to male comrades' sense of self, it did to female detainees'.[18]

When asked what aspect of detention she found the most difficult, one interviewee, who was kept in solitary confinement for a combined period of ten months, responded, 'At first it was food [long pause]. The atmosphere in jail is not good anyway, because you'll be given one blanket. It was winter. The cells are *so* cold. That was the most painful thing there. One blanket – and this linen is so hard, it's not nice, you know, these grey sheets we were using.'[19] In the DPSC's daybooks, the absence of spare clothing, poor bedding, and insufficient washing facilities are often mentioned in young women's testimonies, yet rarely feature in men's. Female interviewees frequently lamented only having the clothes they were wearing at the time of their arrest or the lack of adequate blankets and bedding during the winter months. This focus on clothing and bedding was initially surprising given the seemingly more difficult experiences these women face in detention. Yet these narratives reveal state attempts to dehumanise or defeminise female detainees through a denial of hygiene or attacks against feminine domesticity. Girls' emphasis on keeping themselves and their cells clean suggests that in detention these young women felt the need to maintain or assert the femininity that was being attacked or denied by their imprisoners by emphasising their domesticity and hygiene. In Latin American women's memoirs, Mary Jane Treacy similarly found that female political prisoners strove to affirm their 'normal' femininity in response to warders' gendered attacks against them by 'assert[ing] their dignity and by emphasizing their hygiene and modesty within the filthy conditions of prison life.'[20] Maintaining cleanliness in detention may have been a particularly important means by which female detainees could hold on to their feminine identities as they came under attack from the police's gendered threats and assaults – even though these were markers of a more traditional, normative femininity rather than of the alternative, struggle femininity performed by female comrades in Soweto's streets. Furthermore, keeping clean was for some women the only control over their bodies they had in detention, and may have been a particularly important habit to maintain as a means of countering the loss of control they suffered during intense interrogation.

Another challenge of detention which was felt in an acutely gendered way by female comrades was isolation. Female comrades often described being alone in cells as more difficult than the beatings or torture they endured. While both male and female comrades were at times kept in solitary confinement, statistics

---

[18] Interview with Florence, Diepkloof, 3 March 2015.
[19] Interview with Sibongile, Johannesburg, 9 June 2015.
[20] Treacy, 'Double Binds,' 137; 139.

and interviews suggest that female activists experienced isolation more often than males. This can in part be attributed to state infrastructure: while prisons were accustomed to holding high numbers of male political prisoners in large, communal cells, they often did not have such spaces allocated specifically for females.[21] Consequently, a number of interviewees were kept in isolation throughout lengthy periods in detention. But solitary confinement also held different meanings for female comrades who, having struggled for equality with their male comrades and being eager to be accepted by them, were suddenly separated from them. While their male friends were kept together and could continue discussing strategy, girls and young women were physically, emotionally, and, perhaps most importantly, politically isolated. Consequently, their ability to maintain their sense of empowerment gained through becoming female comrades was threatened as their feelings of camaraderie and ties to a broader community of comrades were severed.

Throughout multiple interviews, Florence repeatedly stated that in the struggle she did not see herself as a girl or a woman but as an activist. Yet when she was detained with a number of her male comrades, and separated from them in prison, this gender-neutral narrative was challenged: 'That was when it dawned for the first time ever that I'm a woman,' she stated. 'We forgot that we're different sexes.'[22] Several interviewees also spoke of the 'social death' of being a female comrade in prison. Florence later stated, 'When you're in a challenging place, you need somebody to talk to. And I was, for me, I was like in a desert, all by myself.'[23] Bessie, a comrade who presented herself in interviews as particularly fearless and tough, also displayed a rare moment of vulnerability when talking about her detention. As a COSAS leader, Bessie experienced particularly harsh and prolonged punishment. She was arrested multiple times: in 1984 she spent six months in 'Sun City'; during the 1985 state of emergency she was held for another two weeks; and again in 1986 she was kept in John Vorster Square, where she spent six months in solitary confinement. While she was beaten and interrogated during her previous spells in detention, at John Vorster Square she was not. Yet she describes the months she spent there as the most difficult, the hardest part being 'the fact that we can't talk to anybody.' She continued, 'That was tough, ya, that tormented me...And that's when one got sick, in my head [sic]. I had the headaches,

---

[21] Evidence from interviews suggests that this was especially the case for those detained in 1985, but that from 1986 onwards, the state became more accustomed to young female political detainees and created communal cells in which to detain them.

[22] Interview with Florence, Diepkloof, 8 May 2014.

[23] *Ibid.*

everything. I was just so scared. I didn't know what was wrong with me.'[24] The difficulty of isolation for female comrades speaks to the collective nature of their empowerment, and the importance of camaraderie – with both each other and their male comrades – to their construction of alternative gender identities and feelings of liberation.

A third strategy used by the state was verbal taunts and threats specifically designed to attack female comrades' political identities. In their research on gender for the TRC, Sheila Meintjes and Beth Goldblatt found that when interrogating female detainees, apartheid security agents sought to purposefully undermine their sense of womanhood, dehumanise them, and destroy their sense of selves. Police were keenly aware of the gendered nature of power in carceral spaces and used this to their advantage. Attacks against female prisoners, 'were all assaults on the sexuality and sexual identity of women,' which were used to 'undermine their identity and integrity as human beings.'[25] As Temma Kaplan writes in regards to women's experiences in Chile, 'By reducing women to their bodies, regarding the female body as despicable, and sexualizing the violence against them, army intelligence attempted to transform a woman's identity from political activist to pathetic victim.'[26] In South Africa, police and prison guards forced female detainees to question their political commitment by casting them as insignificant, dispensable pawns in the male-dominated anti-apartheid struggle, or as sexual deviants who were using politics as a pretext for physical gratification and promiscuity. Interviewees were reluctant to recall the exact words or phrases used by security staff, preferring to just state that they were 'verbally abused' or 'sworn at'. But the specific phrases recalled by a select few women are very illuminating. As one female interviewee recounted, 'Yes, they used to swear at us. "Hey, you fucking bitch. Why are you doing this [being involved in politics]? You are so young. You are looking for men. You are not a comrade. You are not even political. You don't know anything but rubbish".' She later elaborated, 'They would say, "You're not a politician, you're just after men. You don't want to stay in your place".'[27]

Similar taunts were recollected by other female detainees, demonstrating how attempts by the Special Branch to purposefully undermine female prisoners' political identities were widespread. Mamani Kgomotso, a founding member of COSAS, was detained for five and a half months in 1979 and recalled, 'I was literally told that I was a bitch, I've actually joined the struggle

---

24 Interview with Bessie, Johannesburg, 25 April 2014.
25 Meintjes and Goldblatt, 'Gender and the Truth and Reconciliation Commission.'
26 Temma Kaplan, 'Acts of Testimony: Reversing the Shame and Gendering the Memory,' *Signs* 28:1 (2002): 188.
27 Interview with Thobile, Diepkloof, 12 April 2014.

to service these men sexually, nothing else. There's no woman or girl of my age who can be involved in politics.'[28] During the TRC, Thenjiwe Mtintso, the chairperson of the Gender Commission and formerly a commander of MK, attested, 'when they interrogated, they usually started by reducing your role as an activist. They weighted you [sic] according to their own concepts of womanhood.'[29] Some interviewees were keenly aware of how police and guards sought to undermine their gendered political identities. Florence described:

> Now you see, being a woman is…people can use that against you, make you feel that you've got the unfortunate gender politically. They will start telling you things about the opposite sex, brainwashing you, trying to tell you, 'No, they [male comrades] are using you'…They'll be saying those people are using you as a number because you're a woman.[30]

She continued by explaining how the police told her that the ANC were just using women like her as cannon fodder in their struggle. Such verbal attacks were designed to undermine the sense of empowerment female comrades gained from being involved in the struggle and make them question whether their male comrades really did take them seriously as political actors. Numerous interviewees described their isolation in detention or these deliberate attacks against their gendered or political identities as more threatening and damaging than physical abuse. This could be because such gendered attacks endangered their identity as female comrades more than blows alone could. As comrades, these women were prepared for the physical discomforts and pain that came with committing their lives to the struggle. But they were perhaps less prepared for having their sense of selves undermined through systematic attacks against their feminine identities.

Yet assaults on female comrades' gender identities went beyond verbal taunts or abuse. In apartheid's police and prison cells sexual violence was also routinely used against female prisoners. As Inger Agger highlights, sexual torture is not necessarily physical in nature, but includes any physical or psychological attempt to exploit one's sexuality.[31] The torture of women uses cultural norms about respectable femininity to cast women as deviant, often by identifying women's political activity as sexual activity.[32] Physical forms

---

[28] Mamani Kgomotso, in Mazibuko, *Spring Offensive*, 16.

[29] Antjie Krog, *Country of My Skull: Guilt, Sorrow, and the Limits of Forgiveness in the New South Africa* (New York: Three Rivers Press, 1998), 235.

[30] Interview with Florence, Diepkloof, 8 May 2014.

[31] Inger Agger, 'Sexual Torture of Political Prisoners: An Overview,' *Journal of Traumatic Stress* 2:3 (1989): 306.

[32] *Ibid.*, 313–314.

of sexual torture against women are often 'rooted in sadistic fantasies' and include rape, but more commonly stripping, body searches, beatings, and electric shocks.[33] The combination of violence and sexuality breaks down both women's gendered and political identities. It 'takes advantage of shame and guilt in connection with an active, feminine sexuality,' making women feel ashamed for being a 'whore'.[34]

Within apartheid's carceral spaces, the use of sexualised torture varied greatly. The most common form perpetrated against young female detainees was undressing, either when female warders performed routine strip searches or when male police forced girls to take off some or all of their clothing during interrogation. Detainees recall both of these experiences as being particularly humiliating. In her written statement to the DPSC, a fifteen-year-old girl recounted, 'Treatment was bad. Warders used to come and harass us, they used to strip us naked daily and search our bodies.'[35] Another young woman, eighteen-years-old at the time, recounted through similar language, 'The harassment in jail was so bad that they used to come to the cells daily and make us strip and check our bodies. This was too much.'[36] In a similar case, the DPSC recorded the experiences of another young woman: 'At central prison they would have to queue up in the cell while women police would look through the cells – shake out the bed linen and make them undress, made them open their thighs, etc.' The only direct quote taken from the detainee followed: 'It was humiliating.'[37]

Soweto's female comrades endured similar experiences. The majority of those who were detained without trial experienced forced stripping and electric shocks – often to their breasts. As Florence matter-of-factly explained during our first interview, 'They strip you naked. They blindfold you. They take a sack, dampen it, they put it over your head, they tie it. They start beating you.'[38] For female comrades, such experiences of sexualised torture were particularly traumatic. In our second interview, Florence again turned to discussing her distinctly gendered experience of detention and interrogation. Talking about being taken out of her cell for questioning, she recalled, 'when you go into that room with guys and they tell you to take off your clothes, and you are,

[33] Jean Franco, 'Gender, Death and Resistance: Facing the Ethical Vacuum,' in Juan E. Corradi et al (eds), *Fear at the Edge: State Terror and Resistance in Latin America* (Berkeley: University of California Press, 1992), 109.

[34] Agger, 'Sexual Torture,' 313; Treacy, 'Double Binds,' 139.

[35] 'Daybooks: November 1985–May 1986,' AG2523: G5, DPSC, HP.

[36] 'Daybooks: November 1985–May 1986,' AG2523: G5, DPSC, HP.

[37] 'Daybooks: June–August 1986,' AG2523: G6, DPSC, HP.

[38] Interview with Florence, Diepkloof, 8 May 2014.

you know [sighs].' She paused here, and stumbled with her words, discussing how 'a war is a war', before returning to this memory and concluding, 'they traumatised us, those people'.[39]

Many women interviewed shared their experiences of sexualised torture and interrogation methods without being asked specifically to do so. Yet when it came to speaking about these particularly gendered experiences, interviewees often lost the fluency and confidence present in the rest of their narratives. As Goldblatt and Meintjes demonstrate, the very strategy of targeting women's sexual identities during interrogation and torture was based on a belief that women would be unable to talk about and share such experiences.[40] Some female comrades recounted their experiences with brief, formulaic and unemotional language. Admitting to the vulnerability she felt in prison, Lucy – a COSAS leader – stated:

> They would torture me. And I was so scared by that time because when they torture us, they used to strip us naked. As a female comrade, there are about six, seven, eight male police stripping you naked. They touch your breasts. They put…the wet cloth onto your face to cover your head… When you breathe, you breathe that water from that wet cloth…On top, here on the body [motions to her chest], we were naked…And they were doing that every night.[41]

She continued, 'They used to come [to take her to interrogation]…I was so scared that they might rape us, because of the things that happened to other comrades.' Here, Lucy refers to general knowledge and fears of rape in detention rather than to any specific attacks against herself or her fellow female comrades. When asked if she was ever afraid of being raped, another female comrade provided a similar narrative:

> We were! Because you go alone in that room, that room, they used to call it the dark room. You go alone with them. They will take you to the dark room and ask you questions. If you don't want to talk they strip, they tell you to strip your clothes, and you must strip everything. And they will pour you with water, put the electric wires, and start shocking you.[42]

---

[39]   Interview with Florence, Diepkloof, 3 March 2015.
[40]   Beth Goldblatt and Sheila Meintjes, 'Women: one chapter in the history of South Africa? A critique of the Truth and Reconciliation Commission Report,' Draft paper presented at CSVR/History Workshop Conference, 'The TRC: Commissioning the Past,' 13 June 1999.
[41]   Interview with Lucy, Fleurhof, 7 April 2014.
[42]   Interview with Ntebaleng, Diepkloof, 15 April 2014.

Like Lucy, Ntebaleng responds in the collective, answering that 'we' were afraid of rape. She also does not provide details about anyone she personally knew who was raped, but rather testifies generally to the fact that women were sexually assaulted in detention. When asked a similar question, Zanele responded that her and her fellow comrades were also afraid of rape:

> Because others, they tell us that, 'hey, you know, they took me to interrogation and they took me to wherever and they've raped me.' You know? But it never happened to me. But I was waiting for it, because I was asking myself, why would they do that to others? That means that one day that it will come to me. But they usually do that. I can say maybe I was so fortunate.[43]

Meintjes and Goldblatt similarly found that interviewees spoke of their constant fear of rape and knowledge of it happening to other detainees, but rarely of specific attacks against themselves or their friends.[44] They argue that coming forward with personal experiences of rape would have been very challenging for women, not only due to the shame and trauma attached to such experiences but also because being raped by a state official could be seen as a form of collusion or 'selling-out' within the heightened political context of the struggle. The women who testified to being raped in detention before the TRC are likely only a very small sample of those who actually experienced such violence – making it impossible to know how many female detainees were ever raped. Furthermore, state security agents themselves seem to have deliberately fostered this generalised atmosphere of fear and the ever-present threat of sexual violence in detention. For female comrades, such fears of rape would have resonated the same anxieties they felt as girls and young women growing up in Soweto – the very fears that in part motivated their initial involvement in the struggle. Their experiences in detention thus eroded much of the empowerment they had created for themselves through their political activism, reducing them to the feelings of vulnerability and powerlessness they had been struggling against.

Resistance and Redemption

Yet interviewees rarely centred their narratives of detention on their status as vulnerable victims of violence. Rather, the brief moments in which they spoke about the trauma they suffered were generally followed by accounts of their survival, resistance, and triumph in the face of such horrific experiences. In the post-apartheid period, South Africa has witnessed a profusion of struggle

---

[43]   Interview with Zanele, Diepkloof, 12 April 2014.
[44]   Meintjes and Goldblatt, 'Gender and the Truth and Reconciliation Commission.'

memoirs and autobiographies, which are often centred on long periods spent in detention or prison.[45] Many of these works share a similar narrative form, in which prisons are depicted as spaces of pain and humiliation, but also spaces of resistance in which prisoners were able to further their political struggle and exercise agency. This collective culture of remembrance in South Africa, in which former activists are encouraged to tell redemptive, liberating stories, has had tangible effects on female comrades' own recollections of their time spent in detention. Female comrades' accounts of detention follow similar narratives paths, from their arrest, to their torture and imprisonment, and ultimately concluding with their survival and the reinforcing of their political commitment. As with South African prison memoirs, these women's narratives are 'also testimonies of surviving in desperate circumstances, of making meaning from suffering and above all of *active* people somehow able to strategize and resist.'[46] The stories they told of their isolation, humiliation, and physical vulnerability were often followed by accounts of the bonds they developed with their fellow detainees, the political education they received, or their strengthened resolve once they were released. As Jocelyn Alexander writes of African prison writing more broadly, their stories 'forge a narrative arch which – in shorthand – tells of the triumph of the "rebel writer" over oppression.'[47]

Conforming to such narrative conventions, argues Sarah Nuttall, can actually help people coping with trauma to heal in a variety of ways. First, memory itself can be used as a form of resistance, a tool to restore agency to former prisoners.[48] Rather than succumb to the feelings of vulnerability instilled in them in prisons and police cells, female comrades refuse to be cast as weak or helpless. In their narratives of detention, they preference memories in which

[45] See Breyten Breytenbach, The True Confessions of an Albino Terrorist (London: Faber and Faber, 1984); Ruth First, One Hundred and Seventeen Days: An Account of Confinement and Interrogation under South African Ninety-Day Detention Law (London: W.H. Allen, 1975); Mandela, Long Walk to Freedom; Indres Naidoo, Island in Chains: Ten years on Robben Island (London: Penguin, 1982); Albie Sachs, The Jail Diary of Albie Sachs (London: Paladin, 1990).

[46] Don Foster and Donald Skinner, 'Detention and Violence: Beyond Victimology,' in N. Chabani Manganyi and Andre du Toit (eds), Political Violence and the Struggle in South Africa (New York: St. Martin's Press, 1990), 219.

[47] Jocelyn Alexander, 'Political Prisoners' Memoirs in Zimbabwe: Narratives of Self and Nation,' Cultural and Social History 5:4 (2008): 395–396.

[48] Paul Gready, 'Autobiography and the "Power of Writing": Political Prison Writing in the Apartheid Era,' Journal of Southern African Studies 19:3 (1993): 521; Sarah Nuttall, 'Telling "free" stories? Memory and Democracy in South African Autobiography since 1994,' in Sarah Nuttall and Carli Coetzee (eds), Negotiating the Past: The Making of Memory in South Africa (Oxford: Oxford University Press, 1998), 82.

they defied state authority or clearly demonstrated their agency, even in tight corners. In her testimony before the TRC, Sandra Adonis (who became involved in the struggle in 1985 at the age of fifteen), narrated how she was arrested while at home:

> Whilst I was in the bath he [policeman] started shouting from outside, if you do not finish up now, I will come in there and I will fetch you…then I realised that this door could not lock. I said to him, if you dare enter this bathroom I will certainly lay charges against you for attempted rape, because I did not have any clothes on.

While being interrogated, a police officer threatened to hit her. She told the truth commission: 'so I said to him, well I will charge you for assault.'[49] Rather than focusing on any feelings of fear or embarrassment she had during these moments, Sandra centres her narrative on her own defiance and legal awareness.

In constructing narratives of resistance, female comrades also tell very particular stories about how they were initially arrested that cast them as active agents, not passive victims. Rather than being ashamed of being caught or speaking about their fears of what was to come, they cast their arrest as a badge of honour, reframing detention as an affirmation of their political importance. Tonosi, a female comrade from Diepkloof, emphasised how when she was arrested, 'there was eighteen cars that came [sic]. Eighteen.'[50] Florence also depicted her arrest in this self-affirming way. She repeated how she was the first leader in Diepkloof to be arrested following the declaration of the 1985 state of emergency, and how she was the only girl detained with fourteen boys. She highlighted how when the police came for her, she was taken to Protea Police Station in a convoy of four cars, 'just for me'. With pride, she spoke of how she overheard police bragging to their colleagues about how they had finally arrested her, yelling 'that Florence! Did you get that Florence!?' She continued by describing that when she was taken from her cell to be interrogated, guards would chain her at the wrists and ankles, and walk her down the corridor with their guns aimed on her. 'I don't know if Mandela's own child would be treated like that,' she stated. 'That's when I realised how much we've worked.'[51]

Other female comrades focused on their individual agency by highlighting their ability to manipulate their experiences of detention for their own ends. During her detention in Protea Police Station, Bessie explained, 'The only time we could go outside is when we were sick. Sometimes we played sick. Then we'd go to the hospital, and it will be such an experience.' At times, she

[49] Sandra Adonis, TRC Youth Hearings, 22 May 1997.
[50] Interview with Tonosi, Diepkloof, 3 May 2014.
[51] Interview with Florence, Diepkloof, 8 May 2014.

was able to adopt a more stereotypically feminine identity that she used to her advantage with policemen. She described how it was generally black security police who would take her to the doctor. Seeing a teenage girl, 'they would be smiling. You could see that they wanted to, you know?' she said, raising her eyebrows and implying their sexual interest. 'And you would ask for favours,' she described, exploiting the police's obvious desire.[52]

Some women also cast detention and interrogation as a litmus test of their political commitment, focusing on their power to withstand questioning rather than any weakness they displayed. Florence emphasised her strength to not break under pressure. She described how when detained, those who only joined the struggle out of a sense of adventure or for opportunistic purposes would quickly confess under torture. But with comrades like herself who 'joined the organisation for a purpose...they won't break you.'[53] For female comrades, demonstrating their commitment to the struggle through their tolerance of torture was a particularly important marker of their political identity. By emphasising their power to resist pain and the temptation to divulge information under duress, women could demonstrate that they were not merely gossip-prone young women incapable of keeping secrets and susceptible to breaking under interrogation as male comrades sometimes cast them as. Rather, they were committed, serious political actors. Furthermore, by centring their narratives of detention on their political commitment and indispensability to the struggle, female interviewees also countered warders or policemen's taunts that they were nothing but cannon fodder or pawns in the struggle. By highlighting the sacrifice they were prepared to make for the struggle – their willingness to die – they also stake a claim to this central characteristic of comrade culture that was deemed to be exclusively masculine, and borrow the narrative of sacrifice and heroic resistance that is often central to dominant narratives of men's political imprisonment.[54] As Lucy emphasised when speaking about police attempts to make her an informant, 'So I told them straight, I'm not going to betray my comrades...If it's time for me to die now, you better kill me...You know, I was so dedicated to the struggle, whereby I was not scared that even if they kill me...I was really not scared.'[55] By emphasising her lack of fear, Lucy takes control away from the police in her narrative of detention, and refuses to be cast as a victim of intimidation and torture.

[52]   Interview with Bessie, Johannesburg, 25 April 2014.
[53]   Interview with Florence, Diepkloof, 8 May 2014.
[54]   Srila Roy, *Remembering Revolution: Gender, Violence and Subjectivity in India's Naxalbari Movement* (New Delhi: Oxford University Press, 2013), 148.
[55]   Interview with Lucy, Fleurhof, 7 April 2014.

In addition to using memory itself as a form of resistance and a means of restoring one's agency, a second key way in which female comrades' memories of detention match those commonly found in South African prison narratives is in their emphasising of their connections to other prisoners and the bonds of solidarity they forged in carceral spaces. A primary objective of detention and torture is to isolate the victim by deconstructing their cultural identity and attacking the collective dimension of their sense of self.[56] But by emphasising their collective identity as part of the broader struggle, and highlighting the bonds prison created between activists, prisoners can challenge warders' attempts to isolate them from each other and from their political cause. Despite attesting to the hardship their isolation in detention caused, female comrades also spoke of the joy they felt at having even brief moments of communication or connection with their fellow detainees. Several women spoke of how, when kept in large communal cells with other female activists, they would sing political songs to keep their spirits up. Even in solitary confinement, comrades found ways to communicate with those in the cells next to them. As Bessie explained, 'But we could talk through the windows, you know, we'd shout and we gave each other names then we'd talk through the windows. It was tough, but we were motivated by knowing that the struggle continues… And I think we grew stronger day by day when we were [in detention].'[57]

Female detainees also took pride in caring for other, often younger girls in detention. Writing about Latin American women's experiences, Treacy argues that taking on such caring roles not only furthers feelings of solidarity, but also 'allows prisoners to maintain their humanity and therefore to triumph, no matter how harsh their circumstances.'[58] Lucy, the leader of COSAS' women's section in Soweto, spoke of the mothering role she played in prison: 'When I met other comrades during lunch, I can see that some of them were younger than me. I have to try and comfort them because I was the leader to them. Some of them, they were crying…I have to tell them, "No, everything will be fine. Just hold on".'[59]

Treacy's work from Latin America also demonstrates a third way in which conforming to traditional narrative forms can help prisoners cope with trauma: by linking their experiences to a redemptive future, and thus deriving meaning from their suffering.[60] South Africa's female comrades create a narrative

---

[56] Françoise Sironi and Raphaëlle Branche, 'Torture and the Borders of Humanity,' *International Social Science Journal* 54:174 (2002): 539–540.
[57] Interview with Bessie, Johannesburg, 25 April 2014.
[58] Treacy, 'Double Binds,' 134.
[59] Interview with Lucy, Fleurhof, 7 April 2014.
[60] Treacy, 'Double Binds,' 135.

wholeness by linking their memories of detention to the goals of the wider liberation struggle and their hopes for a better future. One woman stated, 'If I die, I will die, but I know that freedom is there.'[61] After describing herself as a 'walking corpse' following her interrogation, Nonkululeko stated, 'but I survived. Because I knew what I wanted…and we are eating the fruits now, of what we wanted then.'[62] Many women spoke of how they found strength in knowing their detention had a political purpose. As Bessie recalled, 'it was tough, but we were motivated by knowing that the struggle continues. I'm here for a just cause. And nothing will deter me.'[63]

Finally, these narratives may also be used by former detainees as a means of reintegrating themselves into a wider community or network of liberation activists. By aligning their personal memories with collective narrative trends, they assert their belonging to a group that is celebrated and venerated in post-apartheid South Africa, a group that also includes the likes of Nelson and Winnie Mandela, Albertina and Walter Sisulu, and many other leaders and struggle icons. This is perhaps more important for female comrades than other groups of former prisoners, in that it allows them to have their con-tributions to the struggle recognised alongside these great men and women, and to contest their marginalisation from history. They do this not only by conforming their narratives to the pain-survival-redemption path, but also by drawing on more specific tropes common to popular prison memoirs. One particular example of this can be found in how former comrades dis-cuss the political education they received in detention. Thanks to Mandela and others' autobiographies, and to Fran Lisa Buntman's seminal work on Robben Island, collective narratives of imprisonment in South Africa today often focus on prisoners' success in transforming carceral spaces from 'hell-holes' into 'universities' – spaces for personal and political development rather than destruction.[64] Khosi, a female comrade from Pimville, spoke about the education she received from her fellow female comrades while in detention: 'actually, when we were arrested, that's where I started to learn more. We had comrades, we were still young when we were there, when we are sitting and they talked.'[65] Similarly, another comrade from Zola who was detained just one week after attending her first COSAS meeting insisted that prison was 'not bad' because it allowed undisturbed time for strategizing and political

[61] Interview with Rethabile, Diepkloof, 1 May 2014.
[62] Interview with Nonkululeko, Diepkloof, 8 April 2014.
[63] Interview with Bessie, Johannesburg, 25 April 2014.
[64] Fran Lisa Buntman, *Robben Island and Prisoner Resistance to Apartheid* (Cambridge: Cambridge University Press, 2003).
[65] Interview with Khosi, Orlando East, 1 May 2014.

discussion. Male comrades too drew on this popular narrative, with one explicitly stating, 'we turned prisons into universities', and other describing jail as 'like a university', where days were filled with political education.[66]

For female comrades, narrating their time in detention in these ways held particular importance in that it allowed them not only to come to terms with their trauma, but also to reassert their struggle femininity and reclaim their feelings of empowerment. In his work on political prisoners' memoirs, Gready emphasises the 'oppositional power' former detainees can claim in writing their own accounts of confinement that counter the state's official narrative and restore political ground to the prisoner.[67] Female comrades' narratives successfully recover their gendered political identities: their emphasis on camaraderie and connection resists state attempts to isolate them; and their focus on moments of agency overshadows any feelings of weakness or helplessness. Yet in addition to regaining control over their narratives from the apartheid state, female comrades are also regaining control from male comrades, their families, and their communities, and countering the negative, disparaging narratives such people have constructed about them. Their narratives of detention and of their ultimate triumph in the face of adversity are thus central to their wider stories of themselves as female comrades. By constantly framing their experiences in terms of their struggle femininity, highlighting their indispensability to the struggle by inserting themselves into male-dominated narratives while also emphasising their female identities and exceptionalism, they reassert their own sense of selves in contrast to any wider perceptions of them as weak, frivolous, or ill-suited to political activity.

'There are things in life that are better left unsaid'

These complete, redemptive narratives help former prisoners to heal and contend with their past experiences. Yet they may also be used by interviewees to shift our attention away from the lingering effects of the traumatic experiences they endured in prison and police cells. As Treacy writes, women's retelling of such experiences can also be used 'to pretend the trauma does not exist, that one has recovered, that all is well.'[68] Buntman agrees that in South Africa, 'the strains of imprisonment tend to be well hidden,' masked beneath these tales of agency and empowerment.[69] This is very much the case for female comrades who, in their desire to be acknowledged as

---

[66] Interview with Themba, Orlando East, 6 April 2015.
[67] Gready, 'Autobiography and the "Power of Writing",' 493.
[68] Treacy, 'Double Binds,' 141.
[69] Buntman, *Robben Island*, 77.

activists, have an overall tendency to downplay emotions or experiences that could be taken as feminine, including weakness, fear, or grief, and to – at least at first – hide from view their lingering trauma.

This raised difficult issues surrounding the ethics of conducting oral history interviews with victims of violence. Most interviewees brought up their experiences of detention without prompting – the time they spent in detention was an essential chapter in their wider life histories. If an interviewee did not themselves mention detention, I would ask them if they were ever arrested or detained. In the rare case that an interviewee responded 'yes' but did not themselves seem to want to elaborate on the topic, I did not press them to do so. I also used the technique of 'circling around' specific or painful questions – asking simply if interviewees had been detained, and what detention was like, rather than requesting specific information about beatings, solitary confinement, or torture. As Jack Douglas highlights, when narrators are comfortable, they will often answer questions without being directly asked.[70] At times interviewees became noticeably upset or sad but continued to narrate their experiences, and in these instances I followed the advice of South African oral historian Sean Field by continuing to listen to their stories until they came to a natural pause. I would then acknowledge their sadness and offer the option to pause or end the interview – an offer no comrade took during my research.[71] Field also reminds us that while oral history can resemble psychotherapy at times, historians are not trained counsellors. 'Oral historians generally do not – and should not – have healing or therapeutic aims,' he argues.[72] Field critiques the TRC for offering 'healing' to South Africans in exchange for their testimony and advises historians against repeating this mistake. Nevertheless, historians can show empathy and listen to the painful narratives shared with them as a way of 'bearing witness' to trauma. Doing so can at times 'offer subtle support to interviewees' efforts to recompose their sense of self and to regenerate agency.' Yet historians must accept that 'there is no "cure" or "closure"' to this pain, and that 'silences and uncomfortable emotions will remain' in the interview.[73]

---

[70]   Jack Douglas, *Creative Interviewing* (Beverly Hills: Sage Publications, 1985), 138. See also Valerie Yow, 'Ethics and Interpersonal Relationships in Oral History Research,' *The Oral History Review* 22:1 (1995): 51–66.

[71]   Sean Field, *Oral History, Community, and Displacement: Imagining Memories in Post-Apartheid South Africa* (New York: Palgrave Macmillan, 2012), 159

[72]   Sean Field, 'Disappointed Remains: Trauma, Testimony, and Reconciliation in Post-Apartheid South Africa,' in Donald A. Ritchie (ed), *Oxford Handbook of Oral History* (Oxford: Oxford University Press, 2011), 150.

[73]   Field, *Oral History, Community, and Displacement*, 153; 162.

Trauma, Field argues, is distinguished from other painful experiences in its 'rupturing of an individual's sense of internal and external worlds.'[74] It refers specifically to 'the self-altering, even self-shattering experiences of violence, injury and harm.'[75] The establishing of South Africa's TRC in 1996 prompted a flourish in academic studies of trauma, memory, and history in the country.[76] Archbishop Desmond Tutu, in his opening address to the TRC, declared, 'every South African has to some extent or other been traumatized. We are a wounded people.'[77] Through studying women's testimonies given before the TRC, scholars have produced a rich body of literature on how women articulate (or in many cases remain silent about) the violence they experienced or witnessed during apartheid.[78] Yet the focus on trauma in the country has overwhelmingly been on the TRC and the collective 'healing' of the nation through the public recollections of traumatic experiences by the select few who testified before the Commission. This has left a large gap in understanding how South Africans deal with trauma in their everyday lives. We know little about the more private cultures of trauma in the country – what is or is not taboo to speak about, who people share their traumatic experiences with, and what forms of therapy or healing people seek on their own. Despite the TRC's promotion of public sharing, it seems that speaking of one's trauma outside of such spaces remains proscribed. As Buntman writes, 'Grappling with the past was and is made all the more difficult because South Africa lacks a culture where addressing past trauma is acceptable.'[79]

---

[74] *Ibid.*, 153.

[75] Leigh Gilmore, *The Limits of Autobiography: Trauma and Testimony* (Ithaca and London: Cornell University Press, 2001), 6.

[76] Richard Wilson, *The Politics of Truth and Reconciliation in South Africa: Legitimizing the Post-Apartheid State* (Cambridge: Cambridge University Press, 2001); Krog, *Country of My Skull*; Pumla Godobo-Madikizela, 'Re-Membering the Past: Nostalgia, Traumatic Memory and the Legacy of Apartheid,' *Peace and Conflict: Journal of Peace Psychology* 18 (2012): 252–267; Pumla Godobo-Madikizela, 'Language Rules: Witnessing about Trauma on South Africa's TRC,' *River Teeth: A Journal of Non-Fiction Narrative* 8 (2007): 25–33; Deborah Posel, 'History as Confession: The Case of the South African Truth and Reconciliation Commission,' *Public Culture* 20:1 (2008): 119–141.

[77] Wilson, *The Politics of Truth and Reconciliation*, 14.

[78] Ross, *Bearing Witness*; Motsemme, 'The Mute always Speak'; Annalisa Oboe, 'The TRC Women's Hearings as Performance and Protest in the New South Africa,' *Research in African Literatures* 38:3 (2007): 60–76; Annie E. Coombes, 'Witnessing History/Embodying Testimony: Gender and Memory in Post-Apartheid South Africa,' *Journal of the Royal Anthropological Institute* 17 (2011): 92–112.

[79] Buntman, *Robben Island*, 77.

Central to the experience of trauma is the difficultly of adequately articulating it. In her seminal work *The Body in Pain*, Elaine Scarry contends that one of the primary purposes of torture and confinement is to deconstruct a detainee's sense of self, world, and language through the infliction of pain. Torture thus makes that pain unspeakable; 'whatever pain achieves, it achieves in part through its unsharability, and it ensures this unsharability through its resistance to language.'[80] Scholars of trauma highlight the exceptional nature of traumatic memories, which are often contradictory and fragmented, and narrated in non-linear or even non-verbal ways.[81] As Roberta Culbertson writes, 'violence, violation, and trauma…live on in the victim survivor in ways that confound ordinary notions of memory and narrative, or to which ordinary narrative is simply inadequate.'[82] Verbal markers of trauma found in victims' testimonies can include a loss or absence of recollections altogether, a form of amnesia, in which they are either unwilling or unable to remember traumatic events; 'intrusion', as memories are recounted as if the survivor is having a flashback or reliving the traumatic event in the present; or a 'dissociation' or distancing from their experiences, as their traumatic memories are compartmentalised, or stored as isolated fragments that are not integrated with the survivor's sense of self.[83] Others may demonstrate such dissociation through a depersonalisation of their own narratives, as survivors testify generally to atrocities committed but not to their specific individual experiences.[84]

These verbal displays of trauma were evident in many interviewees' narratives of their time in detention. Particularly in their accounts of sexualised torture, we can see their dissociation from events as they speak about what happened to 'us', 'you', or 'we' rather than specifically to themselves as individuals. Even the perpetrators of this violence are depersonalised, almost always simply referred to as 'they' by interviewees. The more complete destruction of language through pain was evident in the recollections of several interviewees

80   Elaine Scarry, *The Body in Pain: The Making and Unmaking of the World* (New York: Oxford University Press, 1987), 4; See also Paul Gready, *Writing as Resistance: Life Stories of Imprisonment, Exile, and Homecoming from Apartheid South Africa* (Lanham: Lexington Books, 2003).

81   Judith Lewis Herman, *Trauma and Recovery: From Domestic Abuse to Political Terror* (London: Pandora, 1992), 1; 37.

82   Roberta Culbertson, 'Embodied Memory, Transcendence, and Telling: Recounting Trauma, Re-Establishing the Self,' *New Literary History* 26:1 (1995): 171.

83   Herman, *Trauma and Recovery*, 37–46; Culbertson, 'Embodied Memory, Transcendence, and Telling,' 169–170; Bessel A. Van der Kolk and Rita Fisler, 'Dissociation and the Fragmentary Nature of Traumatic Memories: Overview and Explanatory Study,' *Journal of Traumatic Stress* 8:4 (1995): 510.

84   Kaplan, 'Acts of Testimony,' 180.

whose speech became particularly vague, brief, or distant when talking about detention. Speaking about the four months she spent in solitary confinement, one female COSAS member simply stated, 'Life in jail was not so good. Anyway, it's jail.'[85] Another female interviewee, who was otherwise particularly proficient and fluent during our interviews, spoke about detention with obvious difficulty. When talking about her time in prison, and especially about the physical abuse she suffered, her language lost its eloquence as she began to stumble, struggled to find words, and descended into sparse descriptions. Describing her detention during the state of emergency she narrated, 'That was a tough one. Um [long pause] one was beaten, one was shocked – electric shocks. Um [pause] taken for about four days every time [for interrogation]. You know when they take you, you're going to suffer.'[86] In addition to stalling and struggling to find words, she also speaks in an impersonal tone, using 'one' rather than 'I', similar to the interviewees cited above.

Sometimes, the silence surrounding painful memories was almost total in interviews. While many women included narratives of their detention in their life histories, others did not. Towards the end of an interview with a female comrade from Naledi, I asked:

Emily: Were you ever detained?

Mamosa: Ya (speaking very softly)

Emily: Can you talk about it or no?

Mamosa: No, I can't talk about it.

Emily: Because it's painful?

Mamosa: Ya, it was painful, oh! It was bad, a bad situation.[87]

Such silences around female comrades' experiences in detention are not only created in the specific dynamics of an oral history interview with a white, female outsider. The unsharability of pain was also demonstrated in a different way during an interview with a male comrade who still lives in Diepkloof and has remained close with many of his former comrades. He testified to suffering from particularly brutal abuse during his own interrogation, including stripping and electric shocks. Yet when asked if his female comrades suffered from similar torture in detention he replied, 'no female has told me that she

---

[85] Interview with Sibongile, Johannesburg, 9 June 2015.
[86] Interview with Bessie, Johannesburg, 25 April 2014.
[87] Interview with Mamosa, Naledi, 18 June 2015.

was having these things…never, no.'[88] His testimony illuminates the cultural taboos women face in speaking about detention and suggests that some female interviewees may feel more comfortable sharing their experiences of torture, and particularly that of a sexual nature, with a female outsider than a male insider. Yet we still know too little about private cultures of trauma in South Africa to fully understand the dynamics at play here.

It is also important to briefly acknowledge that male comrades too endured harrowing experiences in apartheid's police and prison cells. Overall, male interviewees were less forthcoming with their personal experiences of abuse or torture than women, perhaps due to the gendered dynamics of speaking to a female researcher. They predominantly spoke about detention within the framework of political resistance – speaking about the prison as a site where their commitment to the struggle was deepened or their education furthered. When men did speak about being interrogated, their narratives were at times even more reticent than those of female interviewees. One interviewee in particular seemed to struggle to find the words to convey his experience: 'And then in 1986 we were re-arrested. I was also re-arrested. And that was a bad one because in that one, we were beaten up. Maybe to describe it, severely beaten up – it's a lousy word to describe that. We were tortured. We were tortured.' Here, Themba became very quiet, and his speech grew increasingly laborious. He continued by simply describing the situation as 'very bad', and repeated simple phrases such as 'we were beaten up', and 'it was difficult'. Throughout his description of detention, he took numerous long pauses, and only spoke very softly despite being a confident narrator throughout the rest of his interview.[89] Themba's narrative of detention was amongst the most fragmented and non-fluent of all former activists interviewed. The narrative he provides is frozen in the sense that it uses the same words and stereotyped phrases over and over again; while his other memories of the struggle are fluent and assured, his detention memories are static and muted.[90] With tears in his eyes he continued, 'And unfortunately, some of those things, we live with them, even today [long pause]. Ya, [sighs] it was a difficult thing, mmm. We were severely beaten up.'

Themba's difficultly to find the language to speak about his interrogation is not only indicative of traumatic memory, but also of the cultural taboos that govern where and with whom men, as well as women, are allowed to share narratives of vulnerability and victimisation. While much emphasis has been

[88] Interview with Moses, Diepkloof, 19 April 2014.
[89] Interview with Themba, Diepkloof Extension, 6 April 2015.
[90] Herman identifies such 'frozen' narratives as a key marker of traumatic memory. Herman, *Trauma and Recovery*, 37–38.

placed on women's difficulty in sharing such stories, Lynne Segal emphasises that 'men too have tended to remain silent about such bodily disintegration and personal trauma.'[91] Due to the prevalence of gendered stereotypes regarding victims and perpetrators, men are often not recognised or are even dismissed as victims of abuse, and are thus particularly reluctant to disclose any traumatic experiences.[92] Furthermore, gendered socialisation encourages men to adopt particularly stoic and strong masculinities, leaving men who do speak about their trauma at risk of being seen as weak, less masculine, or homosexual (particularly in cases of sexual abuse).[93] Having already been de-masculinised by their experiences in detention, Soweto's male comrades may have wanted to protect their gender identities from further destabilisation, and thus not recounted any particularly personal or emotional narratives of abuse to a female outsider during interviews. However, those male comrades who did express feelings of fear or victimisation during interviews complicate existing assumptions about struggle masculinity and demonstrate how it was a gender identity that was fragile and susceptible to attack, and an ideal that young male activists aspired to rather than constantly embodied.

While emphasising prisoner resistance and agency, it is thus important not to lose sight of the physical and psychological pain young people endured in apartheid's carceral spaces. Despite presenting themselves as defiant or empowered, interviewees simultaneously displayed the lasting wounds of their detention. For some, their bodies are constant reminders of the pain they endured; during interviews, I was shown scars and crooked noses resulting from abuse during interrogation and told about lingering health problems such as difficultly hearing and even infertility. As Roy argues, even when people fail to find the language to describe their suffering, 'the pain of torture is literally inscribed on the body where it leaves its mark, and it is the body that remembers.'[94] Some female comrades openly acknowledged the affects detention continues to have on their emotional and mental wellbeing. Nonkululeko concluded our interview by stating, 'Because really, I need counsel [sic]. But I never got counselling. Because sometimes, this thing comes, flashes, you see?'[95]

91 Lynne Segal, 'Gender, War and Militarism: Making and Questioning the Links,' *Feminist Review* 88 (2008): 32.
92 Pauline Oosterhoff, Prisca Zwanikken, and Evert Ketting, 'Sexual Torture of Men in Croatia and Other Conflict Situations: An Open Secret,' *Reproductive Health Matters* 23:23 (2004): 68.
93 Lynn Sorsoli, Frances K Grossman and Maryam Kia-Keating, '"I Keep That Hush-Hush": Male Survivors of Sexual Abuse and the Challenges of Disclosure,' *Journal of Counseling Psychology* 55:3 (2008): 342.
94 Roy, *Remembering Revolution*, 159–160.
95 Interview with Nonkululeko, Diepkloof, 8 April 2014.

Many interviewees oscillated between presenting themselves as active agents and victims in their narratives of detention, drawing equally on the tropes of hero and victim. Such contradictions are not uncommon in the narratives of those who have lived through conflict or violence. Research with Holocaust survivors demonstrates that people tend to conceal 'deep' memories that reveal the true extent of their victimisation and focus instead on 'common' memories of resistance, solidarity, or redemption – using narratives which downplay or negate trauma altogether.[96] As Florence told me, 'there are things in life that are better left unsaid.' Demonstrating a keen awareness of the conflicting narratives interviewees provide, she explained:

> The thing is it's opening [long pause] ya, old wounds if I may say. And you know, the sad part is [long pause] I think most comrades, especially female comrades, they were so damaged inside and we show this face of no, we're strong, we're ok. But deep down inside it's hurting, and we let it out in different ways.[97]

What is particularly interesting here is that Florence highlights the gendered nature of living through traumatic experiences. Perhaps, this is due to these women's desire to be seen as true activists or combatants; their belief that they need to 'become like men' in order to conform to societal notions of political agents causes them to emphasise memories typically seen as masculine such as bravery or empowerment, while downplaying those potentially seen as weak or feminine. Performing struggle femininity – both in interviews and in their day-to-day lives – thus comes at the cost of not being able to discuss more traumatic or vulnerable experiences, as female comrades lose the space for articulating emotional vulnerability.

The other juxtaposition in interviewees' narratives is the tension between pain's destruction of language on the one hand, and one's need to tell their story to reassert their humanity and agency on the other. Judith Herman identifies this as the 'dialectic of trauma': 'the conflict between the will to deny horrible events and the will to proclaim them.'[98] This conflict can be seen in the divergence between my two interviews with Florence. In our first, she spoke extensively about detention without prompting. Her narrative that day was so much more comprehensive and fluent than that of others that it is disproportionately cited in this chapter.[99] Yet in our second, she was nervous and

---

[96]   Lawrence L. Langer, *Holocaust Testimonies: The Ruins of Memory* (New Haven: Yale University Press, 1991), 9; Treacy, 'Double Binds,' 141
[97]   Interview with Florence, Diepkloof, 3 March 2015.
[98]   Herman, *Trauma and Recovery*, 47; 1.
[99]   Interview with Florence, Diepkloof, 8 May 2014.

unsettled. In the ten months in between these two meetings, she seemed to have undergone a stark shift. In 2014, she very much wanted to talk about her experiences, spoke confidently and chronologically, had a clear sense of herself as a historical agent, and seemed to believe in the healing powers of narration. Yet by 2015, she seemed traumatised by her own memories of detention, and unable to recall them in a clear, chronological fashion or without becoming noticeably upset.[100] Nevertheless, she insisted on speaking about detention in our second interview, declining my offers to pause or end the interview. This shift, though particularly clear with Florence, represents the ongoing struggles most female comrades face in dealing with and speaking about their pasts. These women cannot be singularly characterised as empowered or traumatised by their experiences; forcing their narratives into these clear categories denies how their identities and positionalities fluctuate and change day-to-day, or even over the course of a single interview. The difficulties they still face demonstrate how trauma cannot be reconciled or resolved through one interview, or one time-bound process such as the TRC. Their processes of healing are not linear either. Their attempts to give voice to their trauma are complex, and clearly not always palliative or redeeming.

It is important to note that none of the female comrades interviewed for this book provided testimony to the TRC about the abuses they suffered in detention. Many felt as though their experiences were not extraordinary enough to warrant attention on a national stage. But some also expressed their concern with the TRC's conceptualisation of trauma. The commission assumed that testifying to apartheid atrocities would promote a collective 'healing' of the nation, and thus lay the past to rest.[101] Yet interviewees perceived this as a requirement for them to forget and move on from their pasts. For Zanele, the TRC severed the relationship between the past and the present as 'after the TRC, everything just went blank', and people's trauma became a 'closed case'.[102] Similarly, Nonkululeko believed that the commission's main purpose was to promote forgetting – something she could not do.[103] Interviewees' sentiments about the TRC point to the fact that mastering one's trauma through narration is an on-going process, not something that can be achieved in a single interview or by speaking once before a public commission. Female comrades' narratives complicate any clear binary between detention being either horrific and traumatising or empowering and redemptive. They thus highlight some of the problems with previous literature on detention in South Africa. While

[100] Interview with Florence, Diepkloof, 3 March 2015.
[101] Field, *Oral History, Community, and Displacement*, 153.
[102] Interview with Zanele, Diepkloof, 12 April 2014.
[103] Interview with Nonkululeko, Diepkloof, 8 April 2014.

psychological studies painting detainees as victims suffering from PTSD do not pay enough attention to prisoner resistance and resilience, literature focused on resistance at times ignores how triumphant accounts presented in memoirs or testimonies can mask ongoing pain.[104]

Conclusion

The previous chapters in this book have argued that, by joining the struggle and contesting gender norms, female comrades felt empowered against patriarchal restraints, feelings of inferiority, and the physical insecurities that tended to mark African girls' lives. This chapter, in contrast, has highlighted the fragility of this empowerment. In apartheid's carceral spaces, female comrades were forced to come to terms with the vulnerability their age and sex accorded them, as they were isolated, beaten, and tortured. Much of this abuse was distinctly gendered and designed to break down comrades' identities as both girls and dedicated activists: unhygienic living conditions, humiliation through stripping, and sexualised torture were used as means of attacking female comrades' femininity; while isolation and taunts about their dispensability and assumed promiscuity were designed to undermine their political identities and sever their ties to their fellow comrades.

Yet female comrades refuse to be cast entirely as victims in narratives of their detention. Drawing on a narrative path now entrenched in collective memories of political imprisonment in South Africa, they tell stories of their detention that acknowledge their pain and suffering but ultimately conclude with their redemption and renewed feelings of empowerment. Casting their memories in this mould allows them to come to terms with their experiences in a number of ways: it helps to restore agency by highlighting moments of action rather than passive suffering; it attaches a broader meaning and purpose to detention experiences; it helps comrades to rebuild their political sense of selves; and integrates these women into a wider political community of former prisoners. While the narrative style female comrades adopt here is one primarily fashioned by male struggle leaders, there are gendered dimensions to their memories of detention. Perhaps even more so than men, female comrades feel the need to conform their narratives to these dominant stories in order to downplay their weakness or vulnerability and ensure that their involvement in the struggle is acknowledged and taken seriously. By highlighting their

---

[104] Ashraf Kagee and Anthony V. Naidoo, 'Reconceptualizing the Sequelae of Political Torture: Limitations of a Psychiatric Paradigm,' *Transcultural Psychiatry* 41:1 (2004): 46–61; Kalpana Hiralal, 'Narratives and Testimonies of Women Detainees in the Anti-Apartheid Struggle,' *Agenda* 29:4 (2015): 34–44.

importance to the struggle through tales of their arrests, their involvement in prison political culture, or their ability to withstand torture and interrogation, they challenge the stereotyping of girls as too weak, ignorant, or unimportant to have played a key role in the liberation movement.

But in conforming to these dominant narratives of imprisonment, and by casting carceral spaces as sites of political development rather than destruction, they leave little room for sharing their ongoing trauma and any feelings of grief or distress. Yet the redemptive narratives they construct are not tidy enough to fully conceal this. The unsharable nature of trauma means that such experiences are, to an extent, unknowable to the researcher. Rather than forcing survivors' fluctuating and at times contradictory narratives of detention into any set analytical framework, it is perhaps best to let these memories speak for themselves, and understand their disfluent, inconsistent, or conflicting nature as evidence of the enormous difficulties victims face in constructing stories about their past experiences. Female comrades' narratives of detention may be analytically confusing, but listening to them requires appreciation for this confusion, rather than an attempt to classify female comrades according to any neat theories of trauma and healing. As Field contends in his work on violence and trauma in South Africa, we are doing survivors a disservice by 'analytically cutting into their shattered lives' and forcing their stories into academic frameworks.[105]

[105] Field, 'Disappointed Remains,' 148.

7

The Interview: Reflecting on the Struggle

After joining COSAS in 1985, Beatrice became a particularly active young comrade in her home township of Pimville. Throughout the latter half of the 1980s she worked as a women's organiser for the student and youth movement. When negotiations between the apartheid government and the ANC began in 1990, she continued her political participation and is still an active member of the ANC today. During our interview in 2015, my first impression of Beatrice was of a confident and passionate woman who was eager to share her story with a foreign researcher. She spoke about her past with a tangible sense of personal agency and pride in her accomplishments. At times this was expressed in terms of the collective achievements of her generation. Drawing on and contesting wider public memories of the struggle, she argued, 'I think it's, to be honest, normally they say June 16th [1976], that's the era of the people that liberated our country. But it's not true. I'm not saying it because I was there, but I believe it's our era, from 1985, yes, the COSAS leaders, SOSCO, they are the people who liberated this country.' Yet she also clearly believed in the importance of the individual role she played. Discussing male comrades in Soweto, she stated 'I think most of the guys, they would say it's Beatrice; when they talk about Pimville they will talk about me.' Far from overstating her personal importance to the liberation movement, Beatrice was right – when I spoke to male comrades from Pimville they *did* mention her as a key political force in the community.

Towards the end of our interview, I asked Beatrice if she today feels empowered by everything she went through as a teenager. Given my initial impression of her, I expected her answer to be an explicit 'yes'. However, her response was more complex than I anticipated:

> Not exactly, because I'm still struggling now. You can see [laughs, motions around her township home]. I was supposed to have my own house, have my own car, but I'm not driving. It's difficult…But what can I say, at least I have something for my family. But basically, I'm battling, and you wouldn't say that I'm a politician other than that I've donated a lot.

Revisiting this interview, I later found that Beatrice's narrative was not as une-quivocally positive as I had first perceived. Rather, there were traces throughout her reflections that hinted at her more ambivalent relationship with her own past and ongoing struggles in the present. Within a discussion of her former bravery she stated that while she was not scared of engaging in political vio-lence during the 1980s, she *was* scared now – though of what she did not give details. At the end of our conversation she spoke glowingly of one of her son's successful admission into university and another son's nearing completion of his matric. Yet these accomplishments caused her to reflect upon her own unfulfilled goals: 'They are doing well. Even my son is doing well. It's only me that could not further my studies, because these politics. But what can you say? At least I've achieved. I don't regret that much.'[1]

This book is based on the individual narratives of female comrades – stories which these women tell about their pasts as they seek to make sense of their roles in the liberation struggle in the years since. Their narratives are thus a dialogue between the past and the present. They not only tell us about what these women did, but also about how they see themselves today, how they wish to be seen, and how they situate their personal experiences within collective memories of South Africa's liberation movement.[2] This chapter begins by exploring female comrades' lives since the township uprisings, following their trajectories as activists and young women through the transition period and into post-apartheid South Africa. It does so not necessarily to generate new data about the paths taken by this generation of politicised youths, but rather to look at how these women's present lives shape their reflections of the past. To understand how they ascribe meaning to their involvement in the struggle we must appreciate the current successes, pressures, or insecurities they face and how they relate these to their former identities as comrades.[3]

Involvement in the liberation struggle has been a double-edged sword for most female comrades, particularly regarding the legacies of its gender dynam-ics. Most women reported feeling liberated from conventional gender roles in certain ways: they believe they are more aware of gender issues; stand on a more equal footing with men; and have shed the 'inferiority complexes' they once held as young girls. Yet they have also experienced stigma and judgement from some in their communities for their previous breach of gender norms.

---

[1]   Interview with Beatrice, Pimville, 23 May 2015.
[2]   Alessandro Portelli, 'The Peculiarities of Oral History,' *History Workshop Journal* 12:1 (1981): 99–100; Clifford, 'Emotions and Gender in Oral History,' 211.
[3]   James Mark, Anna von der Goltz, and Anette Warring, 'Reflections,' in Robert Gildea, James Mark, and Anette Warring (eds), *Europe's 1968: Voices of Revolt* (Ox-ford: Oxford University Press, 2013), 284–285.

Many find navigating personal, romantic relationships with either activists or non-activists difficult, and they are dismayed at the lack of wider gender transformation in South Africa. As with Beatrice, their narratives are somewhat contradictory. While at first, they seemed to convey pride and reflect positively on their pasts, upon closer examination many testimonies were also cut through with more ambivalent reflections, and expressions of regret, lingering difficulties, or uncertainty. This chapter brings these uncertainties to the fore to explore the various meanings former female comrades attach to their involvement in the liberation struggle, and the links they see in their own lives between their past and presents. It argues that the at times ambiguous nature of these women's reflections are in part a result of their competing needs in the present and reasons for sharing their life histories: their desire to have their involvement in the struggle more widely acknowledged; their struggles for composure; and their attempts to cope with post-apartheid disappointments. These competing needs mean that these women's narratives resist any neat categorisation as empowered or disempowered, affirmational or apologetic. But in blurring these boundaries, female comrades' stories challenge dominant histories of South Africa's liberation struggle and reveal the messy complexities of political participation and its aftermaths.

The Afterlives of Young Women against Apartheid

The township uprisings and the comrade movement did not come to any decisive, abrupt end – making any neat delineation between activists' struggle and post-struggle lives somewhat futile. On 2 February 1990, President FW de Klerk announced the release of Nelson Mandela from prison and the unbanning of liberation movements including the ANC, PAC, and South African Communist Party (SACP). This day marked the beginning of a new political phase in the struggle and the opening of negotiations between the National Party and other political organisations. Yet the struggle was not over. The negotiations coincided with the deadliest period of political violence in the country's history: from 1990 to 1994 an estimated 14,000 people were killed in politically related violence.[4] While much of this violence occurred in KwaZulu-Natal or in the townships on the East Rand, Soweto also experienced continued conflict. Particularly unsettling to student and youth activists in the area was the killing of Vuyani Mabaxa, a young community leader in Diepkloof and key player in the student and youth struggles of the 1980s, by

---

[4]   Gary Kynoch, *Township Violence and the End of Apartheid: War on the Reef* (Woodbridge: James Currey, 2018), 1.

police on 13 October 1991.[5] In response, Soweto students took to the streets. Pupils from many Diepkloof schools including Bopasenatla, Diepdale and Madibane (which many interviewees attended) set up barricades, defended themselves from police birdshot with stones, and attacked delivery vans and local councillors' houses.[6] White-owned newspaper descriptions of Soweto as being once again engulfed by a 'rampage' of youth protest or schools being 'plagued by riots' are nearly indistinguishable from the reports produced at the peak of the township uprisings in the mid-1980s. Meanwhile, the material conditions of many students and youth in Soweto deteriorated further in the early 1990s as poverty, overcrowding, and poor public service provision worsened. Struggles for free and fair education also continued to disrupt schooling and provoke violence between students and teachers.[7]

The unbanning of political organisations prompted some formal changes to student and youth organisations in the country. In April 1990 SAYCO disbanded, its membership absorbed into the now-legal ANC Youth League (ANCYL), which relaunched in December 1991. COSAS, now also unbanned, remained the predominant ANC-aligned student organisation, and continued to organise boycotts and campaign for improved conditions of schools. Yet in Soweto the political participation of some comrades waned after 1990. Marks argues that many within this particular generation of comrades – the '1985 detachment' – lost their sense of purpose when the armed struggle and peoples' war were suspended. They also felt side-lined by the negotiation process and did not see a clear role for themselves in the continued push for non-racial democracy. As some experienced leaders left the movement and a new generation of activists look their place, the youth movement also experienced a swing away from well-organised collective action towards more disorderly and less judicious violence.[8]

Soweto's female comrades faced particularly gendered obstacles to their continued participation in addition to this wider loss of morale or sense of purpose. Fourteen of the twenty-eight female comrades interviewed for this study continued to participate in politics until the country's first democratic elections in 1994. With the unbanning of political parties, many joined the ANCYL or trade unions, while others helped in organising the 1994 elections. Yet for the other half, their participation in the struggle was eventually hampered or constrained by a number of factors: three women recounted that after being released from detention they chose not to continue their political

5   Marks, *Young Warriors*, 1–2.
6   'Soweto schools plagued by riots,' *The Star*, 18 October 1991; 'Poem shows activist's death fears,' *City Press*, 20 October 1991.
7   Marks, *Young Warriors*, 65.
8   *Ibid.*, 73; 5.

activity due to continued police pressure for them to become informers or their parents' concerns for their safety; four were moved outside Soweto by their parents in an attempt to stop their political activities; and another four either became pregnant or left the struggle to find employment to look after children they already had. Sibongile provided a narrative typical of many female comrades: after joining the struggle in 1985 and participating fully for about three years, she fell pregnant in 1988. Her family did not have the resources to support the new child, so she went looking for work. She kept one foot in the struggle, but her participation was not like it was before. When she could she took her baby along to meetings, but her shifts at work meant that she missed most of them.[9]

Other women had more success in retaining their activist commitments while also struggling as new mothers. But this came at a cost. Phumzile also became pregnant around this time, having two sons born in 1991 and 1993. She continued her activism, becoming a deputy chairperson of her local ANCYL branch. Yet doing so required that she leave her children with her mum. 'Ooo it was a mess!' she said.

> When they started at school, I was having a problem because the first day, when I was supposed to go with my child at school, it was not me. It was my grandmother that go with the child to school. I was busy with ANC meetings…I didn't enjoy my children, like to be with them always, even now…When I go home, I am trying to enjoy my life with them and family, you know? But I know that my family is within the ANC. My life, forever.[10]

Some young women decided to take breaks away from activism with the beginning of negotiations. A few reported that they felt tired and drained or needed time for personal introspection and healing after what they had been through. Florence stated that she, 'had to find a way of healing…because there was a lot of damage, physically, psychologically. I couldn't sleep, I had to go through so much. An uh, it took me time, it took me time, and I'm still dealing with it.'[11]

Yet at the time of interviews, almost all women had returned to politics in some form or another and today are engaged in their communities through local ANC branches, the ANC Women's League, or the Each One Teach One Foundation, an organisation created by former COSAS members in Soweto. When speaking about their political lives they rarely drew a clear temporal line between the apartheid and post-apartheid periods or their lives during and after the struggle. Most insisted that today they are 'still struggling' for

[9]   Interview with Sibongile, Johannesburg, 9 June 2015
[10] Interview with Phumzile, Johannesburg, 17 April 2015.
[11] Interview with Florence, Diepkloof, 8 May 2014.

liberation in some form or another. During our interviews from 2014 to 2016, all of these former comrades (male and female) remained deeply loyal to the ANC, refusing to be swayed by rival political parties such as the Economic Freedom Fighters or Democratic Alliance. A palpable feeling of community, support, and friendship endures between Soweto's comrades of the 1980s. Many remain incredibly close to this day. When I was interviewing someone new, previous interviewees would often drop by unexpectedly to say hello. On Saturdays I would often find groups of comrades together at Diepkloof Hall, local *shebeens*, or in each other's houses.

Despite the twenty-five years that have passed since the end of apartheid, most female comrades have seen few tangible changes in their lives in terms of their socio-economic status. Many continue to live in the same township houses they did as school students, often with their parents, children, and grandchildren. The majority did not manage to finish their schooling during the 1980s due to the disruptions caused by their political lives – although a few have returned to school and gained matric certificates since. Most of these women are currently un- or under-employed, although some have found work in both the formal and informal sectors, inside and outside Soweto, ranging from driving *kombis* transporting children to and from school to selling ANC merchandise outside its headquarters in Luthuli House. The struggle thus did not provide a definitive path to a stable job or political career for these women – although it did not necessarily do so for male comrades either. While a few of the men interviewed, and particularly those in leadership positions within COSAS during the 1980s, have since risen to high-ranking positions within the government or private sector, many too still live in Soweto and struggle to find long-term work.

Given the lack of economic transformation in many female comrades' lives, it is not surprising that a number expressed their frustrations with post-apartheid life, lamenting how not enough has changed in terms of people's lived realities, and expressing how democratic South Africa has not lived up to the millenarian expectations they held as young activists. 'When they started negotiations, I had this thing in my mind, this concept that like, we will be having the wealth of the country, as our charter [the Freedom Charter] says,' stated Beatrice. 'But it was not like that.'[12] Speaking in 2014, Zanele, a comrade from Diepkloof, similarly expressed, 'I can say the apartheid is not over. It's not over, not yet over, really. Because…you know as South Africans, most of the people are not working.'[13]

[12] Interview with Beatrice, Pimville, 23 May 2015.
[13] Interview with Zanele, Diepkloof, 12 April 2014.

Several women also expressed disappointment with the next generation of political actors who followed in their wake for not continuing to uphold they key principles set out by Charterist students and youth in the 1980s. They drew a clear line between their own generation of altruistic activists and today's more avaricious politicians. Beatrice continued, 'And the other thing is these different organisations that are emerging now, and people are power hungry. Not like us. Before, when we participated, we participated because we had a wish to help the community. Now people when they participate, they're thinking of money…but before it was not like that.'[14] When I asked Sissy, a comrade from Diepkloof, how she feels looking back now on her time as a comrade, she responded:

> Both pride inside and sadness. I'm proud of participating. I'm proud of risking my life and my family's life for this freedom. On the other hand, I'm sad that what we fought for, I don't think that we did get it. It's like we fought for corruption. We fought for more hardship for the poor of the poorest. We have fought for people that we didn't even know, people who never participated, to come and just grab what was fought for, by people who have died, families who have lost their loved ones.[15]

In terms of wider societal transformations in gender ideologies or women's liberation, former female comrades have also primarily experienced disappointment. On paper, South African women have achieved much since the end of apartheid, and the transition years were widely heralded as a 'success story' in terms of wider gender transformation in the country. Sustained pressure by the women's movement in the early 1990s was successful in placing gender equity high on the agenda for the new government in 1994.[16] When the country's new constitution was ratified in 1996, it was heralded as one of the most progressive in the world when it came to issues of gender and sexuality. Women were guaranteed 30 per cent of parliamentary seats, marital rape was recognised as an offence, domestic violence was subject to harsher sentencing, and women were granted access to abortions.[17] Yet these provisions have done little to address gender inequality on the ground.[18] The gains made by women in post-apartheid South Africa should thus not be overstated,

---

[14]   Interview with Beatrice, Pimville, 23 May 2015.

[15]   Interview with Sissy, Diepkloof, 17 April 2015.

[16]   Hassim, *Women's Organizations and Democracy in South Africa*, 129–169.

[17]   Liz Walker, 'Men Behaving Differently: South African Men since 1994,' *Culture, Health and Sexuality* 7:3 (2005): 227.

[18]   Natasha Erlank, 'ANC Positions on Gender, 1994–2004,' *Politikon: South African Journal of Political Studies* 32:2 (2005): 199.

as women are still more likely than men to live in poverty, be unemployed, and have a lower level of education. Since the end of apartheid, rates of domestic and gender-based violence have increased, with South Africa having the highest per capita rate of reported rape of any country in the world in 1998.[19] The post-apartheid situation is particularly dire for female youth, who suffer disproportionately from these escalating rates of violence both within and outside their personal relationships.[20] Expressing her frustration with the current situation and the rise of sexual violence targeting very young girls, Zanele stated, 'I'm not happy. As things are, I'm not happy. Ok, they are trying to balance the genders. But it is still here, this gender thing.'[21]

Consequences of Comradeship

In addition to these broad disappointments with the post-apartheid state, female comrades also feel as though their participation in the struggle has brought specific, negative consequences to their own lives. Some expressed tentative regret about the choices they made as teenagers. As Thobile from Diepkloof stated:

> I didn't complete even my school, because of the struggle, you understand?...I didn't go to varsity, I didn't do nothing. As today I'm still here at home. If it was not for my commitment to the struggle, maybe I [would have] continued with my school...today, my wish, it was being a police or a soldier. But I'm sitting at home. I'm at home. I'm not working.[22]

Such sentiments were expressed much more strongly by a female comrade who gave testimony to the TRC. Sandra Adonis, who joined the Bonteheuwel Military Wing in the Western Cape in 1985 at the age of fifteen, lamented to the commission, 'I have lost my education and I have lost my childhood...I do not think we [comrades] have gained anything, because we

---

[19] Walker, 'Men Behaving Differently,' 227–228; A spate of rape and femicide cases in August and September 2019 led many gender activists within the country to call on the government to introduce a state of emergency, labelling gender-based violence a national crisis. Anton Katz and Eshed Cohen, 'Gendered Violence: A State of Emergency,' *Daily Maverick*, 9 September 2019.

[20] For more on female youth, gender-based violence, and HIV/AIDS in post-apartheid South Africa see Moffett, 'These women, they force us to rape them'; Jewkes and Morrell, 'Sexuality and the Limits of Agency'; Rachel Jewkes et al., 'Intimate Partner Violence, Relationship Power Inequity, and Incidence of HIV Infection in Young Women in South Africa: A Cohort Study,' *The Lancet* 376:9734 (2010): 41–48.

[21] Interview with Zanele, Diepkloof, 12 April 2014.

[22] Interview with Thobile, Diepkloof, 12 April 2014.

are still in the same position as we use to be [sic], unemployed, homeless, abandoned and there is nobody that looks back and say, these are the people that has fought the struggle [sic].'[23]

In general, Soweto's female comrades did not express such overt regrets. Yet where they did see particularly adverse effects of their political involvement was in their personal relationships with friends, families, and potential romantic partners. Their breaching of gender norms and involvement in political violence, although now more than thirty years in the past, have had lasting effects on how they are viewed by their communities.[24] As Ntebaleng said of her former classmates in Diepkloof, 'They did call us with names, but we didn't care. Up until today, they are still doing that... You will hear them. Even if you go in the street, they will call you names, and you will just look at them and pass.'[25] Khosi too spoke of how women in her neighbourhood continue to '[comment] in corners' about her detention and participation in the struggle. Since the end of apartheid, she has moved from Pimville to Orlando East, where few people know about her comrade past. 'People who know me here in Orlando,' she explained, 'they know me as a nice woman...I would never go around telling people that I'm a comrade...Let's say that I'm in a party, I cannot announce myself as a comrade.' She continued by telling a story about a friend who knew about her past and divulged her former comrade status at a social gathering. She was angry with her friend and chastised her for telling non-politicised women she was a comrade, thinking they would not understand her political commitment, and simply see her as a 'thug'.[26]

These women's involvement in the struggle has also earned them lasting stigmatisation from some of their family members. In exhibiting characteristics associated with both masculinity and femininity, they became stuck

---

[23] Sandra Adonis, TRC Youth Hearings, Athlone, 22 May 1997.
[24] Across many African societies, women returning from participation in civil conflict have endured similar stigmatisation. Viewed with suspicion or fear for their involvement in violence, female combatants may be rejected by their former communities, can experience taunting, teasing, difficultly finding work, and are thought to be less likely to marry. See Tazreena Sajjad, 'Women Guerillas: Marching toward True Freedom? An Analysis of Women's Experiences in the Frontlines of Guerilla Warfare and in the Post-War Period,' *Agenda* 59 (2004): 4–16; Chris Coulter, Mariam Persson, and Mats Utas, *Young Female Fighters in African Wars: Conflict and Its Consequences* (Uppsala: Norkiska Afrikainstitutet, 2008); Myriam Denov, 'Girls in Fighting Forces: Moving Beyond Victimhood,' (Canadian International Development Agency, 2007); Veale, *From Child Soldier to Ex-fighter.*
[25] Interview with Ntebaleng, Diepkloof, 15 April 2014.
[26] Interview with Khosi, Orlando East, 1 May 2014.

in some relatives' eyes in a confused state between girlhood and boyhood, male and female. Both Phumzile and Ntiski expressed that this was only rectified once they had children, and biologically affirmed their femininity. Before becoming pregnant, Phumzile was teased as a 'tom boy' by her friends and family, while Ntiski was told by her father that she would never have children because she was 'a man'.[27]

But what female comrades were most disgruntled with was how their past political involvement has affected how they are perceived by men in their townships. Two thirds of this group of female comrades are not married today and cite their involvement in the struggle as the primary reason for this.[28] The qualities that young women tend to gain through political struggle or conflict, including self-assertiveness, independence, and moral and physical strength, are generally qualities that hinder their prospects as wives.[29] Compared to other young women in their community, female comrades in South Africa were politically aware, empowered against sexual violence and gender discrimination, and were perceived as masculine, aggressive, and independent, and therefore not desirable as romantic partners. During a group interview, women from Diepkloof expressed that men today are not only threatened by female comrades' assertive nature but are also frightened of them because of their past involvement in political violence. When asked about low marriage rates amongst female comrades they responded:

27   Interview with Phumzile, Johannesburg, 17 April 2015; Interview with Ntsiki, Diepkloof, 5 April 2015.
28   Marriage rates amongst female comrades are not actually too dissimilar from those of other women in the country today. In 2008, less than a quarter of African women between the ages of 20 and 45 were married. In her research in Natal during the late 1980s, Campbell found that almost half of her non-political female interviewees were either ambivalent about marriage, or explicitly rejected the idea of marriage. But former female comrades insist that low marriage rates amongst their group are specifically tied to the roles they played in the struggle. See Dorrit Posel, Stephanie Rudwick and Daniela Casale, 'Is Marriage a Dying Institution in South Africa? Exploring Changes in Marriage in the Context of Ilobolo Payments,' *Agenda* 25:1 (2011): 102–111; Campbell, 'Identity and Gender in a Changing Society,' 116.
29   This is something commonly faced by former female activists or fighters in post-liberation contexts. See Victoria Bernal, 'Equality to Die For?: Women Guerrilla Fighters and Eritrea's Cultural Revolution,' *Political and Legal Anthropology Review* 23:2 (2000): 61; West, 'Girls with Guns,' 190; Elise Fredrikke Barth, *Peace as Disappointment: The Reintegration of Female Soldiers in Post-Conflict Societies: A Comparative Study from Africa* (Oslo: International Peace Research Institute, 2002), 24; Modise and Curnow, 'Thandi Modise,' 40.

Nonkululeko: Because males are afraid to approach you. They say, 'ah this one...

Thobile: She's *Siyayinyova*...

Nonkululeko: She's going to stand and be a man in my house.

Thobile: Yes, she's going to tell me to do these things. So they are afraid of us. Even our boyfriends now, they say, 'Eh! I'm afraid of you. You can kill me!'[30]

Nomsa, also from Diepkloof, similarly stated about men in the township today, 'If they know that you are a comrade, they are even scared sometimes to propose to you.'[31]

Conversely, the majority of former male comrades in Soweto *are* married, but not to female comrades. When asked about this discrepancy, female interviewees all provided similar answers. Penelope, a comrade from Jabavu, explained, 'I generally think men do not like women who have an opinion... They want you to be obedient, listen to everything that they say, and you must not object anything...Especially the comrades, I don't know why. I started realising, the more educated a man gets, the more he feels insecure.'[32] When asked why so few female comrades are married, Beatrice replied:

> Because we understand, we can engage, so that's why they [male comrades] don't want [us]....They want to suppress you, always you must be submissive with them...Even though they are comrades...they always want to be the head of the house. So they know you are a comrade, you know everything, you'll be engaging.[33]

Female interviewees openly discussed their rejection by male comrades, as long as none of them were present. For a period in 2015, Musa – a male COSAS leader from Diepkloof – helped to arrange interviews and often accompanied me around Soweto. Without my asking, however, he always made sure to leave the room before the interview started, knowing that his presence would inevitably influence what women recalled to me. Yet during one interview conducted late at night in winter, the power went out, and due to only having one candle Musa remained in the room with myself and two female interviewees, as did another male comrade and their friend, Cecil. When I asked the two women why so many female comrades today are not married, they became awkward, shy, and never provided a definitive answer.

---

30   Group interview with female comrades from Diepkloof, Diepkloof, 27 June 2015.
31   Interview with Nomsa, Diepkloof Extension, 19 April 2014.
32   Interview with Penelope, Jabavu, 12 June 2015.
33   Interview with Beatrice, Pimville, 23 May 2015.

Lindiwe: You ask comrade Musa and comrade Cecil. They will tell you that women comrades are not married. We don't know why. Maybe they can explain [laughs].

Mamosa: And then most of the female comrades, they are not married to the male comrades…But we were there, all of us, we were struggling together but they didn't marry us! [laughs].

Emily: Why?

Mamosa: I don't know, you can ask them. Ask Cecil and comrade Musa.

I then asked Musa his opinion, but he only laughed and said, 'you know, that's why I don't want to sit in the interviews.'[34]

On the other hand, male comrades now involved with non-politicised women are not necessarily happy in their marriages, women explained. Beatrice said that many of her male friends are 'suffering in their marriage because the two parties, they don't understand each other.' She continued, 'You find that most of our comrades, they are married – the males – but they are not happy.' Much of this unhappiness she attributed to wives not understanding the lifestyle activists live and the demands of their continued political work: 'I feel pity for the male comrades, the way they live, the way their wives are handling them. Because they don't understand. For males coming late at home, oh! You'll be a nagging woman [laughs].'[35] Her explanation was supported by one male comrade, who admitted that his marriage was 'not in good standing' because of the amount of time he continues to dedicate to politics. This man has since started dating one of his former fellow comrades, who he was also romantically involved with for a period of time during the struggle. He explained, 'You'll find comrades, male comrades and female comrades… as an adult person now, you can see that there's a link between these two people, you know?' Compared to his estranged wife, his current girlfriend is more understanding of the time he dedicates to politics. 'We have tried to live with different people,' he lamented, 'But they seem not to be satisfied…they need more of our time as their husbands…The female comrades are more accommodative.'[36]

Female comrades also find it difficult to be seriously involved with someone who did not participate in the struggle, or who is not involved in politics now. 'For me, getting involved with somebody who's not political, who doesn't live the lifestyle that I'm living, it's so difficult, flipping difficult,' said Beatrice.

[34] Group interview with female comrades from Naledi, Naledi, 18 June 2015
[35] Interview with Beatrice, Pimville, 23 May 2015.
[36] Interview with Sello, Diepkloof, 14 May 2015.

This is in part because non-politicised men do not necessarily accept the close relationships women still have with their male comrades. Speaking about her current boyfriend, Beatrice stated, 'He wouldn't understand because he'd be seeing guys here, most of the comrades… "Why are these guys with you?" He'll be thinking of something else different.'[37] When asked if she is married, one interviewee told me no, and said that if she was, she would not be participating currently in the Each One Teach One Foundation because her husband would not allow it.[38]

Benefits of Comradeship

Yet despite all this stigma they have been subject to, female comrades otherwise generally looked back on their pasts positively and focused more on the beneficial than the adverse consequences of their involvement in the struggle. Almost all female comrades highlighted specific ways in which their own lives as women, individually and collectively, have improved as a direct result of their past activism, particularly in comparison to other women in their communities. First, although many comrades were unable to finish their schooling because of their political involvement, they stress that their activism provided them with a political and life education that school alone could not. Several women described how their entire outlook on life had shifted as a result. As Penelope said:

> being involved in the struggle opened the horizon, you know? The way you think and the way you do things, and your associations, how you associate with other people. You are always conscious…You no longer live your life here, you know, you also think globally, that there are other things happening around you that you might not be able to see.'[39]

A few women credited their enhanced awareness to having to constantly deal with issues of state surveillance and informers as school students. They claimed that they are more perceptive than other women in their communities and have better critical thinking skills because of this.

A second benefit women reported was the discipline they learned during the struggle, and how this has been carried over into their post-apartheid personal lives. Many bemoaned the current state of township youth and their propensities towards drinking, drug-taking, and teenage pregnancy. Expressing her appreciation for all the struggle taught her, Sibongile stated, 'Sometimes I say thanks to whatever, to join[ing] these things, because when I look at my

[37] Interview with Beatrice, Pimville, 23 May 2015.
[38] Interview with Vicky, Diepkloof, 14 May 2014.
[39] Interview with Penelope, Jabavu, 12 June 2015.

friends, eh! These people, they are drinking, some of them they are dead. I say maybe I was lucky to join the struggle.'[40] Ntsiki articulated similar gratitude to the struggle for keeping her away from drinking and drugs. 'These days, the problem with the kids of today is *Nyaope*,' she said, referring to the addictive street drug prominent in many South African townships since the 2000s. 'And I'll say I don't judge them,' she continued,

> I'm not Jesus…But I would love to see those kids capacitated because I think they're bored…they are unemployed. We fought the struggle for them, there is nothing that they must fight for, everything is here…For me, I can see, because we were busy those days [as youth], there was no time to drink a beer. You must be sober minded because there was a mission in your mind…So these kids today, they don't have a mission…That is why they are sitting around the corners, they are bored.[41]

Female comrades also believe that the discipline they learned through the struggle has empowered them in terms of family planning. Speaking about pregnancy and marriage, one woman explained, 'I learned to have something when I want it, you know? I'm not doing anyone favours, that's what I've learned. To say, I will do it if I want to. Ok, now I want a child, ok, then I'll have a child now…That's what the politics teach you. Do something you know that you can account for.'[42] Speaking more explicitly, Sissy stated that being involved in the struggle was:

> The best thing, because if you look at the situation and compare it, women from the 70s, 80s, 90s, we never had a high rate of young women falling pregnant. And then after the struggle, hey it's like everybody was applying for it. We had *everybody* falling pregnant…So I think participating in the struggle was the best bet for all of us, and that saved us because we never concentrated on relationships.[43]

Beatrice supported this claim that the struggle played a role in preventing unwanted pregnancies, stating that 'most of the comrades that I participated with, they only got one kid, because we're disciplined.'[44] However, there is clearly some nostalgia here clouding the perceptions of interviewees, as many female comrades interviewed *did* become pregnant while teenagers and activists. Speaking about her cohort of female activists, Stompie stated that, 'our first

[40] Interview with Sibongile, Johannesburg, 9 June 2015.
[41] Interview with Ntsiki, Diepkloof, 5 April 2015.
[42] Interview with Nomsa, Diepkloof Extension, 19 April 2014.
[43] Interview with Sissy, Diepkloof, 17 April 2015.
[44] Interview with Beatrice, Pimville, 23 May 2015.

children, all of us, they were [born in] '87, '88, or '89.' She referred to babies born to comrades during this time as *Abantwana bethu base moyeni* ('our kids that came out of nowhere') or *Abantwana base hlathini* (forest babies). She explained how female comrades would tell their parents they were sleeping *emoyeni* (in their hiding places) when they were really visiting their boyfriends.[45]

Furthermore, female comrades also insist that the political education they received through the struggle has helped them to overcome the 'inferiority complex' they felt as girls growing up in Soweto. Bessie expressed that simply participating as a woman in a male dominated environment brought lasting feelings of empowerment: 'Engaging with men, very powerful men, and being one of the few women, it did a lot very fast…I think that made me stronger.'[46] Male comrades too stressed that their efforts to empower female comrades have had lasting effects. Sello, speaking about his former female comrades today, stated, 'they've risen…they are women of their own now. They've overcome that fear of not speaking.'[47] In emphasising their confidence, female comrades drew a clear distinction between themselves and other women of their generation who did not join the struggle. Talking about the authority she has over her co-workers, Khosi stated, 'I'm stronger than them when I talk. And I realised that maybe I've got that thing of, I mean, if I want us to go this way we should and I mean, tough luck.'[48] This belief that the struggle changed them for the better, particularly in comparison to other women, can be seen in other liberation contexts too. In Ethiopia, former young female fighters similarly reported feeling stronger, more confident, and more capable of solving their problems. As one woman stated to an interviewer, 'Before I was afraid of somebody, to do what I want to do but now I have confidence to do everything, I can decide by myself. I can marry who I want; I do not care for someone else (their opinion). All these things I get from being a fighter. I know I can solve whatever problems face me.'[49]

Lastly, female comrades state that their involvement in the struggle also had more direct consequences in terms of their gender identities and relationships with men. As discussed in chapter five, female comrades contend that their adoption of more assertive femininities and direct actions taken against suspected rapists had substantial effects on their susceptibility to sexual violence and helped to overcome their feelings of powerlessness and victimisation. A number of women also stated that their political involvement

[45] Interview with Stompie, Naturena, 25 May 2015.
[46] Interview with Bessie, Johannesburg, 25 April 2014.
[47] Interview with Sello, Diepkloof, 14 May 2014.
[48] Interview with Khosi, Orlando East, 1 May 2014.
[49] Veale, *From Child Soldier to Ex-Fighter*, 51.

has granted them greater authority in their homes and relationships today than is common for most women in the townships, as the following conversation with Zanele demonstrates:

Emily: Did being in the struggle make you feel stronger?

Zanele: Mmm, yes. Because even in my house now I can take some position.

Emily: Against your husband?

Zanele: Yes. He can't rule everything in the house. There's a part that I must take. And I must stand. If this thing, if I don't like this thing, I must stand and say, 'No, we are not going to do that. Because it's going to be like this.'[50]

She continued by describing how the authority most husbands or in-laws have over household affairs does not exist in her home: 'I can fight for my rights,' she stated. A similar narrative emerged from an interview with Khosi. Like Zanele, she insisted that her relationship with her husband is different from most marital relationships in the community because of her experiences as a comrade. She spoke of how her husband sometimes complains about the characteristics she gained during her time in the struggle, such as her strength and sense of authority. Yet she challenges his complaints: 'And I tell him, unfortunately, you cannot show your manhood. I'll jump, because I won't allow anything to happen.'[51] It is unclear here what exactly Khosi means by 'show your manhood', but one interpretation could be that she is speaking about domestic violence. Khosi's reference to 'manhood' can be linked to academic discussions of a post-apartheid 'crisis of masculinity' in South Africa, in which men's ability to control their partners, often through violent means, has become a key determinant of masculinity.[52] When Khosi states she 'won't allow anything to happen,' she may be speaking of her lack of tolerance for such violence.

The positive effects of comradeship on these women's lives are thus subjective, and difficult to measure. While few felt that they have gained in concrete or material ways, or affected any societal-wide shift in gender roles, almost all women interviewed reported personally *feeling* or simply *being* different because of their time as activists. Through the struggle they gained new social skills and networks that have helped them to cope with the pressures and uncertainties of the post-apartheid period. But perhaps most importantly they

[50] Interview with Zanele, Diepkloof, 12 April 2014.
[51] Interview with Khosi, Orlando East, 1 May 2014.
[52] Rachel Jewkes and Katherine Wood, '"Dangerous" Love: Reflections on Violence among Xhosa Township Youth,' in Andrea Cornwall (ed), *Readings in Gender in Africa* (London: The International African Institute, 2005), 96; Moffett, 'These Women, They Force Us to Rape Them,' 129–130.

have gained friendship; the struggle gave them not just political comrades but also lasting personal relationships that help to sustain them in the present. Expressing this less tangible benefit of the struggle, Ntsiki stated, 'that feels you stronger [sic], because sometimes you can live in a big house…but if there's no warmth, there's no love. You can feel it when you are welcomed, the love is not about something that we see, but the way you'll be received, the way things are happening.'[53] Reflections of this type overshadowed discussions of post-apartheid disillusionment or lack of economic change in women's narratives. It is therefore important to include analysis of these more subjective benefits of political activism for women when asking questions about their post-conflict empowerment or disempowerment.

Coming to Terms with the Past: Affirmation and Uncertainty

Despite their current lack of jobs, houses, or husbands, former female comrades are proud of the political commitments they made. When asked if she ever felt as though she missed out on her childhood and youth, one former comrade resolutely stated, 'No! I am so very, very proud today, because I spent most of my teenage [years] fighting for our people. So I did not even feel maybe I've wasted my time. No. I am so proud because now I'm a leader.'[54] The majority of women approached consented enthusiastically to the prospect of being interviewed by a foreign researcher. Their narratives contained more laughter and excitement than pain or hesitancy, as they wove stories which placed themselves at the centre of historical events. Overall, they seemed keen to celebrate their pasts – to focus on their individual involvement, collective accomplishments, and key contributions to South Africa's recent history. Such affirmational narratives may speak to female comrades' sense of empowerment and the benefits they feel they have gained as a result of their political participation. But they likely serve other, more complex purposes too. The life stories comrades tell not only represent an intricate interplay between the past and the present but are also reflective of interactions between private and collective memory. They are a means by which these women historicise themselves, stake claims to post-apartheid citizenship, and come to terms with their pasts.

First, we can see these triumphant narratives as a means by which female comrades seek to have their involvement in the liberation struggle more widely acknowledged. In constructing accounts of the country's past, commemoration

---

[53] Interview with Ntsiki, Diepkloof, 5 April 2015.
[54] Interview with Phumzile, Johannesburg, 17 April 2015.

initiatives, museums, and South Africa's leadership have all made little to no mention of girls' and young women's involvement in any period of the struggle. Beyond a few female MK cadres who left the country as teenagers, or the predominant image of Antoinette Sithole – the sister of Hector Pieterson pictured in anguish alongside him in Sam Nzima's famous photograph of the 1976 uprisings – girls and young women are largely invisible in popular narratives of South Africa's past.

Shireen Ally argues that heroic narratives of resistance have political currency in post-apartheid South Africa, as the 'burgeoning heritage industry transmutes political violence and revolt into marketable histories.' South Africans are thus encouraged to tell narratives that emphasise their victimisation by apartheid violence and their involvement in the fight against it in order to be included in the country's history.[55] Female comrades' life histories fit this mould in many ways. From even their earliest childhood memories they emphasise their subjection to apartheid oppression and their budding resistance against it. Early in our first interview Lucy showed me a scar on her ear from where she was hit by a bullet during the 1976 uprisings. Only seven or eight years old at the time, she recalled standing on a platform or box trying to watch the student protests: 'The police were shooting, I was nearly, they nearly killed me that time! Because I just saw blood,' she described, as she motioned blood running down the side of her face. 'Because even if I was young,' she continued, 'I saw people dying in front of my eyes…Some of them, they were not even comrades at that time, but they were shot, and they got killed. So, that's some of the things that made me to be involved in the struggle.'[56] Such accounts place female comrades centrally within the wider liberation struggle. Their telling constructs images of a 'heroic life' lived by these young women which was marked by intensity and bravery and the transcendence of everyday banalities in favour of a higher cause.[57] But we need to acknowledge the ways in which these narratives are told to particular audiences. They are designed to elicit recognition and approval, not just from me as the immediate interviewer, but also from the potential wider audiences of this work, and particularly from South African publics.[58] They thus draw on common discourses of heroism in order to align with popular images of liberation struggle heroes and to gain credit alongside them.

[55] Shireen Ally, 'Peaceful Memories: Remembering and Forgetting Political Violence in KaNgwane, South Africa,' *Africa* 81:3 (2011): 351.
[56] Interview with Lucy, Fleurhof, 7 April 2014.
[57] Roy, 'The Everyday Life of the Revolution,' 188.
[58] Penny Summerfield, 'Culture and Composure: Creating Narratives of the Gendered Self in Oral History Interviews,' *Cultural and Social History* 1:1 (2004): 69.

By telling positive stories of their political heroism, female comrades also toe the ANC's party line when it comes to collective memories of the struggle. Since the end of apartheid, South Africa has been engaged in at times heated debates about how to best remember its liberation movement. Today, how a person recalls their own or others' involvement in the struggle is a central way in which political candidates position themselves and jockey for power. Yet the dominant narrative of the struggle, which places the ANC as its hegemonic, heroic leader, continues to hold sway in the country, legitimising the continued rule of its central protagonists. Female comrades' narratives at times match those sponsored by the state in their romanticism and triumphalism. They also very much support the political hegemony of the party. The only parent political organisation they speak of is the ANC; there is no mention of affiliation with Black Consciousness or other alternative liberation philosophies in their life histories. Those who aligned themselves to other organisations, such as the Azanian People's Organisation and their student wing the Azanian Students' Movement (AZASM), appear only as adversaries in comrades' accounts of the past. Even when speaking about their post-apartheid disappointments, they were all careful not to openly criticise the ANC or its policies, at most speaking vaguely about corruption or greed. As Wale highlights, comrades who have thus far been excluded from national recognition may try to be included in the ANC's dominant historical narrative by supporting its underlying assumptions. She argues that this form of memory work 'acts as a kind of glue, attempting to add actors' memories into the pre-created memory web, to demonstrate veteran or victim status.'[59] We can thus see female comrades' narratives of ANC-driven success as another means by which they seek to have their involvement in the struggle recognised.

But this struggle for historical recognition is also gendered. Female comrades have been written out of dominant narratives in South Africa. To be included in them they thus need to be particularly forceful in their demonstrations of heroism or allegiance. It is not enough to simply say they were there during the 1980s uprisings – they must place themselves at the very centre of these events and portray themselves as the most loyal of ANC stalwarts. Female interviewees, much more so than male ones, made very clear, strong statements about their individual contributions to the struggle. One woman expressed, 'I'm the one that made Mandela to come out from the prison,' while another sated that 'South Africa wouldn't be where it was today if it weren't for efforts of COSAS…Because we really made this country ungovernable.

---

[59]   Kim Wale, *South Africa's Struggle to Remember: Contested Memories of Squatter Resistance in the Western Cape* (London; New York: Routledge, 2016), 61.

And I for one, was part and parcel of that leadership of COSAS.'[60] Women's claims to such agency are not unique to the South African liberation struggle. Interviewing women who fought in FRELIMO's female detachment in Mozambique as girls, West found that when they spoke about their pasts, they 'most often told not of traumatic events that *happened to them* but, rather, of purposive acts and of epic events *to which they contributed* in defining ways,' presenting themselves as 'central players in the historical drama that defines their times.'[61]

The affirmational narratives that female comrades tell also serve to maintain their individual and collective identities as 'comrades' in the present. As mentioned, thirty years on from the township uprisings, Soweto's comrades remain incredibly close. The bonds of political camaraderie they formed in the 1980s have transformed into an important social and financial support network. These former activists are best friends; they help to raise each other's children and turn to each other for help finding employment. The preservation of these relationships is likely facilitated by sharing positive accounts of the pasts, ones which nostalgically recount their collective heroism and daring adventures. It was when I met with comrades collectively, either during group interviews or at weekend social events, that they tended to tell particularly animated and positive accounts of their pasts that celebrated the roles they played. This was epitomised in a group interview with female comrades from Diepkloof, when several women told me about a time when they punished a suspected rapist. Laughing, they reminded each other of the specifics of the incident, each joining in to add further details to the story: 'we used *sjam-boks!*' proclaimed one woman; 'and umbrellas!' added another. This interview felt akin to a school reunion, with the women excitedly sharing stories and reminding each other of their most audacious or hilarious exploits. On the other hand, the maintenance of comrades' social network may require female comrades to silence memories which paint their male comrades in a negative light and which, if told, could jeopardise their inclusion in the group. We can see this in the example earlier in this chapter, where Mamosa and Lindiwe refuse to comment on male comrades' romantic preferences while two of them were in the room, as well as in much of what is discussed in chapter four.

A third possible function of these women's celebratory narratives is to help former comrades cope with their post-apartheid disappointments or uncertainties. As mentioned in chapter five, there is a palpable sense of nostalgia in many of their reflections; not necessarily a longing to return to the time of

---

[60] Thobile, in group interview with female comrades from Diepkloof, Diepkloof, 27 June 2015; Interview with Florence, Diepkloof, 8 May 2014.

[61] Harry West, 'Girls with Guns,' 185.

the struggle, but a definitive sentimentality for the excitement and sense of agency that women now ascribe to their pasts. As one female comrade stated, 'with COSAS, I felt I had a voice, as a human being, as a South African, and as a woman, even though it was a challenge...I was happier then, because I was part of the happenings, I was free.'[62] As Field argues, such expressions should be read 'neither as trivial nostalgia nor popular romanticism.'[63] Rather, women's idealisation of certain aspects of their pasts allows them to preserve their comrade identity in the present, and hold on to the feelings of potency and agency that came with it. As Dlamini highlights, 'the irony about nostalgia is that, for all its fixation with the past, it is essentially about the present. It is about present anxieties refracted through the prism of the past.'[64] Given the present uncertainties many former comrades face, narrating their pasts positively and wistfully is an important means of coping with insecurity or disillusionment and, for female comrades in particular, their return to more 'normal' gender roles in the wake of the struggle.

Furthermore, positive affirmations of their pasts may help female comrades to justify the choices they made as younger women and help them to manage any present guilt or regret they feel over leaving their children behind, disrupting their families' lives, or not completing their education. By analysing the often positive or idealised accounts that female comrades tell about their former activism more closely, we can see what Michelle Mouton and Helena Pohlandt-McCormick call 'boundary crossings' – ruptures in women's narratives that reveal these uncertainties, insecurities, or moral conflicts. While collectively and at surface level these women construct stories that focus on their agency and empowerment, we can see within their individual narratives evidence of a more conflicted relationship between their past actions and present sense of selves. Mouton and Pohlandt-McCormick argue that in South Africa, 'although involved in a "legitimate" struggle against an oppressive regime, individual people needed to come to terms with personal guilt and wounds that had to be integrated into life stories which struggled for continuity, morality and meaning.'[65] We can see this struggle in interviewees' sometimes conflicting accounts. Chapter five opened with the story of Lucy, a female comrade from Diepkloof who spoke openly and often enthusiastically about her involvement in street-based confrontations

---

[62]   Interview with Florence, Diepkloof, 8 May 2014.
[63]   Field, *Oral History, Community and Displacement*, 53–54.
[64]   Dlamini, *Native Nostalgia*, 16.
[65]   Michelle Mouton and Helena Pohlandt-McCormick, 'Boundary Crossings: Oral History of Nazi Germany and Apartheid South Africa: A Comparative Perspective,' *History Workshop Journal* 48 (1999): 46.

and political action. She laughed as she recalled throwing stones at police vehicles or once beating a suspected rapist with an umbrella, insisting that female comrades engaged equally in such actions as male comrades. Yet later in her interview she divulged:

> Some of the tasks were very hard because you can, maybe you know that as females we have soft spots. When it's time to do that task, you feel for that person, or for those women from Shoprite who buy groceries and I have to take their groceries…Sometimes we feel for that person. You think, maybe it's their last money that that particular person has made their shopping. But we had to do it, you see. And if maybe we are tasked to beat that person, sometimes you feel as a female that, oh! Maybe you've got kids…But there's nothing you can do because we are also [laughs] being tortured and being harassed. So, we just had to do whatever what we had to do by that time.[66]

This idea that women found participating in political violence more difficult than men was also expressed by Bessie, a comrade leader from Dlamini. Speaking about punishing suspected informers she explained, 'I always say, as much as equality is important, as women you have that emotional side to things.' She continued, 'Women attacked targets. They did…I was very active during that time [of the consumer boycott] …Women were in the forefront. But I think there were instances where women would say, "OK…maybe this person has been beaten enough. Let's leave him." Sometimes that comes out.'[67] Another female activist, who spoke particularly unforgivingly about using the necklace against gangsters, admitted to the remorse she feels for attacking buses during a transportation boycott. Like Lucy above, she tied her mixed feelings about the past to ideas of motherhood: 'It was wrong,' she repeated numerous times, 'It was wrong [because] when we were hitting [the buses], it was our parents inside, coming from work…The driver of that target, it was someone's parent…And they have children at home, and a wife. You see?'[68]

In these conflicting memories and oscillations between revolutionary heroism and painstaking introspection, we can see female comrades struggling for what historians of memory call 'composure'. The term, as Alistair Thomson defines it, has a double meaning: 'In one sense we "compose" or construct memories using the public language and meanings of our culture. In another sense we "compose" memories which help us to feel relatively comfortable with our lives, which give

---

[66]   Interview with Lucy, Fleurhof, 7 April 2014.
[67]   Interview with Bessie, Johannesburg, 25 April 2014.
[68]   Interview with female COSAS member 6.

us a feeling of composure.'[69] When female comrades create idealistic narratives of their heroic femininity and revolutionary zeal, we can see them doing the former – fitting their memories to what is already publicly acknowledged in South Africa. Yet in their discussions of soft spots, reluctance, or regret we see the latter – their attempts to align their past actions to their present sense of selves and post-apartheid identities as women, mothers, and community members. This speaks to the particular difficulties women face in trying to achieve composure. As Penny Summerfield argues, the public discourses through which women are constructed and measured are multiple and contradictory, especially during times of conflict. In Europe during the Second World War, women were expected to be mobilised and independent, making equal contributions to the war effort, yet also be at home waiting for men and caring for children.[70] Within liberation contexts such as South Africa, popular constructions of heroic femininity can often position women in equally ambiguous ways, 'expecting them to repudiate the feminine for the sake of political agency but also idealizing feminine…codes of domesticity, motherhood and romance.'[71] We see in the excerpts above how female comrades struggle to conform to both these idealised images. On the one hand they try to challenge their absence from history by stressing their rejection of gender norms and adoption of masculine heroic traits, emphasising or even over-emphasising their individual, personal roles in the township uprisings. Yet on the other hand, they use gender stereotypes to distance themselves from more morally ambiguous forms of violence or to show remorse by discussing women's 'soft spots' or the regret now felt for attacking fellow parents.

While female comrades portray their involvement in the struggle as legitimate, heroic, and ultimately successful in achieving the goals of the liberation movement, they simultaneously seek to come to terms with past decisions and lingering wounds. Yet composure can never fully be achieved, and 'life stories are constantly revised in a continuing search for meaning.'[72] These women's competing needs in the present produce narratives about the past that are at times contradictory and ambiguous. Their struggle for recognition requires a different strategy, and a different way of reflecting on the past, than their struggle for personal healing, introspection, or socio-economic survival and progress. For these reasons, female comrades' memories resist any neat categorisation. In a single life history they celebrate, atone

---

[69]   Alistair Thomson, 'ANZAC Memories: Putting Popular Memory Theory into Practice in Australia,' *Oral History* 18:1 (1990): 25.

[70]   Summerfield, 'Culture and Composure,' 70–71.

[71]   Roy, *Remembering Revolution*, 7.

[72]   Summerfield, 'Culture and Composure,' 69.

for, reject and rework various aspects of their pasts, producing 'powerful but contradictory' memories.[73] Yet it is the ambiguous nature of their narratives which disrupts dominant histories and reveals the messy, complex realities of being involved in South Africa's liberation struggle and contending with this in the post-apartheid period. Theirs is not a glorious account of revolution, nor an idealistic one, but rather a gritty and sometimes painful story of both gendered and political struggle.

Conclusion

Despite the three decades that passed between the end of apartheid and the interviews conducted for this book, female comrades still largely portrayed themselves as activists in the 2010s. They are still politically involved, and they are also still struggling for liberation – be it in their personal lives, township communities, or the country as a whole. While they express great pride in their individual and collective accomplishments, they simultaneously express disappointment with all they were unable to achieve. The end of apartheid meant that their movement was ultimately a successful one, but much of what they dreamed about as young activists has not materialised. Leading anti-apartheid activist Mamphela Ramphele reminds us that 'it is important to move away from the romanticism that tends to dominate the literature [of the struggle]...which paints women as heroines, without due regard of the cost of these struggles to them as individuals and as a group.'[74] Female comrades' involvement in the liberation movement has both helped and hindered their post-apartheid lives, but often in very contradictory ways. They lament not being able to finish their education and earn matric certificates yet are thankful for the political education they received in the struggle and the new outlook this gave them. They resent how they have been stigmatised by men in their communities for their contravention of gender norms yet celebrate their gendered feelings of empowerment such contraventions brought. Such contradictions reflect the complex realities of female activist or combatants' lives post-conflict; lives that are not exclusively positive or negative, empowering or disempowering, but often more ambivalent.

In seeking to come to terms with their pasts and reflect on their former lives, female comrades provide equally complex narratives. At times they portray themselves as heroic leaders of the struggle, elevating their personal

---

[73] Mark et al, 'Reflections,' 284.

[74] Mamphela Ramphele, 'The Dynamics of Gender Politics in the Hostels of Cape Town: Another Legacy of the South African Migrant Labour System,' *Journal of Southern African Studies* 15:3 (1989): 414.

contributions above the local contexts and gender dynamics that constrained them. In doing so they often conform to ANC-sponsored accounts of the past that honour heroism, party loyalty, and disciplined soldiering. In the next moment however, their narratives sometimes starkly shift to atone for or express regret about their involvement in such activities. These contradictions can in part be explained by the competing motives and needs that shape female comrades' testimonies: their attempt to cope with post-apartheid disappointments; their struggle for composure; and their desire to have their stories heard, more widely acknowledged, and incorporated into dominant narratives of the liberation movement. Yet these contradictions also simply reflect the messy realities of being a female comrade and coming to terms with this in the struggle's aftermath. We can analyse these inconsistencies, but we must also acknowledge that these women's lives and narratives do not fit into neat binaries that divide heroes from victims or empowered from disempowered activists.

Conclusion

In the years that have passed between the interviews conducted for this book and the writing of its conclusion, a new generation of young, black female activists have come to the fore in South Africa through the university-based 'Fallist' movements of RhodesMustFall and FeesMustFall, which arose in 2015 and 2016 out of demands to decolonise the country's higher education sector.[1] In many ways these women's activism has diverged from that of their female comrade predecessors: they are slightly older and generally better educated; they self-identify as radical feminists; and they have found a louder and clearer articulation of the multiple inequalities they face through the concept of 'intersectionality'. They have refused to let their involvement in post-apartheid student politics fade into obscurity or be side-lined by the actions of young men, and have taken to journalism, social media, and academic writing to ensure their voices are heard.

Yet there are clear continuities as well as changes between these two groups of young female protestors, despite the thirty years and profound political changes that separate them. Both groups chose not to initially organise separately as women around explicitly gendered issues but joined wider political causes with shared motivations to their male counterparts. Yet once politically active, both groups also found that issues of race and class cannot easily be separated from those of gender and sexuality. While female students have occupied prominent positions in the Fallist movements, they have also encountered misogyny and sexual violence within its ranks. After a female student was raped in a University of Cape Town building occupied by RhodesMustFall activists in 2016, a new effort – EndRapeCulture – was started by the movements' female members. Across several South African campuses

---

[1] See Sandy Ndelu, Simamkele Dlakavu and Barbara Boswell, 'Womxn's and Non-binary Activists' Contribution to the RhodesMustFall and FeesMustFall Student Movements: 2015 and 2016,' *Agenda* 31:3–4 (2017): 1–4, as well as the other articles in this special issue titled 'Feminisms and Women's Resistance within Contemporary African Student Movements'; Healy-Clancy, 'The Everyday Politics of Being a Student in South Africa.'

young women staged protests, often while topless, promoting a 'liberatory construction of the black female body.'[2] Some women even carried *sjamboks* as a symbol of their fight back against rape culture – a characteristic that made these 2016 protests starkly reminiscent of female comrades' use of *sjamboks* against suspected rapists in Soweto in the mid-1980s.[3] Both groups thus initially joined their respective movements in the hopes of affecting political change, yet within them also staged a wider challenge to gender inequality, sexual violence, and patriarchy.

This book has been narrow in its focus, exploring the lives of female comrades from one decade, in one township, in one country. Yet when read alongside literature from other contexts and conflicts, these women's narratives are not anomalous. On the contrary, their experiences, memories, and even exact phrases they use are at times strikingly similar to those of other young female activists or fighters: whether from South Africa in the 1970s or 2010s; other African liberation movements in Mozambique and Algeria; or civil wars in Sri Lanka and Nicaragua. While there were distinctive factors about township life in South Africa during the 1980s that bred this particular form of young women's resistance, there is also clearly something more universal about how marginalised girls and female youth can fight the multiple injustices or inequalities they experience through their involvement in wider political movements.

To understand the ongoing struggles South African girls and female youth face, and the various ways in which they respond to or fight against these, it is imperative to explore the longer history of young women's lives and activism in the country. While historians have elucidated much about African women and youth living under apartheid, girls have been consistently omitted from this scholarship. 'Youth' in the country have subsequently come to be seen as inherently and uniformly male. This book has demonstrated that the generational struggles faced by African boys and young men in South Africa during the 1980s were not experienced by them alone but were also shared by their female counterparts. Girls, too, suffered the declining quality of Bantu education, corporal punishment in schools, and the

---

[2]   Amanda Gouws, '#EndRapeCulture Camapain in South Africa: Resisting Sexual Violence through Protest and the Politics of Experience,' *Politikon* 45:1 (2018): 9.

[3]   Mbali Matandela, 'Rhodes Must Fall: How black women claimed their place,' *Mail & Guardian*, 30 March 2015; Kagure Mugo, 'When Comrades Rape Comrades,' *Mail & Guardian*, 27 November 2015; 'Wits FMF Feminists stand in solidarity with #RUReferencelist protestors,' *Wits Vuvuzela*, 26 April 2016; Amanda Gouws, 'How South Africa's young women activists are rewriting the script,' *The Conversation*, 15 June 2016.

military occupation of township streets. These experiences, combined with curiosity and exposure to already politicised people, could lead both girls and boys to seek out and join political organisations. The feelings of camaraderie, excitement, and agency that attending meetings, marching in rallies, or battling with police could bring were also not exclusive to young men during these years, but were equally important in motivating and sustaining the political actions of young women. Female comrades themselves insist that their generational identities were more important to their politics than their gendered ones; they identify themselves as 'comrades' much more so than they do as 'girls' or 'women'.

Yet it is equally imperative to acknowledge the ways in which female comrades' generational identities, and the injustices they experienced on account of their age, race, and class, intersected with their gender identities and the particular discrimination and violence they faced as girls and young women. Being both young and female in South Africa's townships during the 1980s and early 1990s came with a specific set of fears, concerns, and pressures. Girls often felt as though they were inferior, second-class citizens compared to their male counterparts. Outside school they were much more confined to the domestic space of the home, bearing the burden of domestic work and also their parents' concerns over their safety and respectability. Some were already parents themselves and cared for their own children while they struggled to complete school or find reliable wage labour. And perhaps most significantly, their everyday lives were marked by the relentless fear of sexual violence, which could be perpetrated by almost any man they came across – teachers, fellow students, gangsters, family members, neighbours, or the police.

These experiences shaped the decisions girls made to avoid, ignore, or join political organisations such as COSAS. Deciding to commit one's teenage years to the liberation struggle was neither an inevitable nor uncomplicated decision for young women at the time. Yet female comrades' own recollections demonstrate that it was the defining decision of many women's lives. For most, their mobilisation was not demarcated by a single, grand moment but by an evolving political curiosity, sense of belonging, and dedication. Initially, participation in the struggle brought girls new feelings of freedom, excitement, and camaraderie that were a welcome departure from their often-tedious home lives. Yet with time they found that the struggle could bring more significant benefits too. It could provide them with a sense of self-worth and agency, offer a political education that school could not, and deliver a radical departure from the feelings of subservience and victimhood instilled in them as young women. For many female comrades, it was in their engagement in collective action in township streets where they felt this freedom and agency most acutely, and where they most publicly challenged gender stereotypes and demonstrated their strength and bravery.

We can thus see the intersectional identities and overlapping grievances which led girls and young women to join the struggle and shaped the nature of their political participation. Multiple scholars have recently highlighted how the struggle was not simply or always a revolt against apartheid, but also 'incorporated protests over many immediate and often local social, economic and political issues in addition to the overarching issues of ending the political system of apartheid.'[4] For female comrades, their involvement was not solely about politics and ideology but was also a means by which they could address the injustices and victimisation they faced as young women growing up in apartheid's townships.

However, there are dangers in painting too rosy a picture of female comrades' involvement in the struggle. To do so would be to reproduce dominant but uncritical narratives of the heroism and triumphalism of the liberation movement. Joining the student movement and participating in collective action brought new dangers and hardships to both young men and women's lives, most profoundly in the detention, torture, and subsequent trauma so many activists suffered. This book has demonstrated how these pitfalls of political participation were also deeply gendered and felt differently by young female activists, who struggled to reconcile their private and public lives and experienced particular vulnerabilities. In the aftermath of the struggle, these difficulties have not been confined to the past or easy to resolve; now in their forties or fifties, these women still contend daily with the ongoing trauma, regret, and uncertainty that their involvement in the struggle occasioned. Furthermore, we must acknowledge that the comrade movement was not always the empowering environment for young women that interviewees initially paint it as. Rather, comrade culture was influenced by and operated within wider township gender ideologies, and regardless of the intentions some male comrades may have had to include girls as equals, it remained mired by inequality and discrimination.

This book has begun to fill the gap in our understanding of how young women experienced township life in an era of multiple and overlapping forms of personal and political violence. Much work remains to be done in this field: on other decades, locations, and groups of young women; rural areas; coloured or Indian youth; the LGBTQ+ community; and on quiescent girls and young women during apartheid – an area where research remains incredibly scant. Yet this book has done more than supplement existing knowledge. The narratives

---

[4]   Seekings, 'Whose Voices,' 19.

and perspectives of female comrades also complicate and challenge existing histories of South Africa's liberation struggle in multiple ways.

First, these women's stories have much to teach us about gender, the apartheid era, and the liberation movement. In public accounts of South Africa's history, women are generally depicted in one of two ways: either as 'secondary victims' of apartheid abuses who suffered from the targeting, torturing, or killing of their husbands and sons; or as female activists who joined the struggle *because of* their identities as mothers or wives, fighting to protect or avenge their children or carry forward their husbands' causes in their absence. Yet female comrades' narratives resist both these tropes and provide us with a more complex view of gender and the struggle than the TRC or commemoration initiatives have been able to. In their accounts they are neither secondary nor victims, but instead active agents central to the struggle. They also reveal a form of women's political agency not couched in motherhood or political wifehood but expressed independently from women's relationships within the family. Furthermore, female comrades evidence how women can be engaged in the struggle not primarily as women or organised around issues explicitly relating to gender equality. This demonstrates the need to expand our analysis of women's activism in South Africa beyond women's organisations or movements. In her work on women in the Black Consciousness Movement, Leslie Hadfield poses an important question: 'Do women have to organize around gender directly to have a legitimate political consciousness, a wider gender consciousness, or an impact on the position of women in society?'[5] The lives of female comrades, it would seem, provide a clear 'no' in response.

The narratives of female comrades also help us to further blur the false divides between private and public spheres, and the personal and political, which still too often pervade histories of the liberation movement. Their life histories are dominated by their identities and activities as political actors. Yet central to these are their relationships with their parents or grandparents, their experiences within the domestic sphere, and the relationships they formed with each other. Details about what many may think to be the foundations of political activism – ideology, organisational structure, or leadership – are surprisingly absent from their accounts. Instead they provide us with an insight into how it *felt* to be a comrade, and how young activists were not simply political actors, but also community members, children, students, and friends. They enable us to see how these overlapping identities led young people to engage in a wide range of 'political' activities that were not limited to meetings, protests, and street confrontations, but also included community and

---

[5] Leslie Hadfield, *Liberation and Development: Black Consciousness Community Programs in South Africa* (East Lansing: Michigan State University Press, 2016), 9.

social work. Furthermore, they offer new insight into the challenges of being a comrade: the disrupted home lives; family disputes and parental pressures; and social stigma many young women contended with alongside fears of state repression. This offers an important lesson to future research: that we need to work against rigid boundaries that separate activism from quiescence, or histories of the liberation struggle from social histories of township life, in order to better understand both topics.

Finally, as the previous chapter demonstrated, female comrades' narratives also challenge the temporal divides in histories of the liberation struggle. February 1990 or April 1994 held little significance in their life histories. It was difficult to pin down exactly when their involvement in the struggle came to an end, and many see themselves as 'still struggling' today, or apartheid as being far from over. In many ways this is because what they were 'struggling' for in the 1980s involved so much more than non-racial democracy. The poor quality of education, violence in schools, and pervasive threat of sexual abuse in the townships were not automatically bettered with the end of apartheid. As Dlamini reminds us, 'There are many South Africans for whom the past, the present and the future are not discrete wholes, with clear splits between them.'[6]

The stories female comrades tell are complex and contradictory. Their narratives do not combine to make up a single, homogenous story. Instead, each woman has her own narrative that often contradicts others, or even contains ambiguities and discrepancies within itself. At the end of this book we are left with more inconsistencies than clear answers: female comrades were considered equals within the comrade movement yet were clearly discriminated against; they were both empowered and disempowered as women through their activism; they were brave and tough yet vulnerable. But these complexities talk back to dominant narratives which tend to paint the liberation struggle as unified, linear, and triumphant. They reveal a messier but likely more honest and raw account of *both* the benefits and pitfalls of being a young comrade. As Gqola writes:

> When we talk about how gloriously revolutionary the 1980s were, we are right. But what are the connections between the down-playing of women's roles in the struggle and what the experience of the role was? To revisit the history of activism means taking seriously the fact that women had experiences that sometimes complicated narrow retellings of the struggle.[7]

---

[6]   Dlamini, *Native Nostalgia*, 12.
[7]   Gqola, 'Cult of Femininity,' 120.

Female comrades' narratives conform to neither the 'victimology' that often portrays black South Africans as 'pathetic objects of colonialism, racism, oppression, poverty, patriarchy, and capitalism', nor to accounts that celebrate and romanticise the struggle as the teleological triumph of good over evil.[7]

Historians have long acknowledged the absence of female youth from histories of the township uprisings. Yet the lives of African girls and young women in South Africa remain little understood. Here, female comrades give us their version of events. Some readers may find gaps in the book, relating to political ideology, organisational structure, or the lives of young women beyond this small cohort of activists. Yet the book reflects the views of the township uprisings as they are recollected by the girls and young women who participated in them. In sharing their stories, these women have not only added their contributions to existing histories of the liberation struggle but have also renegotiated these histories and challenged how we think about gender, generation, violence, and memory in South Africa.

---

[7] Bozzoli, *Women of Phokeng*, 239.

Bibliography

Primary Sources

Individual Oral History Interviews

Most interviewees expressed their wish to have their real names used in this research. Some, as indicated below, wished to be identified using a preferred nickname or requested pseudonymisation. Given the sensitive nature of much of their recollections, only interviewees' first names have been used here and certain biographical details (such as date of birth, occupation, etc.) have been left out.

* = pseudonym

** = preferred nickname

Amahle,* interviewed in her home in Jabavu, 10 June 2015. Amahle first became involved in student activism in White City, Jabavu in 1990, then aged fourteen.

'ATV',** interviewed in his yard in Diepkloof, 2 May 2015. 'ATV' first became involved in the struggle as a school student in Diepkloof around 1986–1987, then aged fourteen or fifteen.

Beatrice, interviewed in her home in Pimville, 23 May 2015. Beatrice joined the student struggle in Pimville around 1985, then aged around sixteen.

Bessie, interviewed in a café in Johannesburg, 25 April 2014. Bessie joined COSAS in Dlamini in 1979, then aged around fourteen. She played a key leadership role in the organisation in Soweto.

Bongani, interviewed in a café in Johannesburg, 4 June 2015. Bongani joined the student struggle in Diepkloof around 1986–1987, then aged thirteen or fourteen.

Bongo, interviewed in his home in Diepkloof, 5 April 2015. Bongo first engaged in the struggle by pamphleting as a young boy in the early to mid-1980s, then joined COSAS once he entered secondary school in 1986, then aged around fifteen.

'Boy George',** Interviewed in his friend's home in Pimville, 17 May 2015. 'Boy George' was recruited into the student movement in Pimville around 1986, then aged seventeen or eighteen.

Carol, interviewed in her home in Diepkloof, 18 April 2015. Carol joined her school's SRC and then became active in COSAS/SOSCO around 1990, then aged fourteen.

Cecil, interviewed in his friend's home in Naledi, 18 June 2015. Cecil was active in student politics in Naledi through the mid- to late 1980s.

Florence, interviewed in her home in Diepkloof, 8 May 2014 and 3 March 2015. Florence joined COSAS in Diepkloof around 1984, then aged fifteen or sixteen.

Joshua, interviewed in his home in Diepkloof, 12 May 2014. Joshua joined COSAS in Diepkloof in 1980, then aged seventeen.

Khosi, interviewed in her home in Orlando East, 1 May 2014. Khosi joined the student struggle in Pimville in the mid-1980s around the age of sixteen.

Lindiwe, interviewed in her home in Naledi, 18 June 2015. Lindiwe joined the student struggle in Naledi as a teenager in the mid-1980s.

Lucy, interviewed in her home in Fleurhof, 7 April 2014 and 18 February 2016. Lucy became involved in COSAS in Diepkloof in the mid-1980s in her early teens, and later played a leadership role within the organisation.

Lulama, interviewed in her home in Diepkloof, 8 May 2014. Luluama was active in the student struggle in Diepkloof. She joined in 1986, then aged around seventeen.

Makgane, interviewed in his office in Sandton, 17 April 2014, and a different office in Illovo, 3 July 2015. Makgane was a key leader of the student and youth movements in Diepkloof and wider Soweto from the early 1980s through to the 1990s.

Mamosa, interviewed in her friend's home in Naledi, 18 June 2015. Mamosa became involved in student and youth politics in Naledi as a teenager in the mid-1980s.

Max, interviewed in his home in Pimville, 17 May 2015. Max became involved in COSAS in Pimville in the mid-1980s, then in his late teens.

Moses, interviewed in his home in Diepkloof, 19 April 2014. Moses became involved in COSAS in Diepkloof in 1984, then around age eighteen.

Musa, interviewed in his parents' home in Diepkloof 8 May 2014, at his friend's house in Pimville, 17 May 2015, again in his parents' home in Diepkloof, 13 June 2015, and lastly at Diepkloof Hall, 14 February 2016. Musa joined the student struggle in Diepkloof in 1985, then around age fifteen. He became a key leader of the movement in Diepkloof and wider Soweto.

Nomsa, interviewed in her home in Diepkloof Extension, 19 April 2014. Nomsa joined her school's SRC and then became active in SOSCO in Diepkloof in 1986, then aged fourteen.

Nonkululeko, interviewed in her home in Diepkloof, 8 April 2014, and her new home in Orlando East, 18 February 2016. Nonkululeko joined the student struggle in Diepkloof in 1985, then around the age of fifteen.

Ntebaleng, interviewed in her home in Diepkloof, 15 April 2014. Ntebaleng joined the student struggle in Diepkloof in the mid-1980s when she was around the age of eighteen or nineteen.

Ntsiki, interviewed in her home in Diepkloof, 5 April 2015. Ntsiki joined COSAS in Diepkloof in her late teens in the mid-1980s.

Patrick, interviewed in his office in Diepkloof, 12 May 2014. Patrick joined the student struggle in Diepkloof in the mid- to late 1980s around the age of sixteen or seventeen.

Paul, interviewed in his home in Diepkloof, 2 May 2015 and 14 February 2016. Paul was active in student and youth politics in Diepkloof. He first joined the struggle in the mid-1980s around the age of fourteen.

Penelope, interviewed at June 16 Memorial Acre, White City, Jabavu, 12 June 2015. Penelope joined SOSCO in White City, Javavu in the late 1980s around the age of sixteen.

Phumzile, interviewed in my car in Johannesburg, 17 April 2015. Phumzile became involved in the student struggle in Diepkloof in the mid-1980s, then aged fifteen or sixteen.

Rethabile,* interviewed in her home in Diepkloof, 1 May 2014. Rethabile joined the student struggle in Diepkloof in 1989, then aged sixteen.

Sello, interviewed at the Each One Teach One offices, Diepkloof, 14 May 2014, and in his home in Orlando East, 18 February 2016. Sello joined COSAS in Diepkloof in 1984, then aged around fifteen.

Shirley, interviewed in her home in Orlando West, 3 May 2014. Shirley joined the student struggle in Orlando West in the mid-1980s, then around the age of sixteen.

Sibongile, interviewed in her office in Johannesburg, 9 June 2015. Sibongile joined her school's SRC and then became active in the student struggle in Orlando West in 1985, then aged around seventeen. She was also active in Zola, where she lived.

Siphiwe, interviewed in his friend's home in Pimville, 17 May 2015. Siphiwe was first recruited into the struggle in Dlamini at the age of fourteen in 1984 or 1985. He later became active in the student struggle in Pimville from 1987.

Sipho, interviewed at his friend's office in Diepkloof, 9 April 2015. Sipho joined COSAS in Diepkloof in 1983, then aged around fifteen.

Sissy, interviewed in her home in Diepkloof, 17 April 2015. Sissy was active in student and youth organisations in Diepkloof from the mid-1980s, having joined in her late teens.

Stompie 'Black Diamond', interviewed in a library in Naturena, 29 May 2015. Stompie joined the student struggle in 1984 around the age of eighteen and was mostly active in Zondi and Zola.

Susan, interviewed in Diepkloof Hall, 16 May 2015. Susan joined the student struggle in Diepkloof in the mid-1980s, then aged around fifteen or sixteen.

'Takazov',** interviewed in his friend's yard in Diepkloof, 2 May 2015. 'Takazov' was active in COSAS in Diepkloof in the early 1990s, having joined around the age of fourteen.

Tandeka, interviewed in a café in Cresta, Randburg, 25 April 2014. Tandeka joined the student struggle in Orlando West in 1987, then aged around nineteen.

Teboho, interviewed in his home in Orlando East, 6 April 2015. Teboho joined SOSCO in Diepkloof when he started secondary school in 1986, then aged around fourteen.

Thabisile, interviewed in her office in Johannesburg, 25 May 2015. Thabisile joined the student struggle in White City, Jabavu in the mid- to late 1980s when in her mid-teens.

Themba, interviewed in his home in Diepkloof, 6 April 2015. Themba was active in student and youth organisations in Diepkloof from 1984. He joined the struggle around the age of seventeen.

Thobile, interviewed in her home in Diepkloof, 12 April 2014. Thobile joined the student struggle at school in Diepkloof in 1986, then aged around fifteen.

Tonosi, interviewed in her home in Diepkloof, 3 May 2014. Tonosi joined the student struggle in Diepkloof in 1986, then aged seventeen.

Vicky, interviewed in her home in Diepkloof, 14 May 2014. Vicky joined her school's SRC and then became active in COSAS in Diepkloof around 1983, then aged eighteen.

'Voice',** interviewed outside his workplace in Diepkloof, 9 April 2015. 'Voice' joined COSAS in the early 1980s in Diepkloof as a teenager and secondary school student.

Zanele, interviewed in her friend's home in Diepkloof, 12 April 2014. Zanele became active in the student struggle in Diepkloof in the mid-1980s, around the age of fifteen or sixteen.

Zintle, interviewed in her home in Windsor West, 17 April 2015. Zintle was not a comrade but grew up in Soweto during the late 1980s.

Zobi, interviewed in his home in Diepkloof, 5 June 2015. Zobi joined COSAS in Diepkloof in 1988, then aged thirteen or fourteen.

Group Oral History Interviews

Group Interview with Male Comrades from Pimville (Max, Boy George, and Siphiwe), conducted in Max's home in Pimville, 17 May 2015.

Group Interview with Female Comrades from Naledi (Lindiwe and Mamosa), conducted in Lindiwe's home in Naledi, 18 June 2015.

Group Interview with Female Comrades from Diepkloof (Thobile, Lucy, Lulama, and Nonkululeko), conducted in Thobile's home in Diepkloof, 27 June 2015.

Archival Sources

University of the Witwatersrand Historical Papers Research Archive (HP)

AG2918 – KAIROS
AG2523 – Detainees Parents Support Committee (DPSC)
AD1790 – Congress of South African Students (COSAS)
AG3245 – Centre for the Study of Violence and Reconciliation (CSVR)
AC623 – South African Council of Churches
AG2413 – Human Rights Commission

South African History Archive, Johannesburg

AL2425 – South African Youth Congress (SAYCO)
AL2431 – United Democratic Front (UDF)

Truth and Reconciliation Commission (Online)

Sandra Adonis, TRC Youth Hearings, Athlone, 22 May 1997, https://www.justice.gov.za/trc/special/children/adonis.htm, accessed 7 September 2014.

Sheila Meintjes and Beth Goldblatt, 'Gender and the Truth and Reconciliation Commission,' submission to the Truth and Reconciliation Commission, May 1996, https://www.justice.gov.za/trc/hrvtrans/submit/gender.htm, accessed 10 August 2014.

Centre for the Study of Violence and Reconciliation (Online)

Graeme Simpson, 'Women and Children in Violent South African Townships,' 1993, https://www.csvr.org.za/%20index.php/publications/1620-women-and-children-in-violent-south-african-townships.html, accessed 3 February 2015.

Graeme Simpson, 'Jack-asses and Jackrollers: Rediscovering Gender in Understanding Violence,' 1992, https://www.csvr.org.za/publications/1547-jack-asses-and-jackrollers-rediscovering-gender-in-understanding-violence, accessed 29 November 2014.

Steve Mokwena, 'The Era of the Jackrollers: Contextualising the rise of youth gangs in Soweto,' 1991, https://www.csvr.org.za/publications/1805-the-era-of-the-jackrollers-contextualising-the-rise-of-the-youth-gangs-in-soweto, accessed 29 November 2014.

Joanna Ball, 'The Ritual of the Necklace,' 1994, https://www.csvr.org.za/publications/1632-the-ritual-of-the-necklace.html, accessed 30 January 2015.

Miscellaneous Primary Sources

South African Institute of Race Relations, *Survey of Race Relations 1984* (Johannesburg, 1985).

Cries of Freedom: Women in Detention in South Africa (London, Catholic Institute for International Relations, 1988).

Other Online Sources

Each One Teach One Foundation, http://www.eotof.org.za/, accessed 29 August 2016.

Human Rights Watch, 'South Africa: The State Response to Domestic Violence and Rape,' November 1995, https://www.hrw.org/report/1995/11/01/violence-against-women-south-africa/state-response-domestic-violence-and-rape, accessed 10 November 2014.

'The Conflict between the AZAPO and the UDF – popular violence in the 1980s and 1990s,' *South African History Online*, September 2012, http://www.sahistory.org.za/topic/war-between-azapo-and-udf-popular-violence-1980s-and-1990s, accessed 14 June 2015.

Periodicals

Business Day
City Press
Daily Maverick
Mail & Guardian
Sunday Tribune
The Citizen
The Conversation

The Sowetan
The Star
The Weekly Mail
Wits Vuvuzela

Printed Primary Sources

Breytenbach, Breyten. *The True Confessions of an Albino Terrorist* (London: Faber and Faber, 1984).
Brittain, Victoria, and Abdul S. Minty (eds), *Children of Resistance: On Children, Repression and the Law in Apartheid South Africa. Statements from the Harare Conference* (London: Kliptown Books, 1988).
First, Ruth. *One Hundred and Seventeen Days: An Account of Confinement and Interrogation under South African Ninety-Day Detention Law* (London: W.H. Allen, 1975).
Mandela, Nelson. *Long Walk to Freedom* (Boston; London: Little, Brown & Co, 1994).
Naidoo, Indres. *Island in Chains: Ten years on Robben Island* (London: Penguin, 1982).
Sachs, Albie. *The Jail Diary of Albie Sachs* (London: Paladin, 1990).
Tlhabi, Redi. *Endings and Beginnings: A Story of Healing* (Johannesburg: Jacana, 2012).
—— *Khwezi* (Johannesburg: Jonathan Ball, 2017).

Secondary Sources

Unpublished

Campbell, Catherine. 'Identity and Gender in a Changing Society: The Social Identity of South African Township Youth.' (PhD thesis, Department of Psychology, University of Bristol, 1992).
Carter, Charles. 'Comrades and Community: Politics and the Construction of Hegemony in Alexandra Township, South Africa, 1984–1987' (DPhil thesis, University of Oxford, 1991).
Goldblatt, Beth and Sheila Meintjes. 'Women: one chapter in the history of South Africa? A critique of the Truth and Reconciliation Commission Report.' Draft paper presented at CSVR/History Workshop Conference, 'The TRC: Commissioning the Past,' 13 June 1999.
Johnson, Rachel E. 'Making History, Gendering Youth: Young Women and South Africa's Liberation Struggles after 1976.' (PhD thesis, Department of History, University of Sheffield, 2010).
Kunz, Rahel, and Ann-Kristin Sjoberg, 'Empowered or Oppressed? Female Combatants in the Colombian Guerrilla: The Case of the Revolutionary Armed Forces of Colombia – FARC.' Paper presented at the Annual Convention of the International Studies Association, New York, February 2009, 1–33.
Moosage, Riedwaan. 'The Impasse of Violence: Writing Necklacing into a History of the Liberation Struggle in South Africa.' (Master's thesis, University of the Western Cape, 2010).

Noble, Vanessa. 'Doctors Divided: Gender, Race and Class Anomalies in the Production of Black Medical Doctors in Apartheid South Africa, 1948–1994.' (PhD thesis, History and Women's Studies, University of Michigan, 2005).

Seekings, Jeremy. 'Quiescence and the Transition to Confrontation: South African Townships, 1978–1984.' (DPhil thesis, University of Oxford, 1990).

Shai, Phambili Nwabisa. 'Constructions of Femininity in the Context of Sexual Relationships among Women living in the Rural Eastern Cape Province, South Africa.' (PhD thesis, Department of Public Health, University of the Witwatersrand, 2018).

Wells, Julia C. 'The History of Black Women's Struggle against Pass Laws in South Africa, 1900–1960.' (PhD thesis, Columbia University, 1982).

Published

Agger, Inger. 'Sexual Torture of Political Prisoners: An Overview.' *Journal of Traumatic Stress* 2:3 (1989): 305–318.

Alexander, Jocelyn. 'Political Prisoners' Memoirs in Zimbabwe: Narratives of Self and Nation.' *Cultural and Social History* 5:4 (2008): 395–409.

Alison, Miranda. 'Cogs in the Wheel? Women in the Liberation Tigers of Tamil Eelam.' *Civil Wars* 6:4 (2003): 37–54.

Ally, Shireen. 'Peaceful Memories: Remembering and Forgetting Political Violence in KaNgwane, South Africa.' *Africa* 81:3 (2011): 351–372.

Ashforth, Adam. 'Weighing Manhood in Soweto.' *Codesria Bulletin* 3–4 (1999): 51–58.

—— *Witchcraft, Violence, and Democracy in South Afric* (Chicago: University of Chicago Press, 2005).

Barth, Elise Fredrikke. *Peace as Disappointment: The Reintegration of Female Soldiers in Post-Conflict Societies: A Comparative Study from Africa* (Oslo: International Peace Research Institute, 2002).

Beall, Jo, Shireen Hassim, and Alison Todes. 'African Women in the Durban Struggle, 1985–1986: Towards a Transformation of Roles?' In G. Moss and I. Obery (eds), *South African Review 4*, (Johannesburg: Raven Press, 1987), 93–103.

—— '"A Bit on the Side"?: Gender Struggles in the Politics of Transformation in South Africa.' *Feminist Review* 33 (1989): 33–47.

Bernal, Victoria. 'Equality to Die For?: Women Guerrilla Fighters and Eritrea's Cultural Revolution.' *Political and Legal Anthropology Review* 23:2 (2000): 61–76.

—— 'From Warriors to Wives: Contradictions of Liberation and Development in Eritrea.' *Northeast African Studies* 8:3 (2001): 129–154.

Bhana, Deevia. '"Girls are not free" – In and Out of the South African School.' *International Journal of Educational Development* 32:2 (2012): 352–358.

Bonner, Philip. '"Desirable or Undesirable Basotho Women?" Liquor, Prostitution and the Migration of Basotho Women to the Rand, 1920–1945.' In Cherryl Walker (ed), *Women and Gender in Southern Africa to 1945* (London: James Currey, 1990), 221–250.

Bonner, Philip, and Lauren Segal. *Soweto: A History* (Cape Town: Maskew Miller Longman, 1998).

Bonnin, Debby. 'Claiming Spaces, Changing Places: Political Violence and Women's Protests in KwaZulu-Natal.' *Journal of Southern African Studies* 26:2 (2000): 301–316.

Bose, Sumantra. *States, Nations, Sovereignty: Sri Lanka, India and the Tamil Eelam Movement* (New Delhi: Sage Publications, 1994).

Bozzoli, Belinda. 'Marxism, Feminism and South African Studies.' *Journal of Southern African Studies* 9:2 (1983): 139–171.

—— 'Why were the 1980s "Millenarian"? Style, Repertories, Space and Authority in South Africa's Black Cities.' *Journal of Historical Sociology* 13:1 (2000): 78–110.

—— *Theatres of Struggles and the End of Apartheid* (Athens: Ohio University Press, 2004).

Bozzoli, Belinda, with Mmantho Nkotsoe. *The Women of Phokeng: Consciousness, Life Strategy, and Migrancy in South Africa, 1900–1983* (London: James Currey, 1991).

Bradford, Helen. '"We are now the men": Women's Beer Protests in the Natal Countryside, 1929.' In Belinda Bozzoli (ed), *Class, Community and Conflict: South African Perspectives* (Johannesburg: Ravan Press, 1987), 292–323.

Bray, Rachel, Imke Gooskens, Sue Moses, Lauren Kahn, and Jeremy Seekings. *Growing Up in the New South Africa: Childhood and Adolescence in Post-Apartheid Cape Town* (Cape Town: HSRC Press, 2010).

Bridger, Emily. 'From "Mother of the Nation" to "Lady Macbeth": Winnie Mandela and Perceptions of Female Violence in South Africa, 1985–91.' *Gender & History* 27:2 (2015): 446–464.

—— 'Soweto's Female Comrades: Gender, Youth and Violence in South Africa's Township Uprisings, 1984–1990.' *Journal of Southern African Studies* 44:4 (2018): 559–574.

Brooks, Alan, and Jeremy Brickhill. *Whirlwind before the Storm: The Origins and Development of the Uprising in Soweto and the Rest of South Africa from June to December 1976* (London: International Defence and Aid Fund, 1980).

Bundy, Colin. 'Street Sociology and Pavement Politics: Aspects of Youth and Student Resistance in Cape Town, 1985.' *Journal of Southern African Studies* 13:3 (1987): 303–330.

Buntman, Fran Lisa. *Robben Island and Prisoner Resistance to Apartheid* (Cambridge: Cambridge University Press, 2003).

Burman, Sandra, and Pamela Reynolds (eds), *Growing Up in a Divided Society: The Contexts of Childhood in South Africa* (Johannesburg: Ravan Press, 1986).

Burton, Andrew, and Helene Charton-Bigot (eds), *Generations Past: Youth in East African History* (Athens: Ohio University Press, 2010).

Buur, Lars, and Steffen Jensen. 'Introduction: Vigilantism and the Policing of Everyday Life in South Africa.' *African Studies* 63:2 (2004): 139–152.

Campbell, Catherine. 'The Township Family and Women's Struggles.' *Agenda* 6 (1990): 1–22.

—— 'Learning to Kill? Masculinity, the Family and Violence in Natal,' *Journal of Southern African Studies* 18:3 (1992): 614–628.

Carter, Charles. '"We Are the Progressives": Alexandra Youth Congress Activists and the Freedom Charter, 1983–85.' *Journal of Southern African Studies* 17:2 (1991): 197–220.

Cherry, Janet. '"We were not afraid": The Role of Women in the 1980s Township Uprising in the Eastern Cape." In Nomboniso Gasa (ed), *Women in South African History: They remove boulders and cross rivers* (Cape Town: HSRC Press, 2007), 281–313.

—— 'The Intersection of Violent and Non-Violent Strategies in the South African Liberation Struggle.' In Hilary Sapire and Chris Saunders (eds), *Southern African Liberation Struggles: New Local, Regional and Global Perspectives* (Cape Town: UCT Press, 2012), 142–161.

Chikane, Frank. 'Children in Turmoil: The Effects of the Unrest on Township Children.' In Sandra Burman and Pamela Reynolds (eds), *Growing up in a Divided Society: The Contexts of Childhood in South Africa* (Johannesburg, Ravan Press, 1986), 333–344.

Clifford, Rebecca. 'Emotions and Gender in Oral History: Narrating Italy's 1968.' *Modern Italy* 17:2 (2012): 209–221.

Cock, Jacklyn. *Colonels and Cadres: War and Gender in South Africa* (Cape Town: Oxford University Press, 1991).

Comaroff, Jean, and John Comaroff. 'Reflections on Youth: From the Past to the Postcolony.' In Alcinda Manuel Honwana and Filip de Boeck (eds), *Makers and Breakers: Children and Youth in Postcolonial Africa* (Oxford: James Currey, 2005), 19–30.

Coombes, Annie E. 'Witnessing History/Embodying Testimony: Gender and Memory in Post-Apartheid South Africa.' *Journal of the Royal Anthropological Institute* 17 (2011): 92–112.

Cooper, Frederick. 'Conflict and Connection: Rethinking Colonial African History.' *The American Historical Review* 99:5 (1994): 1516–1545.

Coulter, Chris. 'Female Fighters in the Sierra Leone War: Challenging the Assumption?' *Feminist Review* 88 (2008): 54–73.

Coulter, Chris, Mariam Persson, and Mats Utas. *Young Female Fighters in African Wars: Conflict and Its Consequences* (Uppsala: Norkiska Afrikainstitutet, 2008).

Culbertson, Roberta. 'Embodied Memory, Transcendence, and Telling: Recounting Trauma, Re-Establishing the Self.' *New Literary History* 26:1 (1995): 169–195.

Delius, Peter, and Clive Glaser. 'Sexual Socialisation in South Africa: A Historical Perspective.' *African Studies* 61:1 (2002): 27–54.

Denov, Myriam. 'Girls in Fighting Forces: Moving Beyond Victimhood.' (Canadian International Development Agency, 2007).

Dietrich Ortega, Luisa Maria. 'Looking Beyond Violent Militarized Masculinities: Guerrilla Gender Regimes in Latin America.' *International Feminist Journal of Politics* 14:4 (2012): 489–507.

Diseko, Nozipho J. 'The Origins and Development of the South African Student's Movement (SASM): 1968–1976.' *Journal of Southern African Studies* 18:1 (1992): 40–62.

Dlamini, Jacob. *Native Nostalgia* (Johannesburg: Jacana, 2009).

—— *Askari: A Story of Collaboration and Betrayal in the Anti-Apartheid Struggle* (New York: Oxford University Press, 2015).

Douglas, Jack. *Creative Interviewing* (Beverly Hills: Sage Publications, 1985).

Duff, Sarah Emily. *Changing Childhoods in the Cape Colony: Dutch Reformed Church Evangelicalism and Colonial Childhood, 1860–1895* (Basingstoke: Palgrave Macmillan, 2015).

Erlank, Natasha. 'ANC Positions on Gender, 1994–2004.' *Politikon: South African Journal of Political Studies* 32:2 (2005): 195–215.

Field, Sean. 'Disappointed Remains: Trauma, Testimony, and Reconciliation in Post-Apartheid South Africa.' In Donald A. Ritchie (ed), *Oxford Handbook of Oral History* (Oxford: Oxford University Press, 2011), 142–159.

—— *Oral History, Community, and Displacement: Imagining Memories in Post-Apartheid South Africa* (New York: Palgrave Macmillan, 2012).

Filippi, Natacha. 'Women's Protests: Gender, Imprisonment and Resistance in South Africa (Pollsmoor Prison, 1970s–90s).' *Review of African Political Economy* 43:149 (2016): 436–450.

Foster, Don, and Donald Skinner. 'Detention and Violence: Beyond Victimology.' In N. Chabani Manganyi and Andre du Toit (eds), *Political Violence and the Struggle in South Africa* (New York: St. Martin's, 1990), 205–233.

Franco, Jean. 'Gender, Death and Resistance: Facing the Ethical Vacuum.' In Juan E. Corradi, Patricia Weiss Fagen, Manuel Antonio Garretón (eds), *Fear at the Edge: State Terror and Resistance in Latin America* (Berkeley: University of California Press, 1992), 104–118.

Gaitskell, Deborah. '"Christian Compounds for Girls": Church Hostels for African Women in Johannesburg, 1907–1970.' *Journal of Southern African Studies* 6:1 (1979): 44–69.

—— 'Housewives, Maids or Mothers: Some Contradictions of Domesticity for Christian Women in Johannesburg, 1903–39.' *The Journal of African History* 24:2 (1983): 241–256.

George, Abosede. *Making Modern Girls: A History of Girlhood, Labor, and Social Development in Colonial Lagos* (Athens: Ohio University Press, 2014).

Gilmore, Leigh. *The Limits of Autobiography: Trauma and Testimony* (Ithaca and London: Cornell University Press, 2001).

Glaser, Clive. 'The Mark of Zorro: Sexuality and Gender Relations in the Tsotsi Subculture on the Witwatersrand.' *African Studies* 51:1 (1992): 47–68.

—— '"We must infiltrate the Tsotsis": School Politics and Youth Gangs in Soweto, 1968–1976.' *Journal of Southern African Studies* 24:2 (1998): 301–323.

—— *Bo-Tsotsi: The Youth Gangs of Soweto, 1935–1976* (Oxford: James Currey, 2000).

—— 'Soweto's Islands of Learning: Morris Isaacson and Orlando High Schools under Bantu Education, 1958–1975.' *Journal of Southern African Studies* 41:1 (2015): 159–171.

—— 'Learning Amidst the Turmoil: Secondary Schooling in Soweto, 1977–1990.' *South African Historical Journal* 68:3 (2016): 415–436.

—— 'Youth and Generation in South African History.' *Safundi* 19:2 (2018): 117–138.

Godobo-Madikizela, Pumla. 'Language Rules: Witnessing about Trauma on South Africa's TRC.' *River Teeth: A Journal of Non-Fiction Narrative* 8 (2007): 25–33.

—— 'Re-Membering the Past: Nostalgia, Traumatic Memory and the Legacy of Apartheid.' *Peace and Conflict: Journal of Peace Psychology* 18 (2012): 252–267.

Gordon, Hava Rachel. 'Gendered Paths to Teenage Political Participation: Parental Power, Civic Mobility, and Youth Activism.' *Gender & Society* 22:1 (2008): 31–55.

Gouws, Amanda. '#EndRapeCulture Campaign in South Africa: Resisting Sexual Violence through Protest and the Politics of Experience.' *Politikon* 45:1 (2018): 3–15.

Gqola, Puma Dineo. 'How the "cult of femininity" and violent masculinities support endemic gender based violence in contemporary South Africa.' *African Identities* 5:1 (2007): 111–124.

—— *Rape: A South African Nightmare* (Johannesburg: MFBooks Joburg, 2015).

Gready, Paul. 'Autobiography and the "Power of Writing": Political Prison Writing in the Apartheid Era.' *Journal of Southern African Studies* 19:3 (1993): 489–523.

—— *Writing as Resistance: Life Stories of Imprisonment, Exile, and Homecoming from Apartheid South Africa* (Lanham: Lexington Books, 2003).

Hadfield, Leslie. *Liberation and Development: Black Consciousness Community Programs in South Africa* (East Lansing: Michigan State University Press, 2016).

Harris, Verne. '"They Should Have Destroyed More": The Destruction of Public Records by the South African State in the Final Years of Apartheid, 1990–94.' *Transformation* 42 (2000): 29–56.

Hassim, Shireen. 'The Limits of Popular Democracy: Women's Organisations, Feminism and the UDF.' *Transformation: Critical Perspectives on Southern Africa* 51:1 (2003): 48–73.

—— 'Nationalism, Feminism and Autonomy: The ANC in Exile and the Question of Women.' *Journal of Southern African Studies* 30:3 (2004): 433–456.

—— *Women's Organizations and Democracy in South Africa: Contesting Authority* (Madison: University of Wisconsin Press, 2006).

Healy-Clancy, Meghan. *A World of Their Own: A History of South African Women's Education* (Charlottesville: University of Virginia Press, 2013).

—— 'The Everyday Politics of being a Student in South Africa: A History.' *History Compass* 15:3 (2017): 1–12.

—— 'The Family Politics of the Federation of South African Women: A History of Public Motherhood in Women's Antiracist Activism.' *Signs* 42:4 (2017): 843–866.

Heffernan, Anne. *Limpopo's Legacy: Student Politics and Democracy in South Africa* (Suffolk: James Currey, 2019).

Herman, Judith Lewis. *Trauma and Recovery: From Domestic Abuse to Political Terror* (London: Pandora, 1992).

Hiralal, Kalpana. 'Narratives and Testimonies of Women Detainees in the Anti-Apartheid Struggle.' *Agenda* 29:4 (2015): 34–44.

Hirson, Baruch. *Year of Fire, Year of Ash: The Soweto Revolt, Roots of a Revolution?* (London: Zed Books, 1979).

Hlongwane, Ali Khangela, Sifiso Mxolisi Ndlovu, and Mothobi Mutloatse. *Soweto '76: Reflections on the Liberation Struggles* (Johannesburg: Pan Macmillan, 2006).

Hofmeyr, Isabel. *'We spend our years as a tale that is told': Oral Historical Narrative in a South African Chiefdom* (Portsmouth: Heinemann, 1994).

Honwana, Alcinda, and Filip de Boeck (eds), *Makers & Breakers: Children and Youth in Postcolonial Africa* (Oxford: James Currey, 2005).

Houston, Gregory. 'The ANC's Internal Underground Political Work in the 1980s.' In SADET (eds), *The Road to Democracy in South Africa*, volume 4 part 1 (Pretoria: UNISA, 2010), 133–222.

Houston, Gregory, and Bernard Magubane. 'The ANC Political Underground in the 1970s.' In SADET (eds), *The Road to Democracy in South Africa*, volume 2 (Pretoria: UNISA, 2007), 371–451.

Hunter, Mark. *Love in the Time of AIDS: Inequality, Gender, and Rights in South Africa* (Bloomington: Indiana University Press, 2010).

——— 'The Bond of Education Gender, the Value of Children, and the Making of Umlazi Township in 1960s South Africa.' *The Journal of African History* 55:3 (2014): 467–490.

Hynd, Stacey. 'Trauma, Violence, and Memory in African Child Soldier Memoirs.' *Culture, Psychiatry and Medicine* (2020), forthcoming special issue.

Hyslop, Jonathan. 'School Student Movements and State Education Policy, 1972–87.' In William Cobbett and Robin Cohen (eds), *Popular Struggles in South Africa* (London: James Currey, 1988), 183–209.

——— *The Classroom Struggle: Policy and Resistance in South Africa 1940–1990* (Pietermaritzburg: University of Natal Press, 1999).

Jewkes, Rachel, and Robert Morrell. 'Gender and Sexuality: Emerging Perspectives from the Heterosexual Epidemic in South Africa and Implications for HIV Risk and Prevention.' *Journal of the International AIDS Society* 13:6 (2010): 1–11.

——— 'Sexuality and the Limits of Agency among South African Teenage Women: Theorising Femininities and Their Connections to HIV Risk Practises.' *Social Science & Medicine* 74:11 (2012): 1729–1737.

Jewkes, Rachel, and Katherine Wood. '"Dangerous" Love: Reflections on Violence among Xhosa Township Youth.' In Andrea Cornwall (ed), *Readings in Gender in Africa* (London: The International African Institute, 2005), 95–102.

Jewkes, Rachel, Kristin Dunkle, Mzikazi Nduna, and Nwabisa Shai. 'Intimate Partner Violence, Relationship Power Inequity, and Incidence of HIV Infection in Young Women in South Africa: A Cohort Study.' *The Lancet* 376:9734 (2010): 41–48.

Johnson, Rachel. '"The Girl About Town": Discussions of Modernity and Female Youth in Drum Magazine, 1951–1970.' *Social Dynamics* 35:1 (2009): 36–50.

Johnson, Shaun. '"The Soldiers of Luthuli": Youth in the Politics of Resistance in South Africa.' In Shaun Johnson (ed), *South Africa: No Turning Back* (Bloomington and Indianapolis: Indiana University Press, 1989), 94–152.

Kagee, Ashraf, and Anthony V. Naidoo. 'Reconceptualizing the Sequelae of Political Torture: Limitations of a Psychiatric Paradigm.' *Transcultural Psychiatry* 41:1 (2004): 46–61.

Kampwirth, Karen. *Women and Guerrilla Movements: Nicaragua, El Salvador, Chiapas, Cuba* (University Park: The Pennsylvania State University Press, 2002).

Kaplan, Temma. 'Acts of Testimony: Reversing the Shame and Gendering the Memory.' *Signs* 28:1 (2002): 179–199.

Konate, Dior. 'Ultimate Exclusion: Imprisoned Women in Senegal.' In Florence Bernault (ed), *A History of Prison and Confinement in Africa* (Portsmouth: Heinemann, 2003), 155–164.

Krige, Jana, and Marcelyn Oostendorp. '"Too late for tears, dear sister": Constructing victims and perpetrators of rape in the advice column "Dear Dolly" from 1984 to 2004.' *Stellenbosch Papers in Linguistics Plus* 46 (2015): 7–23.

Krog, Antjie. *Country of My Skull: Guilt, Sorrow, and the Limits of Forgiveness in the New South Africa* (New York: Three Rivers Press, 1998).

Kynoch, Gary. *Township Violence and the End of Apartheid: War on the Reef* (Woodbridge: James Currey, 2018).

Langa, Malose, and Gillian Eagle. 'The Intractability of Militarised Masculinity: A Case Study of Former Self-Defence Unit Members in the Kathorus Area, South Africa.' *South African Journal of Psychology* 38:1 (2008): 152–175.

Langer, Lawrence L. *Holocaust Testimonies: The Ruins of Memory* (New Haven: Yale University Press, 1991).

Lee, Rebekah. *African Women and Apartheid: Migration and Settlement in Urban South Africa* (London: IB Tauris, 2009).

Lissoni, Arianna, and Maria Suriano. 'Married to the ANC: Tanzanian Women's Entanglement in South Africa's Liberation Struggle.' *Journal of Southern African Studies* 40:1 (2014): 129–150.

Lodge, Tom, and Bill Nasson. *All Here and Now: Black Politics in South Africa in the 1980s* (London: C. Hurst and Company, 1992).

Magaziner, Daniel R. *The Law and the Prophets: Black Consciousness in South Africa, 1968–1977* (Athens: Ohio University Press, 2010).

—— 'Pieces of a (Wo)man: Feminism, Gender and Adulthood in Black Consciousness, 1968–1977.' *Journal of Southern African Studies* 37:1 (2011): 45–61.

Mager, Anne. *Gender and the Making of a South African Bantustan: A Social History of the Ciskei* (Portsmouth, NH: Heinemann, 1999).

Mager, Anne, and Gary Minkley. 'Reaping the Whirlwind: The East London Riots of 1952.' In Philip Bonner, Peter Delius and Deborah Posel (eds), *Apartheid's Genesis: 1935–1962* (Johannesburg: Witwatersrand University Press, 1993), 229–251.

Mark, James, Anna von der Goltz, and Anette Warring. 'Reflections.' In Robert Gildea, James Mark, and Anette Warring (eds), *Europe's 1968: Voices of Revolt* (Oxford: Oxford University Press, 2013), 283–325.

Marks, Monique. *Young Warriors: Youth Politics, Identity and Violence in South Africa* (Johannesburg: Witwatersrand University Press, 2001).

Maynes, Mary Jo. 'Age as a Category of Historical Analysis: History, Agency, and Narratives of Childhood.' *The Journal of the History of Childhood and Youth* 1:1 (2008): 114–124.

Mazibuko, Nokuthula. *Spring Offensive* (Limpopo: Timbila Publishing, 2006).

McClintock, Anne. '"No Longer in Future Heaven": Women and Nationalism in South Africa.' *Transition* 51 (1991): 104–123.

McDowell, Linda. *Gender, Identity and Place: Understanding Feminist Geographies* (Cambridge: Polity Press, 1999).

McRobbie, Angela, and Jenny Garber. 'Girls and Subcultures.' In Stuart Hall and Tony Jefferson (eds), *Resistance through Rituals: Youth Subcultures in Post-war Britain* (London: Routledge, 2003), 209–222.

Meintjes, Sheila. 'Political Violence and Gender: A Neglected Relation in South Africa's Struggle for Democracy.' *Politikon* 25:2 (1998): 97–104.

Merrett, Christopher. 'Detention without Trial in South Africa.' *Africa Today* 37:2 (1990): 53–66.

Miescher, Stephan F. *Making Men in Ghana* (Bloomington: Indiana University Press, 2005).

Minkley, Gary, and Ciraj Rassool. 'Orality, Memory, and Social History in South Africa.' In Sarah Nuttall and Carli Coetzee (eds), *Negotiating the Past: The Making of Memory in South Africa* (Oxford: Oxford University Press, 1998), 88–99.

Modise, Thandi, and Robyn Curnow. 'Thandi Modise: A Woman in War.' *Agenda* 43 (2000): 36–40.

Moffett, Helen. '"These women, they force us to rape them": Rape as Narrative of Social Control in Post-Apartheid South Africa.' *Journal of Southern African Studies* 32:1 (2006): 129–144.

Moletsane, Relebohile. 'South African Girlhood in the Age of AIDS: Towards Girlhood Studies?' *Agenda* 21:7 (2007): 155–165.

Morrell, Robert. 'Corporal Punishment and Masculinity in South African Schools.' *Men and Masculinities* 4:2 (2001): 140–157.

Morrell, Robert, and Relebohile Moletsane. 'Inequality and Fear: Learning and Working inside Bantu Education Schools.' In Peter Kallaway (ed), *History of Education under Apartheid, 1948–1994: The Doors of Learning and Culture Shall be Opened* (Cape Town: Peter Lang, 2002), 224–242.

Motsemme, Nthabiseng. 'The Mute Always Speak: On Women's Silences at the Truth and Reconciliation Commission.' *Current Sociology* 52:5 (2004): 909–932.

Mouton, Michelle, and Helena Pohlandt-McCormick. 'Boundary Crossings: Oral History of Nazi Germany and Apartheid South Africa: A Comparative Perspective.' *History Workshop Journal* 48 (1999): 41–63.

Naidoo, Kumi. 'The Politics of Youth Resistance in the 1980s: The Dilemmas of a Differentiated Durban.' *Journal of Southern African Studies* 18:1 (1992): 143–165.

Ndelu, Sandy, Simamkele Dlakavu, and Barbara Boswell. 'Womxn's and Nonbinary Activists' Contribution to the RhodesMustFall and FeesMustFall Student Movements: 2015 and 2016.' *Agenda* 31:3–4 (2017): 1–4.

Niehaus, Isak. 'Towards a Dubious Liberation: Masculinity, Sexuality and Power in South African Lowveld Schools, 1953–1999.' *Journal of Southern African Studies* 26:3 (2000): 387–407.

Nordstrom, Carolyn. *Girls and Warzones: Troubling Questions* (Uppsala: Life and Peace Institute, 1997).

Ntombela, Sithabile, and Nontokozo Mashiya. '"In my time, girls…": Reflections of African Adolescent Girl Identities and Realities across Two Generations.' *Agenda* 23:79 (2009): 94–106.

Nuttall, Sarah. 'Telling "free" stories? Memory and Democracy in South African Autobiography since 1994.' In Sarah Nuttall and Carli Coetzee (eds), *Negotiating the Past: The Making of Memory in South Africa* (Oxford: Oxford University Press, 1998), 75–88.

Oboe, Annalisa. 'The TRC Women's Hearings as Performance and Protest in the New South Africa.' *Research in African Literatures* 38:3 (2007): 60–76.

Ocobock, Paul. *An Uncertain Age: The Politics of Manhood in Kenya* (Athens: Ohio University Press, 2017).

Oosterhoff, Pauline, Prisca Zwanikken, and Evert Ketting. 'Sexual Torture of Men in Croatia and Other Conflict Situations: An Open Secret.' *Reproductive Health Matters* 23:23 (2004): 68–77.

Passerini, Luisa. *Fascism in Popular Memory: The Cultural Experience of the Turin Working Class* (Cambridge: Cambridge University Press, 1987).

Patai, Daphne. 'U.S. Academics and Third World Women: Is Ethical Research Possible?' In Sherna Berger Gluck and Daphne Patai (eds), *Women's Words: The Feminist Practice of Oral History* (New York: Routledge, 1991), 137–154.

Pohlandt-McCormick, Helena. *'I Saw a Nightmare—': Doing Violence to Memory: The Soweto Uprising, June 16 1976* (New York: Columbia University Press, 2007).

Portelli, Alessandro. 'The Peculiarities of Oral History,' *History Workshop Journal* 12:1 (1981): 96–107.

—— *The Death of Luigi Trastulli and Other Stories: Form and Meaning in Oral History* (New York: State University of New York Press, 1991).

—— *The Text and the Voice: Writing, Speaking, and Democracy in American Literature* (New York: Columbia University Press, 1994).

Posel, Deborah. 'The Scandal of Manhood: "Baby Rape" and the Politicization of Sexual Violence in Post-Apartheid South Africa.' *Culture, Health and Sexuality* 7:3 (2005): 239–252.

—— 'History as Confession: The Case of the South African Truth and Reconciliation Commission.' *Public Culture* 20:1 (2008): 119–141.

Posel, Dorrit, Stephanie Rudwick, and Daniela Casale. 'Is Marriage a Dying Institution in South Africa? Exploring Changes in Marriage in the Context of Ilobolo Payments.' *Agenda* 25:1 (2011): 102–111.

Ramphele, Mamphela. 'The Dynamics of Gender Politics in the Hostels of Cape Town: Another Legacy of the South African Migrant Labour System.' *Journal of Southern African Studies* 15:3 (1989): 393–414.

—— 'The Dynamics of Gender within Black Consciousness Organisations: A Personal View.' In Barney Pityana, Mamphela Ramphele, Malusi Mpumlwana, and Lindy Wilson (eds), *Bounds of Possibility: The Legacy of Steve Biko and Black Consciousness* (Cape Town: David Philip, 1991), 214–227.

Ross, Fiona. *Bearing Witness: Women and the Truth and Reconciliation Commission in South Africa* (London: Pluto Press, 2003).

Roy, Srila. 'The Everyday Life of the Revolution: Gender, Violence and Memory.' *South Asia Research* 27:2 (2007): 187–204.

—— 'The Grey Zone: The "Ordinary" Violence of Extraordinary Times.' *Journal of the Royal Anthropological Institute* 14:2 (2008): 316–333.

—— *Remembering Revolution: Gender, Violence and Subjectivity in India's Naxalbari Movement* (New Delhi: Oxford University Press, 2013).

Rueedi, Franziska. '"Siyayinyova!": Patterns of Violence in the African Townships of the Vaal Triangle, South Africa, 1980–86.' *Africa* 85:3 (2015): 395–416.

Russell, Diana E. H., and Mary Mabaso. 'Rape and Child Sexual Abuse in Soweto: An Interview with Community Leader Mary Mabaso.' *South African Sociological Review* 3:2 (1991): 62–83.

SADET. *The Road to Democracy in South Africa*, Volumes 1–7 (Johannesburg: Unisa Press, 2005–2017).

Sajjad, Tazreena. 'Women Guerillas: Marching toward True Freedom? An Analysis of Women's Experiences in the Frontlines of Guerilla Warfare and in the Post-War Period.' *Agenda* 59 (2004): 4–16.

Sandwell, Rachel. '"Love I Cannot Begin to Explain": The Politics of Reproduction in the ANC in Exile, 1976–1990.' *Journal of Southern African Studies* 41:1 (2015): 63–81.

Sapire, Hilary. 'Township Histories, Insurrection and Liberation in Late Apartheid South Africa.' *South African Historical Journal* 65:2 (2013): 167–198.

Sapire, Hilary, and Chris Saunders (eds), *Southern African Liberation Struggles: New Local, Regional and Global Perspectives* (Claremont, South Africa: UCT Press, 2013).

Saunders, Chris. 'Liberation Struggles in Southern Africa: New Perspectives.' *South African Historical Journal* 62:1 (2010): 1–6.

Scarry, Elaine. *The Body in Pain: The Making and Unmaking of the World* (New York: Oxford University Press, 1987).

Seekings, Jeremy. 'Gender Ideology and Township Politics in the 1980's.' *Agenda* 10 (1991): 77–88.

—— *Heroes or Villains? Youth Politics in the 1980s* (Johannesburg: Raven Press, 1993).

—— 'The "Lost Generation": South Africa's "Youth Problem" in the Early 1990s.' *Transformation* 29 (1996): 103–125

—— 'Beyond Heroes and Villains: The Rediscovery of the Ordinary in the Study of Childhood and Adolescence in South Africa.' *Social Dynamics* 32:1 (2006): 1–20.

—— 'Whose Voices? Politics and Methodology in the Study of Political Organisation and Protest in the Final Phase of the "Struggle" in South Africa.' *South African Historical Journal* 62:1 (2010): 7–28.

Segal, Lynne. 'Gender, War and Militarism: Making and Questioning the Links.' *Feminist Review* 88 (2008): 21–35.

Seidman, Gay W. '"No Freedom without the Women": Mobilization and Gender in South Africa, 1970–1992.' *Signs* 18:2 (1993): 291–320.

—— 'Guerrillas in Their Midst: Armed Struggle in the South African Anti-Apartheid Movement.' *Mobilization* 6:2 (2001): 111–127.

Simpson, Thula. '"Umkhonto We Sizwe, We Are Waiting for You": The ANC and the Township Uprising, September 1984 – September 1985.' *South African Historical Journal* 61:1 (2009): 158–177.

—— *Umkhonto we Sizwe: The ANC's Armed Struggle* (Cape Town: Penguin Books, 2016).

Sironi, Françoise, and Raphaëlle Branche. 'Torture and the Borders of Humanity.' *International Social Science Journal* 54:174 (2002): 539–548.

Sitas, Ari. 'The Making of the "Comrades" Movement in Natal, 1985–91.' *Journal of Southern African Studies* 18:3 (1992): 629–41.

Sjoberg, Laura, and Caron E. Gentry. *Mothers, Monsters, Whores: Women's Violence in Global Politics* (London: Zed Books, 2007).

Sorsoli, Lynn, Frances K. Grossman, and Maryam Kia-Keating. '"I Keep That Hush-Hush": Male Survivors of Sexual Abuse and the Challenges of Disclosure.' *Journal of Counseling Psychology* 55:3 (2008): 333–345.

Straker, Gill. *Faces in the Revolution: The Psychological Effects of Violence on Township Youth in South Africa* (Cape Town: David Philip, 1992).

Summerfield, Penny. 'Culture and Composure: Creating Narratives of the Gendered Self in Oral History Interviews.' *Cultural and Social History* 1:1 (2004): 65–93.

Suttner, Raymond. *The ANC Underground in South Africa* (Johannesburg: Jacana Media, 2008).

Taft, Jessica K. 'The Political Lives of Girls.' *Sociology Compass* 8:3 (2014): 259–267.

Thomas, Lynn M. "'Ngaitana (I will circumcise myself)": The Gender and Generational Politics of the 1956 Ban on Clitoridectomy in Meru, Keny.' *Gender & History* 8:3 (1996): 338–363.

—— *Politics of the Womb: Women, Reproduction, and the State in Kenya* (Berkeley: University of California Press, 2003).

—— 'The Modern Girl and Racial Respectability in 1930s South Africa.' *The Journal of African History* 47:3 (2006): 461–490.

Thompson, Paul. *The Voice of the Past: Oral History* (Oxford: Oxford University Press, 1978).

Thomson, Alistair. 'ANZAC Memories: Putting Popular Memory Theory into Practice in Australia.' *Oral History* 18:1 (1990): 25–31.

—— *Anzac Memories: Living with the Legend* (Clayton: Monash University Press, 1994).

Tonkin, Elizabeth. *Narrating Our Pasts: The Social Construction of Oral History* (Cambridge: Cambridge University Press, 1992).

Treacy, Mary Jane. 'Double Binds: Latin American Women's Prison Memoirs.' *Hypatia* 11:4 (1996): 130–145.

Twum-Danso, Afua. 'The Political Child.' In Angela McIntyre (ed), *Invisible Stakeholders: Children and War in Africa* (Pretoria: Institute for Security Studies, 2005): 7–30.

Unterhalter, Elaine. 'The Impact of Apartheid on Women's Education in South Africa.' *Review of African Political Economy* 48:17 (1990): 66–75.

—— 'Remembering and Forgetting: Constructions of Education Gender Reform in Autobiography and Policy Texts of the South African Transition.' *History of Education* 29:5 (2000): 457–472.

—— 'The Work of the Nation: Heroic Masculinity in South African Autobiographical Writing of the Anti-Apartheid Struggle.' *The European Journal of Development Research* 12:2 (2000): 157–178.

Van der Kolk, Bessel A., and Rita Fisler, 'Dissociation and the Fragmentary Nature of Traumatic Memories: Overview and Explanatory Study.' *Journal of Traumatic Stress* 8:4 (1995): 505–525.

Van Kessell, Ineke. *'Beyond our Wildest Dreams': The United Democratic Front and the Transformation of South Africa* (Charlottesville: University Press of Virginia, 2000).

Veale, Angela. *From Child Soldier to Ex-fighter: Female Fighters, Demobilisation and Reintegration in Ethiopia* (Pretoria: Institute for Security Studies, 2003).

Vince, Natalya. *Our Fighting Sisters: Nation, Memory and Gender in Algeria, 1954–2012* (Manchester: Manchester University Press, 2015).

Viterna, Jocelyn. *Women in War: The Micro-processes of Mobilization in El Salvador* (Oxford: Oxford University Press, 2013).

Vogelman, Lloyd, and Gillian Eagle. 'Overcoming Endemic Violence against Women in South Africa.' *Social Justice* 18:1 (1991): 209–229.

Wale, Kim. 'Falling through the Cracks of South Africa's Liberation: Comrades' Counter-Memories of Squatter Resistance in the 1980s.' *Journal of Southern African Studies* 42:6 (2016): 1193–1206.

—— *South Africa's Struggle to Remember: Contested Memories of Squatter Resistance in the Western Cape* (London; New York: Routledge, 2016).

Walker, Cherryl (ed), *Women and Gender in Southern Africa to 1945* (London: James Currey, 1990), 221–250.

Walker, Cherryl. *Women and Resistance in South Africa* (London: Onyx Press, 1982).

Walker, Liz. 'Men Behaving Differently: South African Men since 1994.' *Culture, Health and Sexuality* 7:3 (2005): 225–238.

Waller, Richard. 'Rebellious Youth in Colonial Africa.' *The Journal of African History* 47:1 (2006): 77–92.

West, Harry G. 'Girls with Guns: Narrating the Experience of War of Frelimo's "Female Detachment".' *Anthropological Quarterly* 73:4 (2000): 180–194.

Wilson, Richard. *The Politics of Truth and Reconciliation in South Africa: Legitimizing the Post-Apartheid State* (Cambridge: Cambridge University Press, 2001).

Wood, Elisabeth Jean. 'The Emotional Benefits of Insurgency in El Salvador.' In Jeff Goodwin, James M. Jasper, and Francesca Polletta (eds), *Passionate Politics: Emotions and Social Movements* (Chicago: University of Chicago Press, 2001), 267–281.

Xaba, Thokozani. 'Masculinity and its Malcontents: The Confrontation between "Struggle Masculinity" and "Post-Struggle Masculinity" (1990–1997).' In Robert Morrell (ed), *Changing Men in Southern Africa* (Scotsville: University of Natal Press, 2001), 105–124.

Yang, Mayfair Mei-Hui. 'From Gender Erasure to Gender Difference: State Feminism, Consumer Sexuality, and Women's Public Sphere in China.' In Mayfair Yang (ed), *Spaces of their Own: Women's Public Sphere in Transnational China* (Minneapolis: University of Minnesota Press, 1999), 35–67.

Yow, Valerie. 'Ethics and Interpersonal Relationships in Oral History Research.' *The Oral History Review* 22:1 (1995): 51–66.

Index

Related James Currey titles on South & Southern Africa

Archaeology and Oral Tradition in Malawi: Origins and Early History of the
Chewa
Yusuf M. Juwayeyi

Manhood, Morality & the Transformation of Angolan Society: MPLA Veterans
& Post-war Dynamics
John Spall

Peacemaking and Peacebuilding in South Africa: The National Peace Accord,
1991–1994
E.D.H. Carmichael

The Vaal Uprising of 1984 & the Struggle for Freedom in South Africa*
Franziska Rueedi

Marikana: A People's History*
Julian Brown

Peacemaking and Peacebuilding in South Africa: The National Peace Accord,
1991–1994*
E.D.H. Carmichael

*forthcoming